IMAGES
of America

SANGER

On the Cover: The view in this 1914 photograph of Sanger is looking east toward the foothills. Sanger's once famous opera house can be seen in the center, to the right of the steeple. Sanger's First Baptist Church, built in 1892, is at left center. The dark horizontal line across the photograph at the east edge of town is the Kings River Lumber Company's flume, nearing the end of its 54-mile journey from the lumber mill. On the horizon are Jesse Morrow Mountain (left) and Campbell Mountain (right). (Courtesy of Pop Laval Foundation.)

IMAGES
of America

SANGER

Scott Haugland, Ken Marcantonio, Hal Shaw,
and the Sanger Historical Society

ARCADIA
PUBLISHING

ISBN 978-1-4671-3018-9

Published by Arcadia Publishing
Charleston, South Carolina

Printed in the United States of America

Library of Congress Control Number: 2013931095

For all general information, please contact Arcadia Publishing:
Telephone 843-853-2070
Fax 843-853-0044
E-mail sales@arcadiapublishing.com
For customer service and orders:
Toll-Free 1-888-313-2665

Visit us on the Internet at www.arcadiapublishing.com

This book is dedicated to the citizens of Sanger, and the pioneers who came before us, who made Sanger what it is today.

Contents

FOREWORD

Growing up in Sanger, I remember packinghouses stretched along Academy Avenue. They were busy all summer long, often operating until 10:00 or 11:00 p.m. to pack all of the fruit grown in the area. Many high school students worked in the summertime at these packing sheds to make money for school clothes and possibly to buy their first car.

Sanger was a great place in which to grow up. Families knew their neighbors and looked out for each other. There were two small family movie theaters, which you could walk to from home. One theater ran English-language movies and the other ran Spanish-language movies. The original Sanger library, built using Carnegie Corporation funds, was a local gathering place.

Our history represents the many phases of American life. Sanger started as a lumber town, has a rich American Indian heritage, and prospered through the agriculture bounty in the area. I grew up with farming and packinghouses, which provided opportunities for my family's trucking business. Agriculture continues to be a major force in our region, and I look forward to new opportunities that will inevitably come as Sanger grows.

—Judith G. Case, Fresno County Supervisor
District 4

ACKNOWLEDGMENTS

We wish to thank those who offered their wisdom and guidance as we researched material for this book. We truly appreciate the time, advice, and assistance given by Dick Sheppard of the *Sanger Herald*, Bob Bosserman and Jim Walton of the Sanger Historical Society, and Melissa Scroggins of the Fresno County Library. We also would like to thank Dorothy Marcantonio for graciously loaning her dining room to us, which was used as our "project office." Every effort was made to ensure the accuracy of facts presented in this publication, and any errors certainly were not intentional. Unless otherwise noted, all images appearing in this book were graciously provided by the Sanger Historical Society's Depot Museum archives.

INTRODUCTION

In 1887, while attending a Yard Masters Convention in San Francisco, Joseph Sanger Jr. was informed by Southern Pacific Railroad officials that a depot and town site in Fresno County were being named in his honor. The Sanger Depot was built in 1887, at the southwest corner of Seventh and L Streets along the Southern Pacific tracks, which ran from Fresno to Porterville. Shortly after, Sanger became ill and his railroad career ended. After living as an invalid for many years, he passed away, having never visited the small town named in his honor.

Following the building of the depot, the Southern Pacific Railroad sold parcels to early settlers eager to establish homes and businesses near the new station. The railroad's presence seemed to give Sanger a new life, encouraging families to settle here with hopes of gaining employment in the booming lumber industry. The town of Sanger was officially founded in 1888 with the establishment of a post office. The railroad had come to the area to provide shipping for grain and other agricultural products. By 1890, Sanger businesses provided the residents with not only the necessities, but luxuries, too. Sanger's 13 saloons proved to be very popular with residents and with the cowboys from the surrounding ranches who came to town on Saturday nights. The town grew and prospered and was officially incorporated in 1911. One little-known fact is that early Sanger had a Chinatown, more than likely a result of the Southern Pacific Railroad construction.

Rumors began to spread about the Kings River Lumber Company's plans to build a flume to ship lumber from the nearby forest to the valley floor. Sanger and other nearby towns, such as Fresno and Centerville, hoped to be chosen for the terminus for the flume. Sanger offered the lumber company 65 acres of prime land near the railroad. The lumber company accepted the offer and chose Sanger as the terminus of the flume and location for its large finishing mill. Until this time, there had been minimal interest in Sanger. Word of the lumber company's decision spread like wildfire, and the town boomed overnight. Lots once selling for a few hundred dollars sold for thousands.

In 1866, pioneer Mary Jane Hazelton planted the area's first orange trees, followed by Harvey Akers setting out the first vineyard. Several sawmills were established in Millwood, Converse Basin, and, later, Hume Lake. Virgin redwood was being shipped to Sanger via the world's longest lumber flume. Although most people think that entire logs were shipped down the flume, in reality, the logs were "rough-cut" and dried in the nearby forests, then the lumber was shipped to Sanger. A large finishing mill awaited the lumber's arrival in Sanger. The lumber industry fueled the local economy. One of the products of the mill was the lumber used to build the crates needed to ship fruit and produce from the packinghouses via the railroad.

Ownership of the lumber company eventually changed to the Hume-Bennett Lumber Company and, later, the Sanger Lumber Company. Unfortunately, the companies never made a profit. In the early 1920s, after many years of struggle, the lumber era came to a close. Fortunately for Sanger, agriculture quickly replaced the lumber industry. Packinghouses sprang up in and around Sanger. Fruit from Sanger was being shipped around the country.

In 1926, Pres. Calvin Coolidge designated the General Grant tree in Kings Canyon as the nation's Christmas tree. In 1949, Sanger was also designated the nation's Christmas tree city by the US Post Office Department. In 1952, the General Grant tree became the only living shrine to those who gave their lives in service to America. To this day, the Sanger Chamber of Commerce sponsors The Trek to the Tree each December. Hundreds of people travel each year from Sanger via tour buses and private vehicles to Grant Grove. The annual memorial ceremony is held at the base of the General Grant tree. A wreath in placed at the tree's base in memory of fallen soldiers.

Eventually, with the closing of the packinghouses, reduced rail traffic ended the need for the depot in Sanger, and it was closed. Later, Jack Tanney and his brother, learning that the former depot was the oldest building in Sanger, purchased it with visions of possibly using the building as a restaurant. As part of the purchase agreement with the railroad the Tanney brothers were required to move the building off Southern Pacific property within 30 days. After abandoning their vision for the depot, the brothers donated the building to the Sanger Historical Society. On December 7, 1977, the building was moved to its current location, near Sanger's Civic Center. The former Southern Pacific depot is now home to the Sanger Historical Society's Depot Museum.

In this book, we hope to tell the story of Sanger. We expect that you will find our efforts interesting and informative as we introduce you to long-forgotten people and events, such as the Native Americans who lived and thrived in the valley for millennia, and the pioneers and visionaries who recognized the great potential the land offered. The book also documents the people who came to build a better life and the community they created.

The year 2013 is the 125th anniversary of the founding of Sanger. Most of the newer residents in Sanger have no idea that their town was once the terminus to the world's longest lumber flume. We feel that this book will spark great interest in the history of the area and in how Sanger came to be. We hope that it will encourage residents to not only remember, but to treasure our local history. We believe that this book will encourage folks to preserve our fading history and learn from those that came before us. As the Sanger Historical Society motto states, "A town with a future, needs to remember its past."

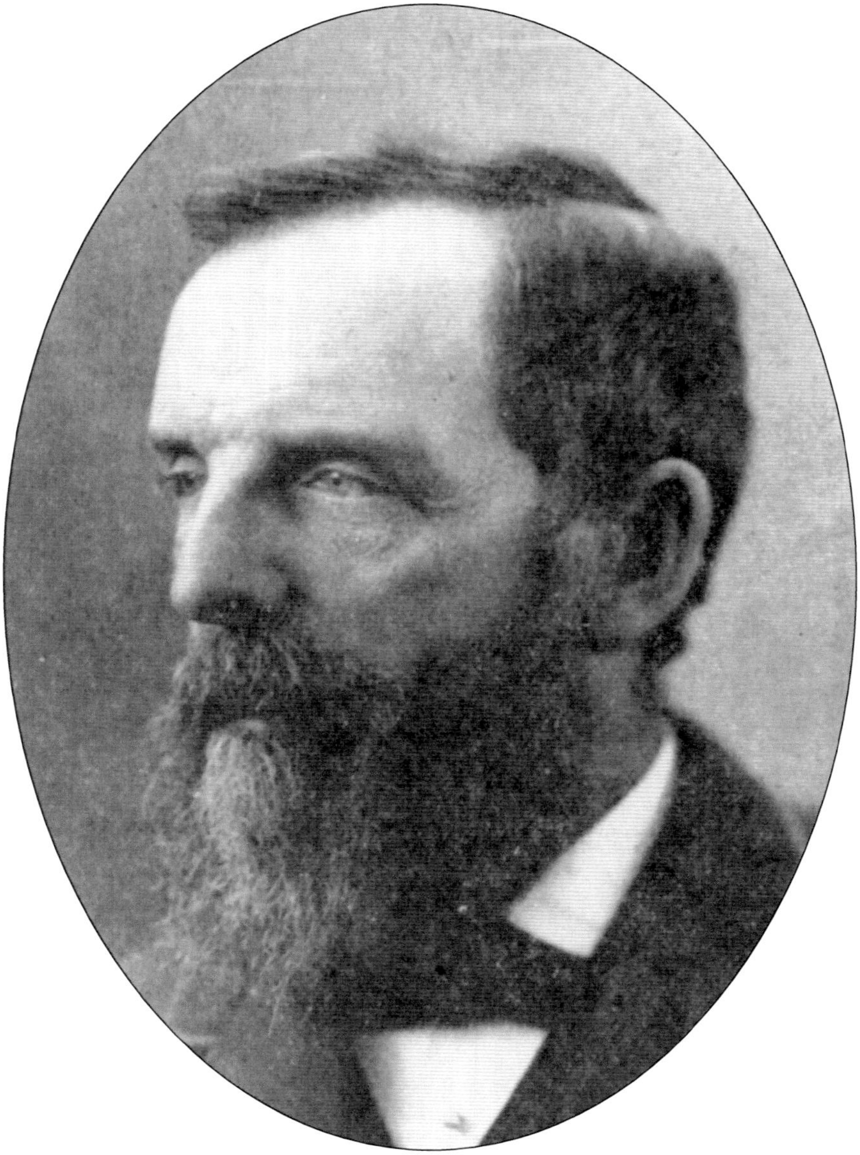

For years, "Who named Sanger?" has been an often-asked question, and the answers have always been evasive and unsubstantiated. The most popular rumor was that a member of the original town survey party was named Sanger, and that the town was named for him about 1887. At various times, residents would attempt to ascertain the facts concerning the naming of the town, but always to no avail—until the golden jubilee edition of the *Sanger Herald* was planned. The Post Office Department in Washington was consulted, and contact was made with Alice B. Sanger, who knew the history of how Sanger got its name. In 1887, her father, Joseph Sanger Jr., then secretary and treasurer of the Railroad Yardmasters Association, attended its annual convention in San Francisco. At that meeting, a group of railroad officials informed him that they had named a town in Fresno County for him. Sanger died without having seen the town that bore his name. (Caption and photograph from the 1938 golden jubilee edition of the *Sanger Herald*, reprinted courtesy of the *Sanger Herald*.)

One

Native Americans

The General Grant tree is estimated to be between 1,500 and 2,000 years old. Yet, when it was barely a seedling, there were people living in and around Sanger. They called themselves Yokuts, meaning "the people." They were unique among California's Indians, because they consisted of 50 distinct tribes with their own territories and dialects. They occupied the entire San Joaquin Valley and lower foothills from north of the Fresno River to the Tehachapi Pass. Some tribal names are still familiar, such as Chukchansi, Tachi, and Choinumni. Others, like the Gawia, Yokud, and Wowol, are known only to students of Native American culture in California.

The Yokuts were present to see the first Spanish expeditions into their valley. It was in the period from 1805 to 1808 that Gabriel Moraga led Spanish soldiers to explore the Central Valley. Moraga's names for the rivers, towns, and valley are still in use today. The Sacramento, San Joaquin, Merced, and Kings Rivers, along with many others, were named by Moraga. From these, we get the names for Sacramento, Merced, and the San Joaquin Valley, among others.

By the time of the Moraga expeditions of 1805 and 1806, the Yokut population was estimated to be between 15,000 and 20,000. The Spanish called the Yokuts *tulerenos*, people of the rush marshes, because of the abundance of the tule marshes along the streams and lakes.

The Yokuts saw famed mountain man and explorer Jedediah Smith trap beaver along the Kings River as he made his way along the foot of the Sierras, heading north. Smith had just made the first documented east-west crossing of the Sierras, from the Great Salt Lake to San Gabriel. Exposure to these newcomers had a devastating impact on the tribal populations.

The Yokuts had no resistance to the diseases carried by these explorers. Many tribes were brought into the mission system, where they lost their culture and never returned to their tribal villages.

In the 1820s, smallpox was ravaging the missions. Many Yokuts, trying to escape the disease, fled to the valley, unknowingly bringing the disease with them. By the time of his expedition in 1834, Joseph Walker reported that the Yokuts had left the valley and were living in the foothills, trying to escape the plagues. Later explorers recorded seeing whole villages of corpses of Indians killed by the diseases. By the time of the California Gold Rush, exposure to smallpox, measles, and scarlet fever had decimated the Yokut population. The Federal Census of 1910 lists only 533 Yokuts, from a prior population of 15,000 or 20,000.

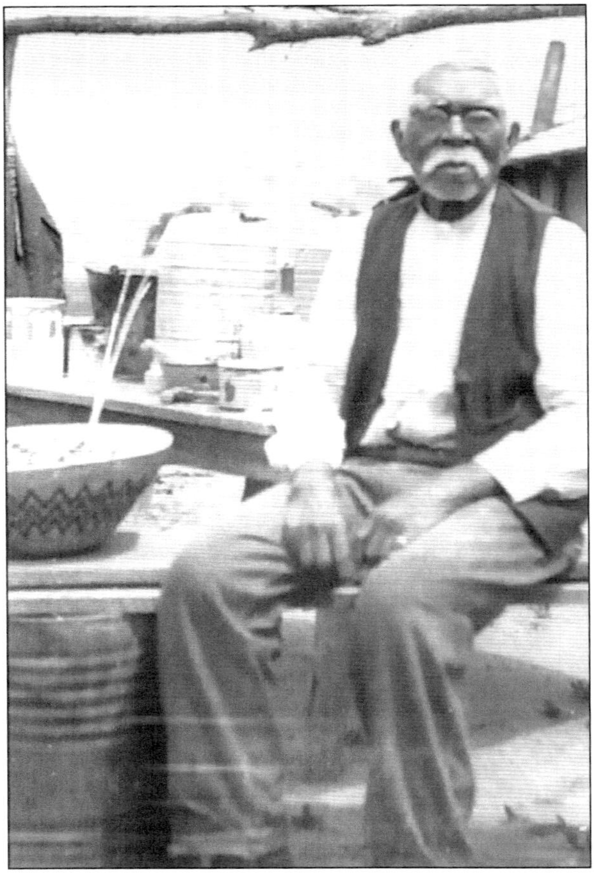

Shown here is Dick Sampson, husband of Mary Sampson and the father of three children—Frank, Annabel, and Maggie. He is wearing western dress. Before the arrival of white men, Yokut men often went naked or wore a small loincloth. In the winter, they wore robes made of animal skins, often rabbits.

Posing at an acorn granary is Sally Edd (left). The diet of the Yokuts consisted of a variety of seeds, acorns, and even buckeyes. The acorns could be stored for years in granaries such as this one. Not all acorns were equal, though. The Yokuts preferred those from the black oaks, which grow at the higher elevations of the surrounding foothills. No one else in the image is identified.

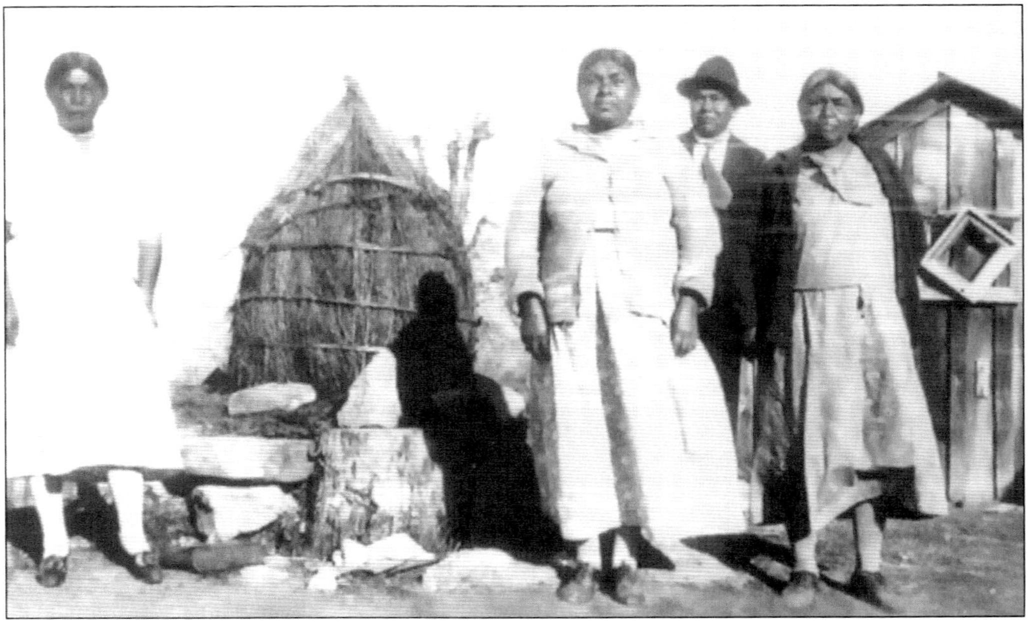

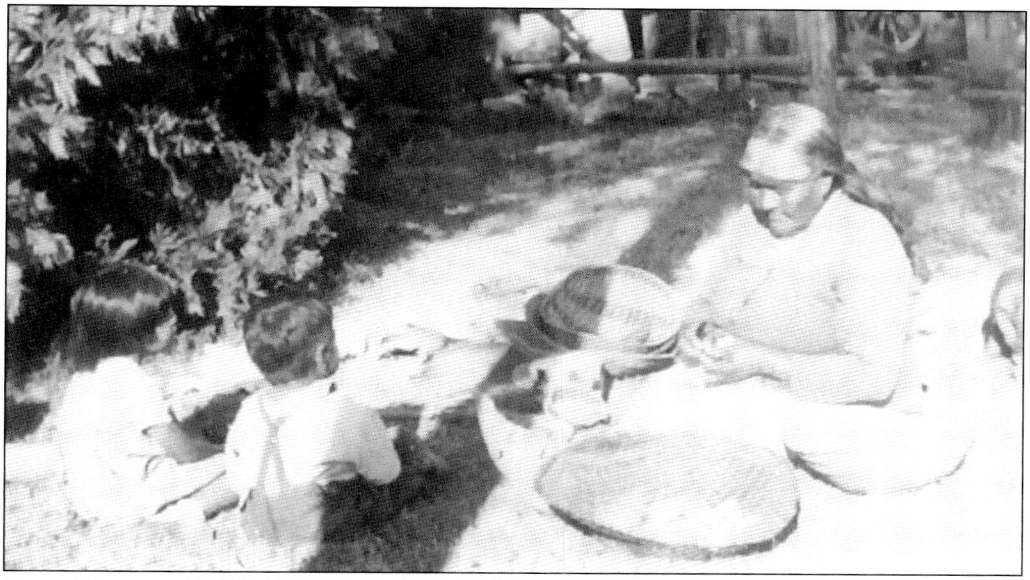

Bessie Edison and Willie Davis sit with an unidentified woman. Although the valley and foothill oaks produced millions of tons of acorns, they could not be eaten until they were processed. The tannins in the pulp had to be leached away to make them eatable. Bedrock mortars can still be found along the streams and rivers near Sanger, where the acorns were ground for processing.

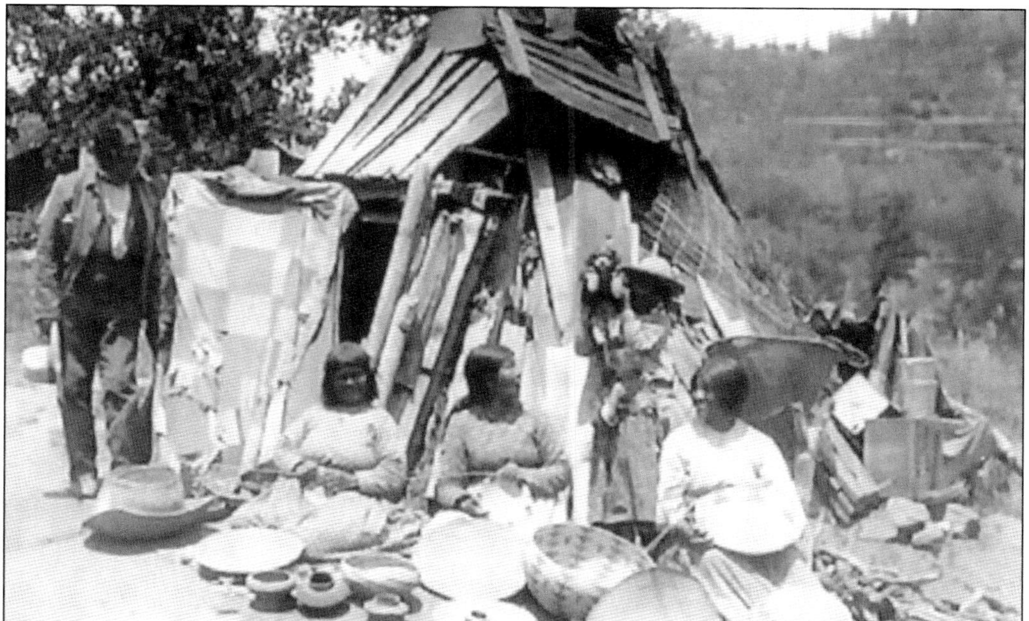

After the arrival of white homesteaders to the area, the Yokuts lived in dwellings like the one shown here. Original Yokut dwellings consisted of a round shallow pit with slabs of wood arranged into a teepee-style hut. This was adequate to protect them from the cold winter rains. When the weather improved, they spent their days outdoors.

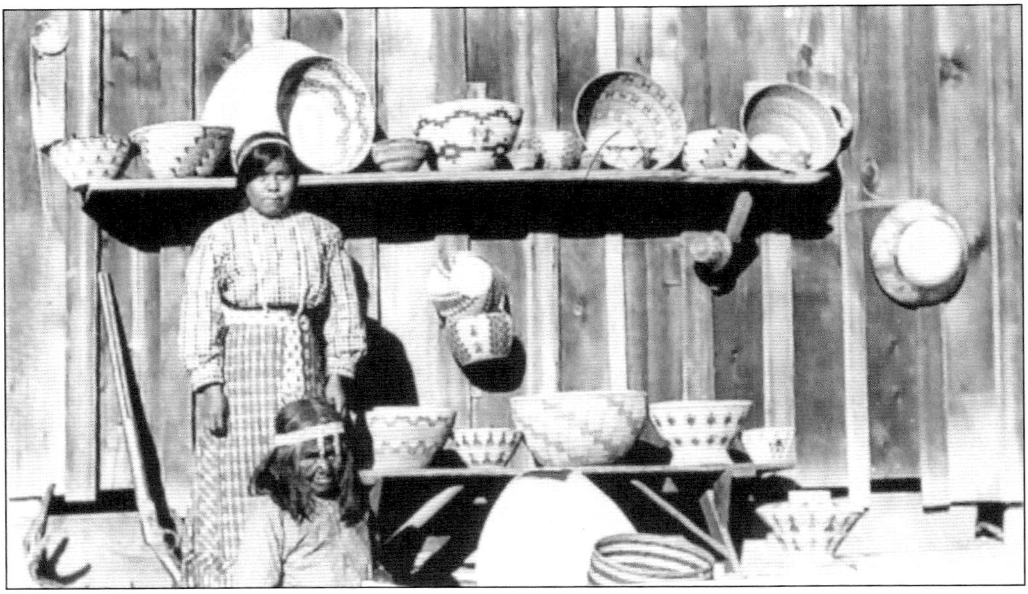

Lizzie Chapa and her unidentified granddaughter proudly display their baskets in front of their home. From their earliest years, Yokut girls learned the fine art of basket weaving from their mothers. The beautiful baskets were used for gathering, storage, and cooking. The weave was so tight that the baskets could hold water.

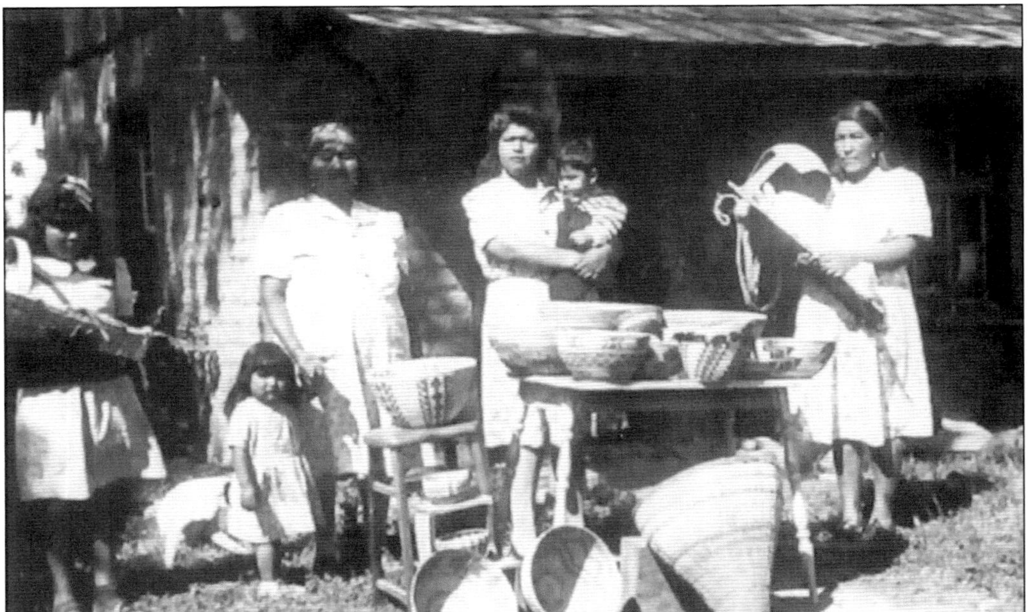

Shown here are, from left to right, Mary Lou Davis (holding Wilma Cisco in cradle), grandma Julia Davis (holding hands with Irene), Gloria Cisco (holding Billy), and Myrtle Davis (holding McArthur in cradle). The designs on cradles for girls and those for boys were quite different. The designs on cradles for girls emphasized weaving; for boys, the designs encouraged them to become good hunters.

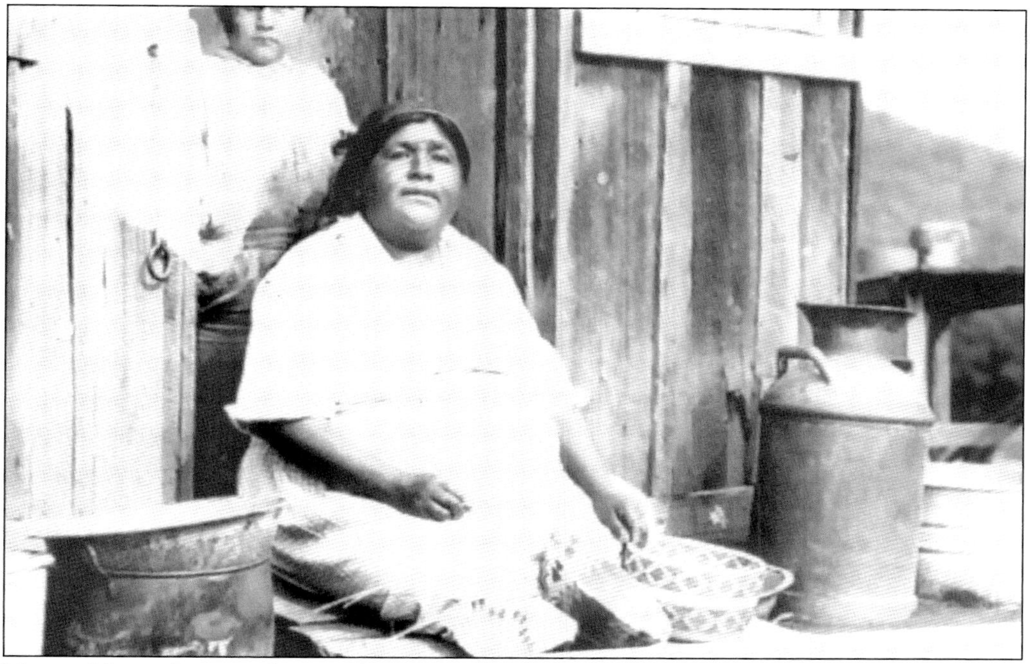

Minnie Hancock is seen here with one of her children. Minnie and her husband, Ben, had 15 children. She was recognized as a master when it came to basketry. Baskets were an important part of California Indian culture, and great pride was taken in their construction. Many of Hancock's baskets can be seen in the collection housed in the Sanger Depot Museum.

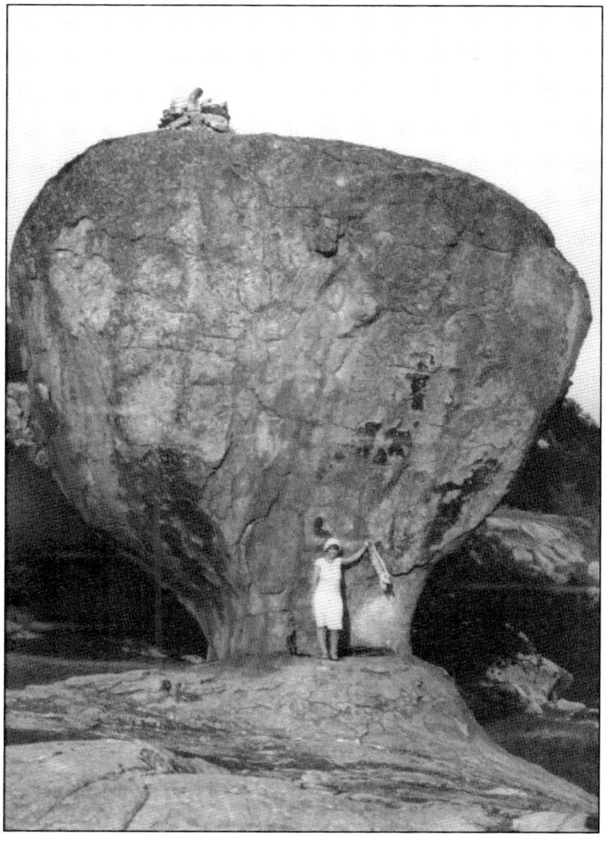

This 1934 photograph shows Jug Rock, which is located east of Sanger and north of Jesse Morrow Mountain. Jug Rock, or Wa-Ha-Lish, is a sacred site of the Choinumni tribe. The presence of grinding holes and other artifacts establish that the Choinumni tribe has been in this area for more than 6,000 years, according to the *Handbook of North American Indians* and the *Handbook of the Indians of California*. This site is private property, and is not open to the public.

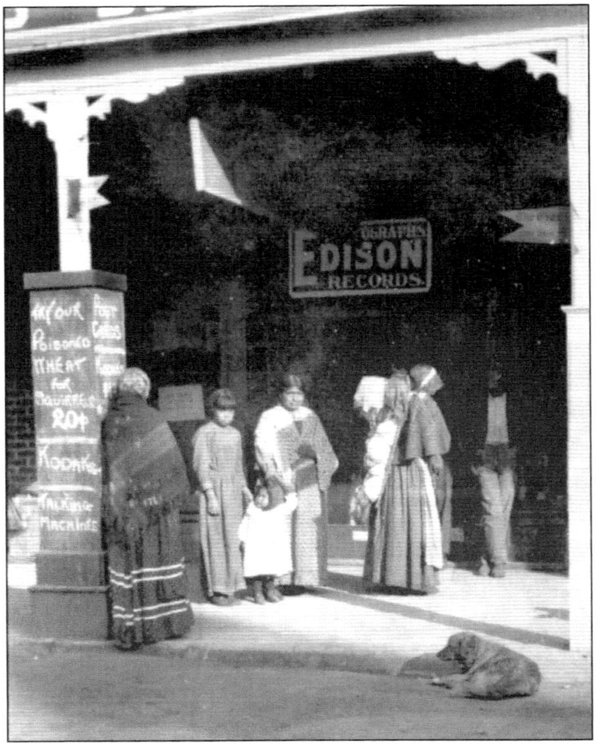

Established in 1888, this was one of the first drugstores in Sanger. Seen here in a 1905 photograph, the store changed hands and became O.A. Brehler Drug Store. Local Indians would come down from the foothills and be amazed at the variety of goods available. They often had a shortage of cash, but, more often than not, Mr. Brehler would barter baskets and other woven items for merchandise.

Oscar and May Sayre Brehler are seen here with a portion of their very large collection of handwoven baskets made by local Indians. The Brehlers left many of these baskets to their stepson, Jack Sayre, who donated many of them to the Sanger Historical Society's Depot Museum. The museum has provided a home to display the beautifully arranged baskets, along with large photographs of the Indian weavers.

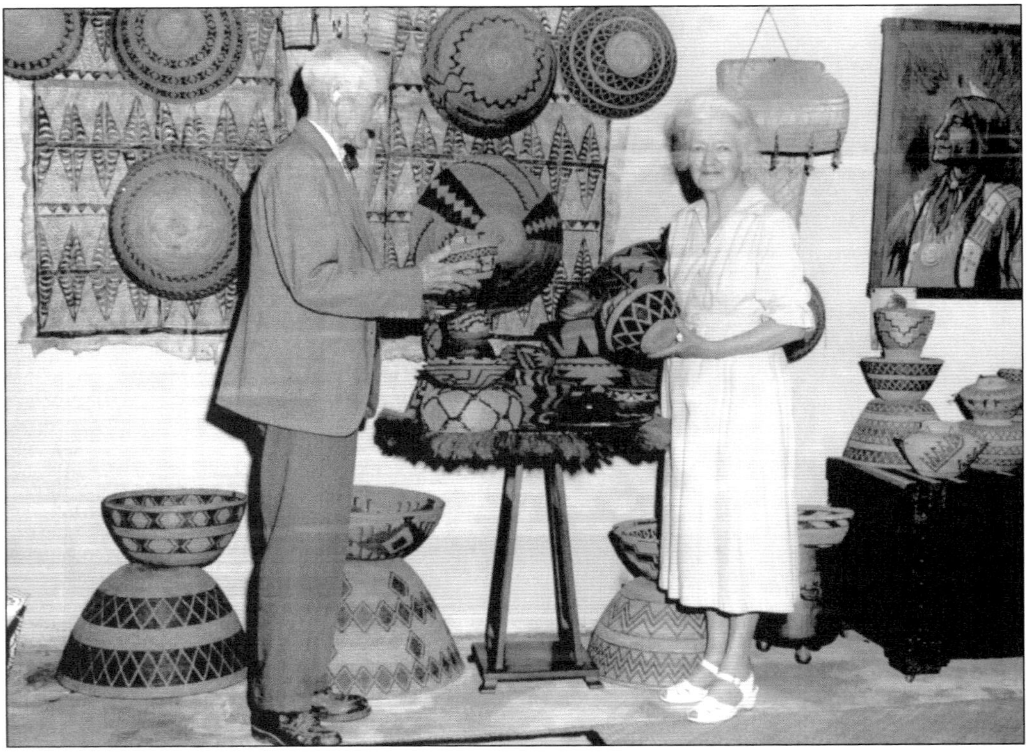

Two

Cattlemen and Dry Farming

In the 1850s, cattlemen ruled this section of the Central Valley. Yank Hazelton is credited with bringing some of the first cattle to his homestead on the Kings River. Henry Akers and Jesse Morrow were other prominent cattlemen. Gabriel Moore, a former slave from Alabama, operated a cattle ranch near Centerville in 1853.

Cattlemen did not get along with sheepmen. When A.Y. Easterby gave a friend, Moses Church, permission to bring 2,000 sheep to his Fresno property, a confrontation was bound to happen. Instead of bringing his sheep to Easterby's, Church set up camp in the Centerville area. According to Church, Hazelton approached him with drawn pistol and told him to be gone by nine o'clock the next morning. Church claimed that when he returned to his camp, all his belongings had been burned. Hazelton's version of events was that Church was camped on his land and that he had warned him to leave, but that Church had ignored him. Regardless of which version of the story was true, Church left to join Easterby and became an important player in the developing agricultural industry.

There was also friction between cattlemen and grain farmers. The entire valley was considered open range. With cattle roaming freely, grain growers had to fence their land to keep the cattle from destroying their crops. The 1874 election for a seat in the state legislature pitted the cattlemen, represented by Thomas Fowler, against the grain growers and farmers, represented by Lindsey Tipton. The farming interests outnumbered the cattle interests, and the farmers won the seat. The "no fence law" was passed; now, it was the cattlemen who had to fence their livestock.

The new law was a boon to the grain and wheat farmers. More farmers flocked to the area, and their farms grew larger and larger. At that time, the farming was all on dry land and depended on the annual rainfall. With the almost desert-like conditions found in the San Joaquin Valley, the need for water was great.

With the development of canals, irrigation provided ample water from the Kings River to vast areas of farmland, allowing for great diversity in crops. Hazelton's oranges and Akers's grape vines could now be grown in large farming operations. Grain and wheat were replaced with the much more lucrative citrus and grape industries, and cattle ranching moved from the valley floor to the foothills.

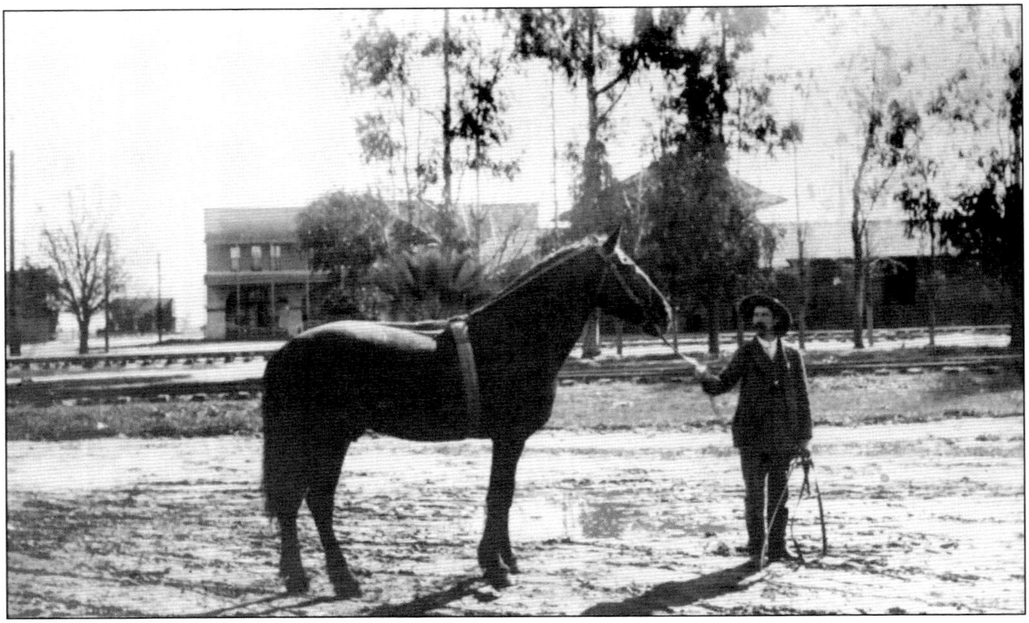

In the above photograph, Leon Akers is seen in front of the Sanger depot. The Sanger Hotel is on the left. Leon's grandfather, Henry Akers, and his wife, Delilah, had led a wagon train from Austin, Texas, in 1852. They set up a homestead near Scottsburg (Centerville) and went into the cattle business. Among the members of that wagon train were a slave, Gabriel Bibbard Moore, his wife, Mary, and son, Ephraim. Moore's owners, William and Richard Glenn, were also on the wagon train. Moore was born a slave in Alabama in 1812. The Glenns owned him when they lived in Arkansas. Little else is know of his years as a slave. Soon after reaching Scottsburg, he obtained his freedom. The 1857 tax rolls list him as a farmer with $3,000 in assets. He was the first black cattle rancher in the San Joaquin Valley. The below photograph shows Gabriel Moore's new gravestone in the Akers cemetery, northeast of Sanger.

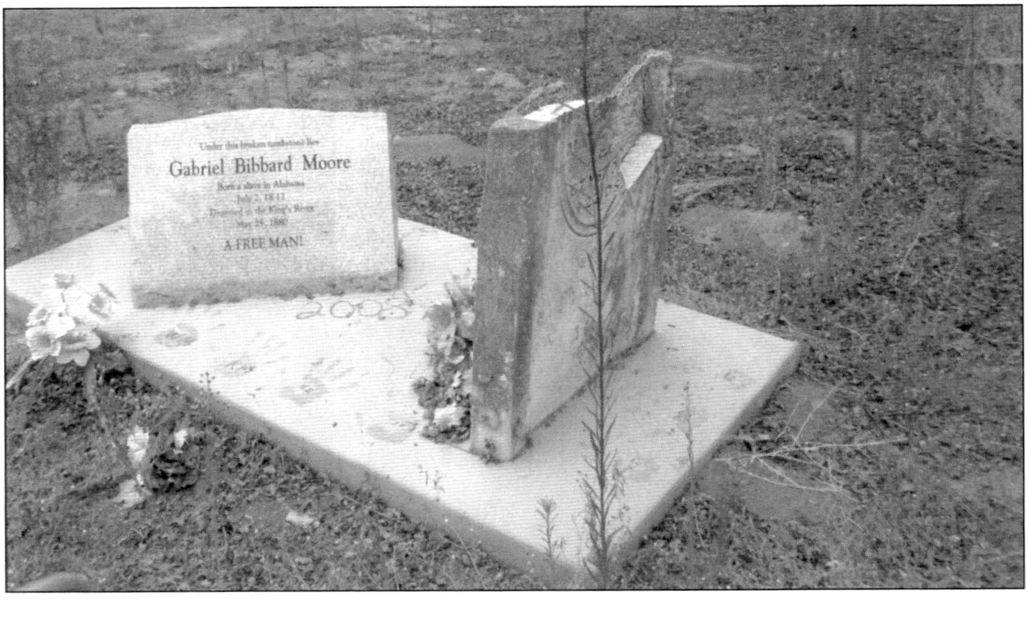

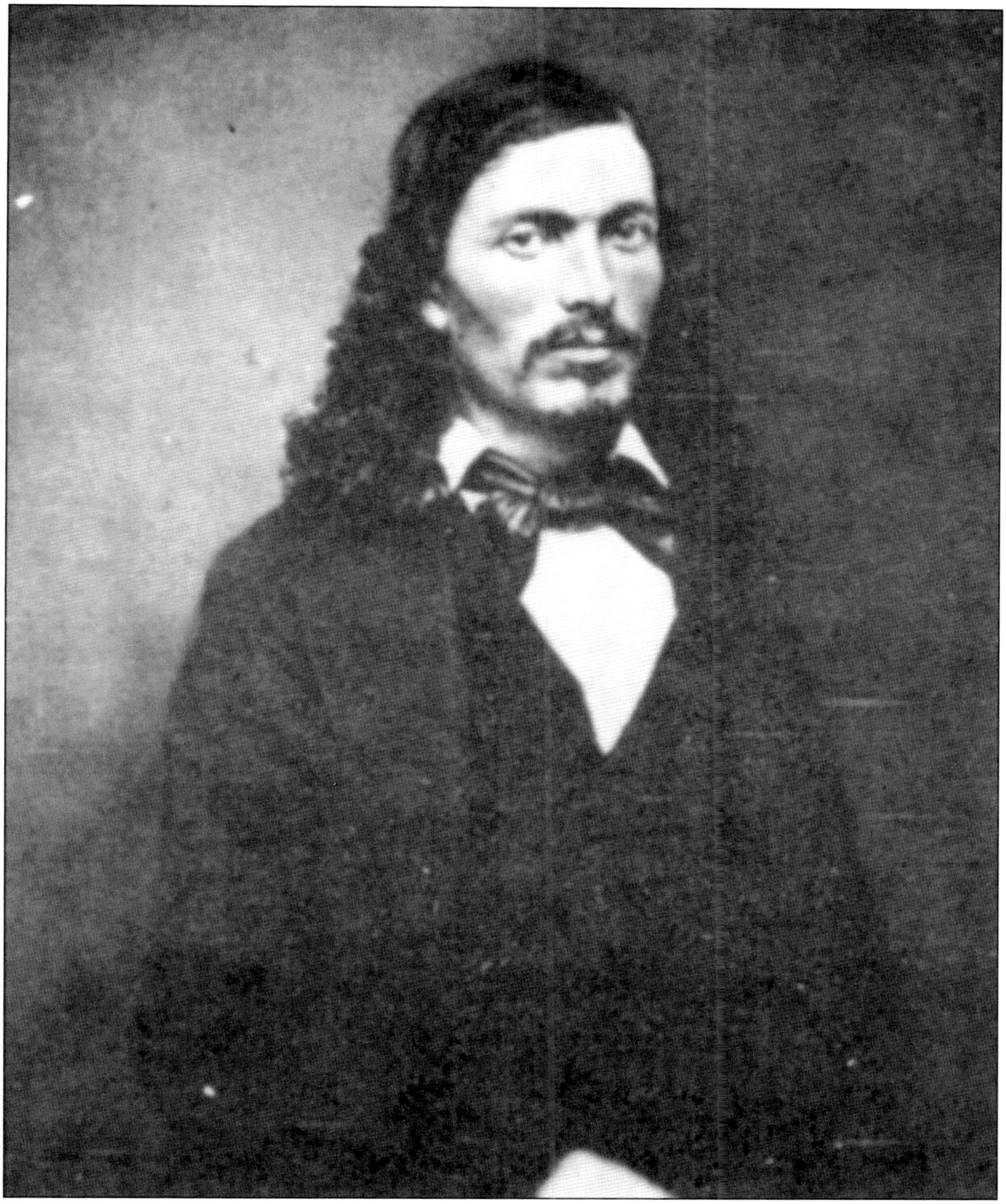

William Hazelton was born in 1824 in Coeymans, Albany County, New York. He arrived in the Sanger area in 1853 and filed his claim on a quarter section of land and started ranching. He had experience as a faro dealer and used that skill to "break the bank" gambling. He put the money in his saddlebags, mounted his horse, and rode to Mexico, where he bought his first herd of cattle. Hazelton and Mary Jane Akers were married in 1857 under a large oak tree on Akers's land near the original Hazelton homesite. They had five children of their own—Clara, Lindsay, Wesley, Henry, and Huckabay—and then they adopted seven more—Laura, Sophia, Fiske, Catherine, John, Cecelia Kimble, and Edward.

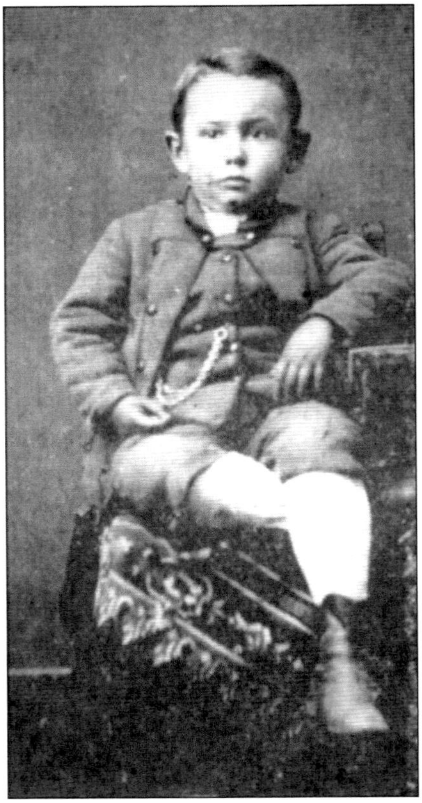

J.W. "Spike" Simpson was born a few years before Sanger became a city. Spike and his brother Frank became excellent ranchers and worked many roundups together over the years. There were many years when they rounded up cattle and drove them into the nearby Sierras during the summer months.

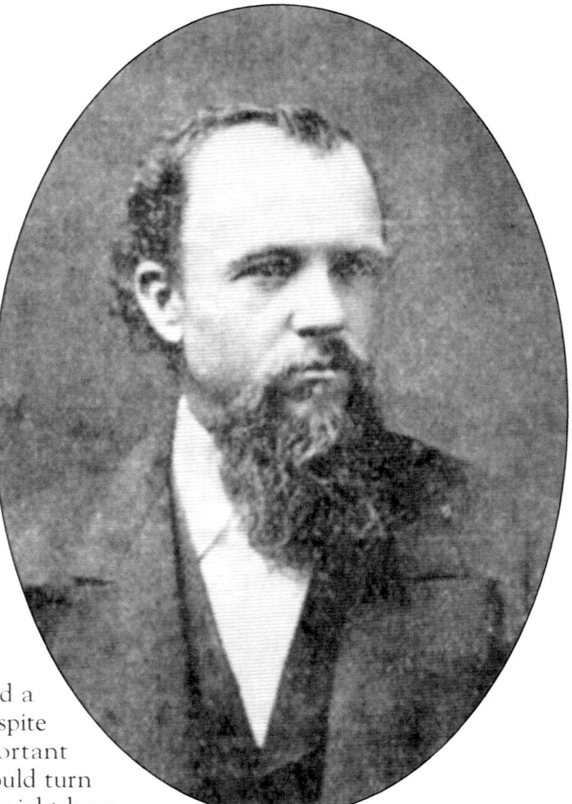

M.M. Jacks, a rancher in the area, played a large role in the development of Sanger despite not living in the city. He was an important leader among the earlier settlers, who would turn to Jacks to help solve any problems they might have.

H.M. Woods was a prominent sheep- and cattleman in Centerville, east of Sanger. In those early years, Centerville was the center of ranching in the area and in the foothills. Woods also provided advice with regards to the infant grape industry. He has been credited with establishing the first vineyard in Mount Hammell country.

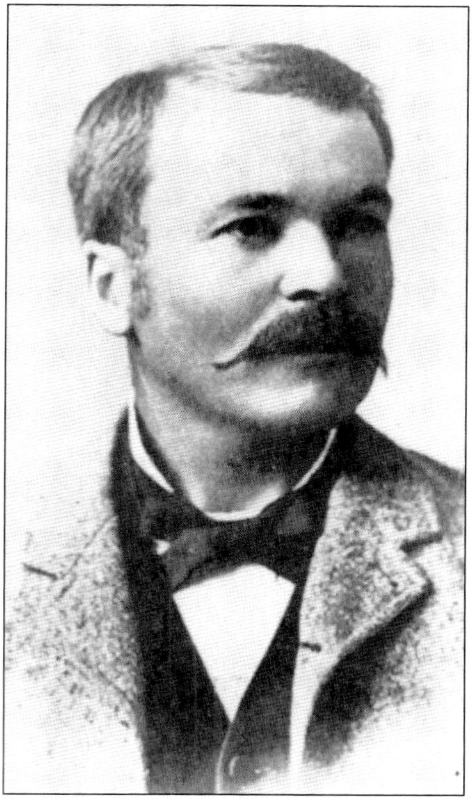

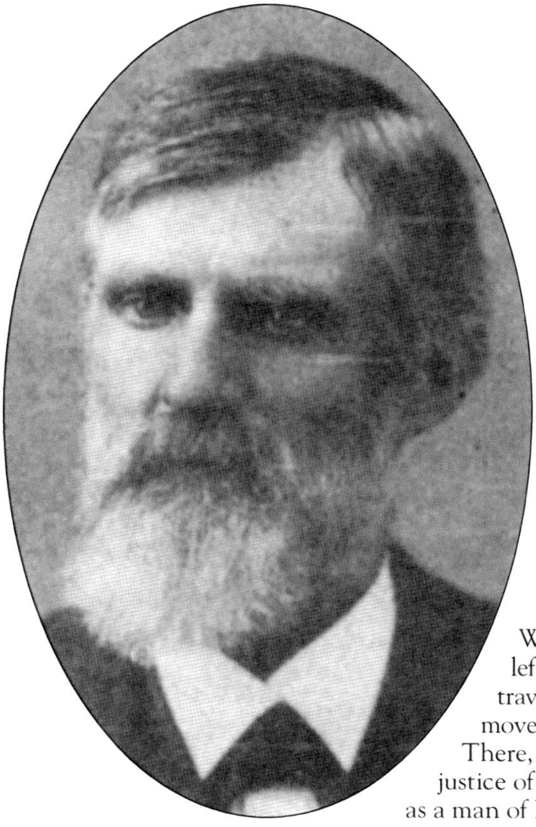

William Deakin and his wife, Elizabeth Leasley, left England to settle in Salt Lake City. Later, they traveled the Mormon Trail to San Bernardino. They moved once again, settling in Centerville in 1855. There, William farmed, raised cattle, and served as justice of the peace. Over the years, he was recognized as a man of leadership throughout Fresno County.

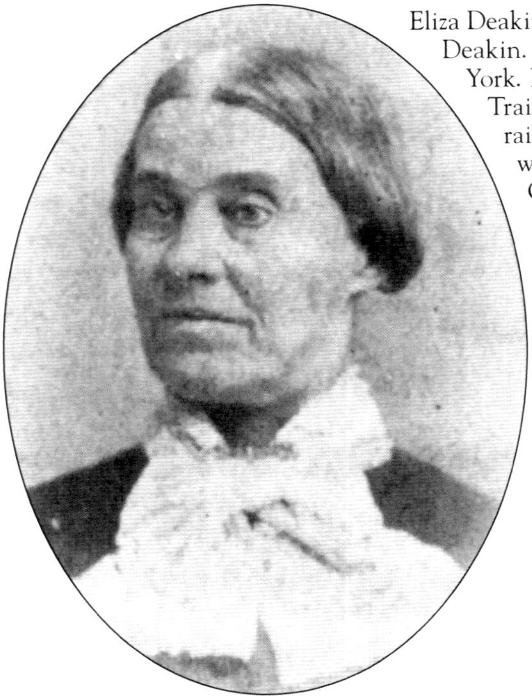

Eliza Deakin was the only child of William and Elizabeth Deakin. In 1861, she married Peter W. Fink from New York. Fink had arrived In the Sanger area in 1852. Trained as a journeyman, Fink turned to cattle-raising on the Kings River near Sanger. He also worked as a teamster and drove stock between Centerville and Stockton. He and Eliza had six children, who also prospered in the Sanger area.

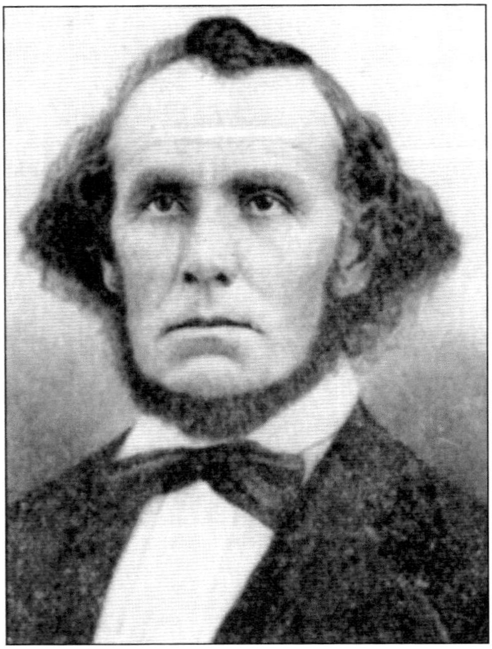

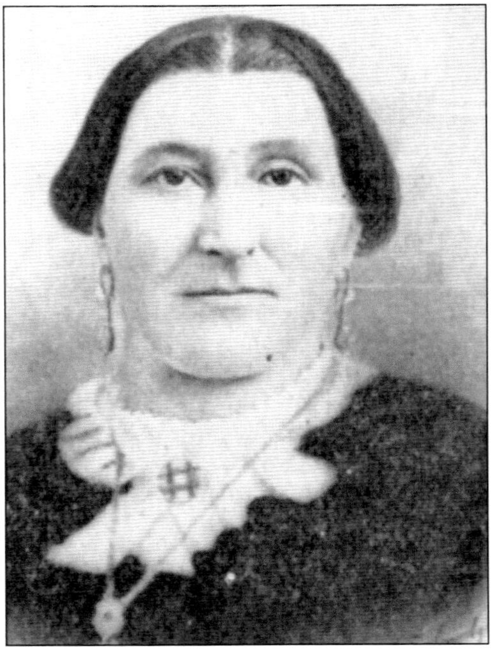

Herman Henry Hanke and his wife, Eliza M., came from Prussia in the 1850s and settled in Northern California with their nine children. Later, they moved into the Sanger area, and, for $1 an acre, bought 2,452 acres of bottomland to raise cattle and sheep. In 1883, their son William moved into the area, where he ranched, was a county supervisor, and was a director of the Bank of Sanger.

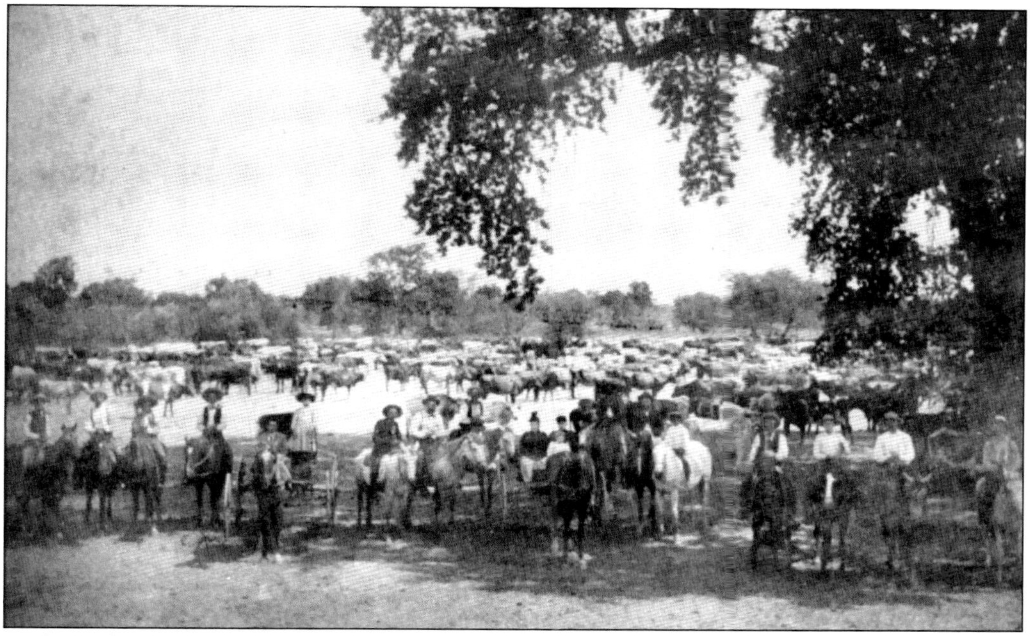

In the early 1880s, stock raising was time consuming, but on this day, the Hankes are enjoying a picnic with neighbors and friends. William Hanke moved into the area to help his mother manage the ranch and farm the 700 acres of grain they had planted. Among his credits were building the first house in the area and opening the first butcher shop. Later, he would help survey for the City of Sanger.

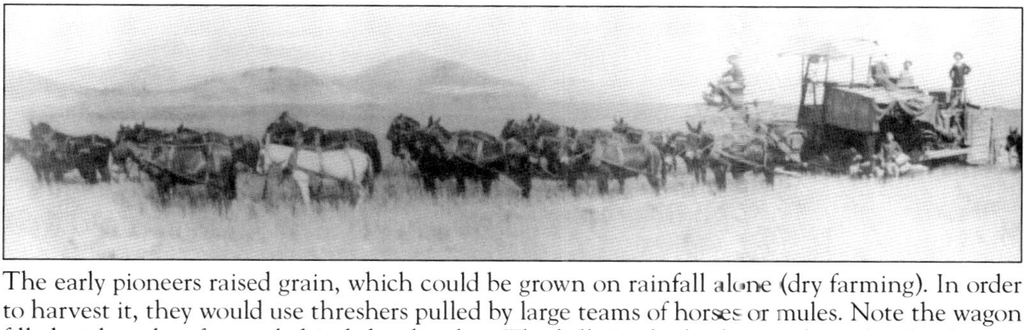

The early pioneers raised grain, which could be grown on rainfall alone (dry farming). In order to harvest it, they would use threshers pulled by large teams of horses or mules. Note the wagon filled with sacks of grain behind the thresher. The hills in the background can be clearly seen just east from Sanger.

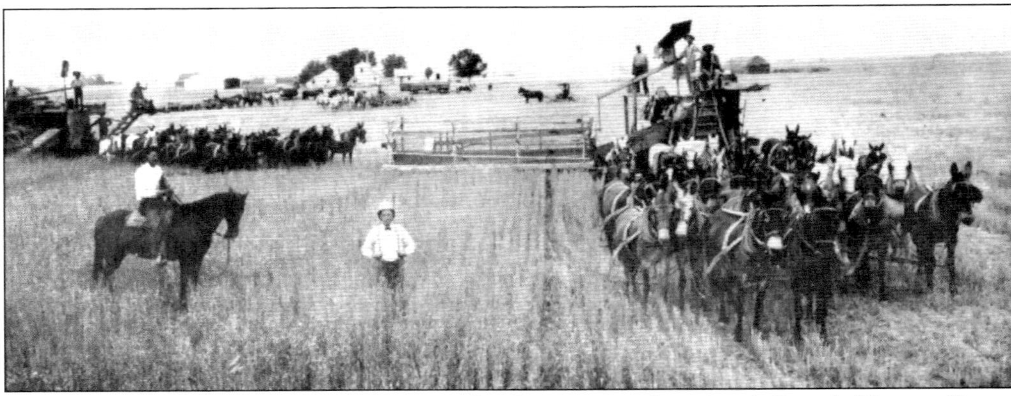

In this 1890 photograph, a 36-horse team pulls a harvester at the Waverly Ranch. Teams of horses harvested the ranch's 5,000 acres of grain. The crop was then hauled to the six grain houses in Sanger. William Radley, sitting on the horse at left, was the manager of the ranch for many years. Hector Burness is standing near him. By 1938, this ranch had changed over to Waverly Vineyards, which was partly owned and managed by Bert Zook.

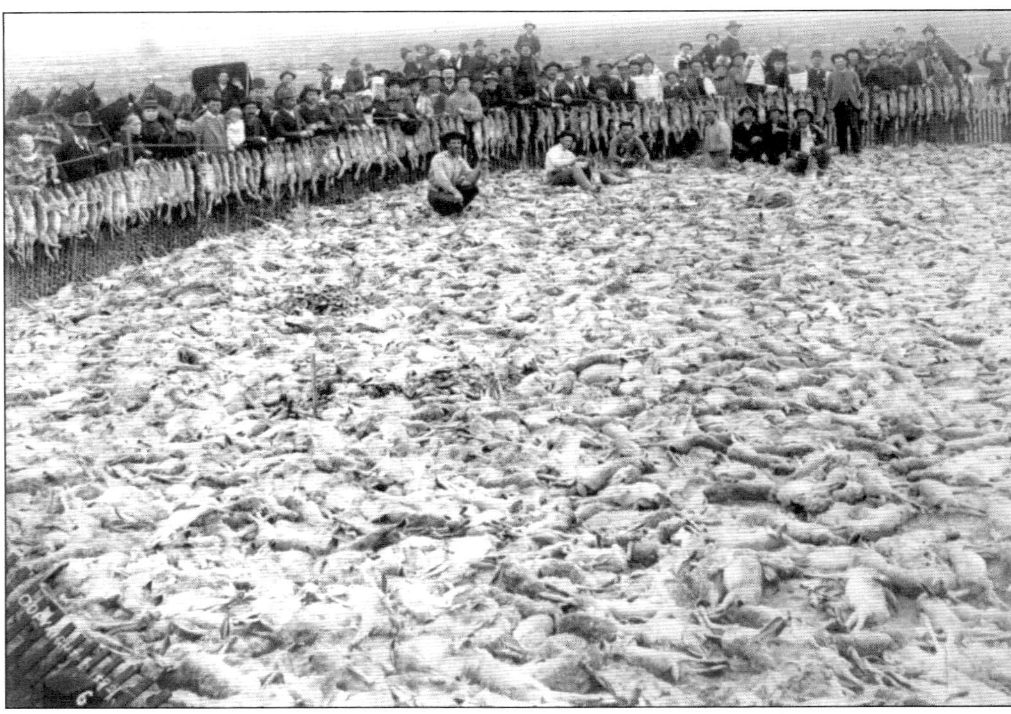

In this 1880s photograph, John C. Cavanah, one of Sanger's pioneers, can be seen participating in a rabbit drive in the Madera area, though his position in the image is not specified. These drives were intended to reduce the large number of jackrabbits that were plaguing the crops of farmers and ranchers. He farmed and operated threshers in the Fairview area just north of Sanger.

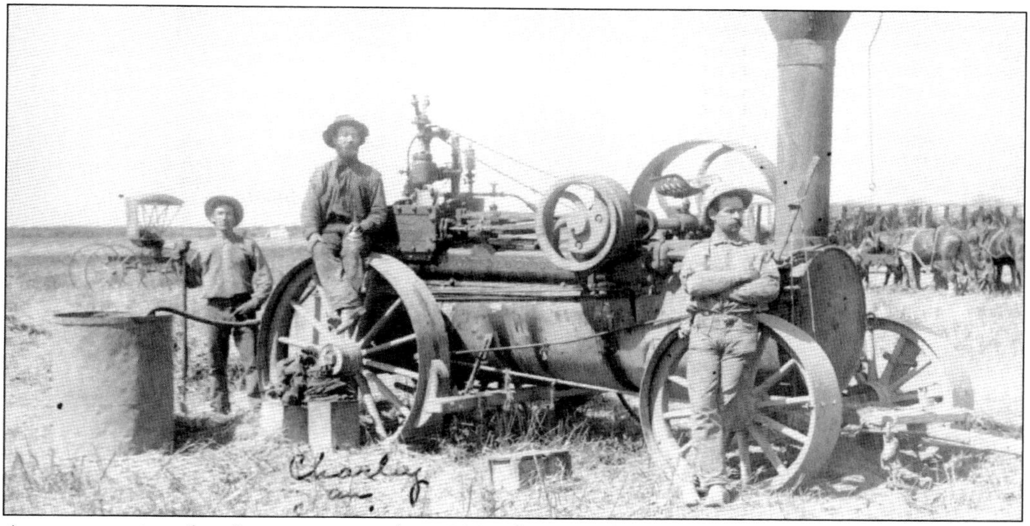

A steam engine thresher is seen in this 1890s photograph. The horses in the background were used to bring the straw to the thresher. J. Charlie Cavanah, sitting on the wheel, was the engineer. He and his wife, Martha Jane (Worsham), came to California from Missouri in 1872 and settled near Sanger (Squaw Valley) before the railroad was built. Later, after his wife died, he remarried and moved to the Sanger area.

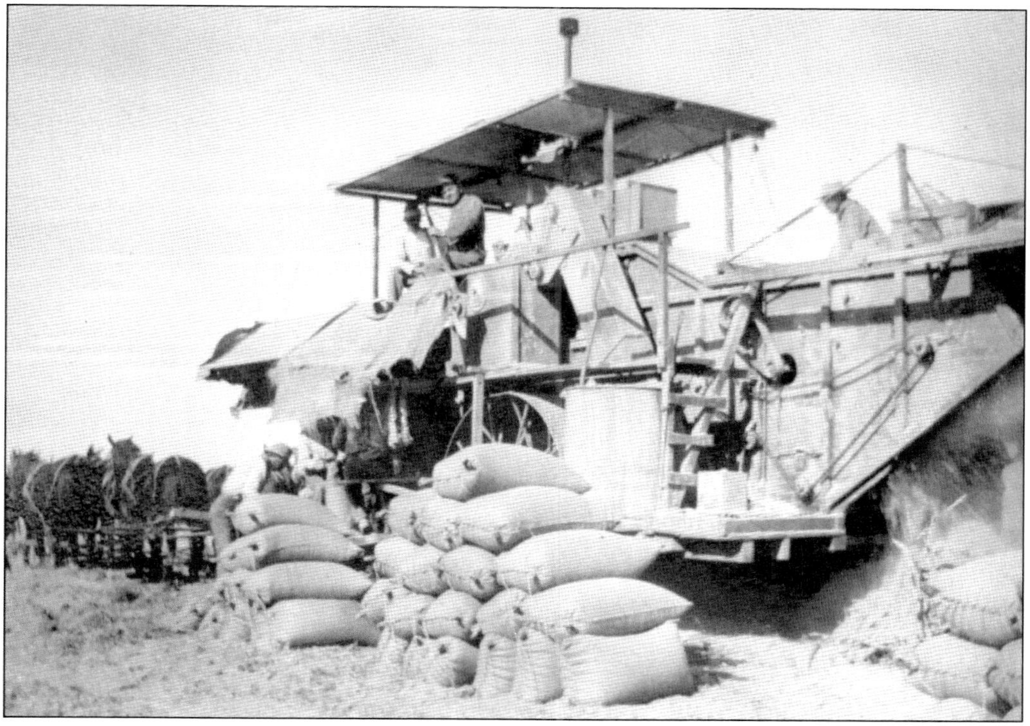

Grain was a crop that could be harvested and processed in the fields. Large teams of horses or mules provided the labor to cut the grain and at times to haul the grain to the thresher. These bags of grain would be hauled to Sanger and stored in the many silos near the railroad. From there, they would be shipped to mills in cities or to ports to be sent overseas.

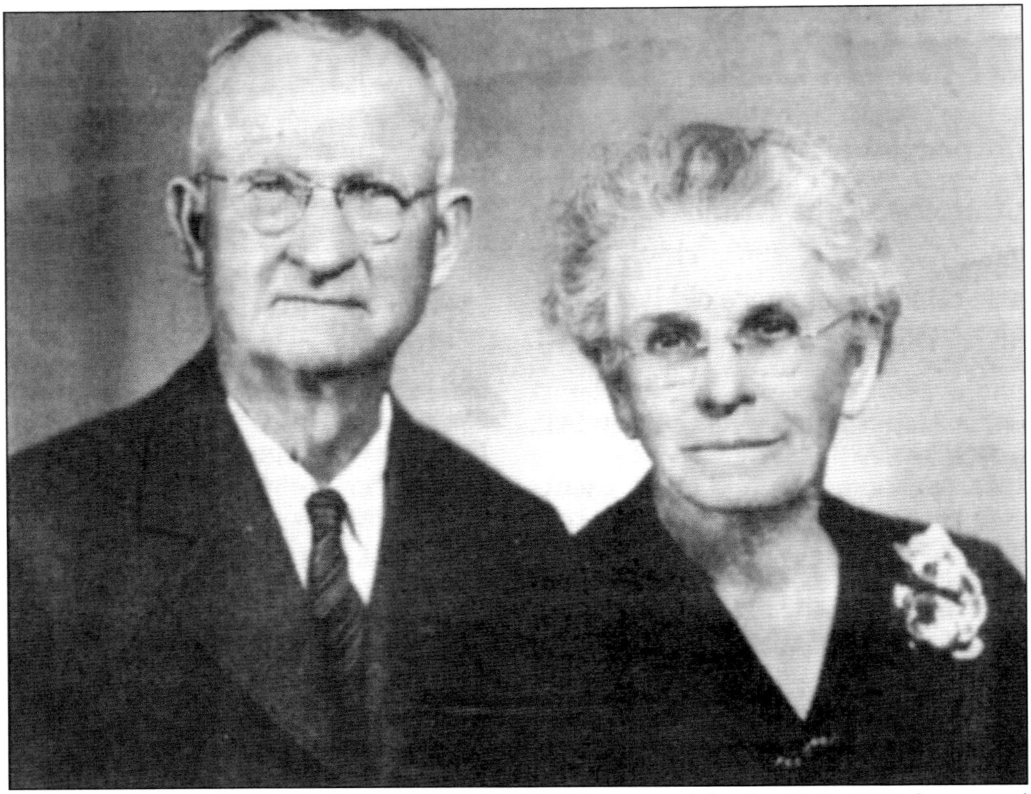

Burton Elwood came to California in 1869 in a covered wagon with his family. In 1879, they moved to the Piedra area, and Burton married Commillia, who was from Visalia. Burton purchased and homesteaded land in the Piedra area east of Sanger. The cattle ranch had 2,880 acres, and today, the Burton heirs still own land and raise cattle in the area. Elwood Road in the area connects Piedra with Highway 180. Burton and Commillia Elwood are seen here in 1888.

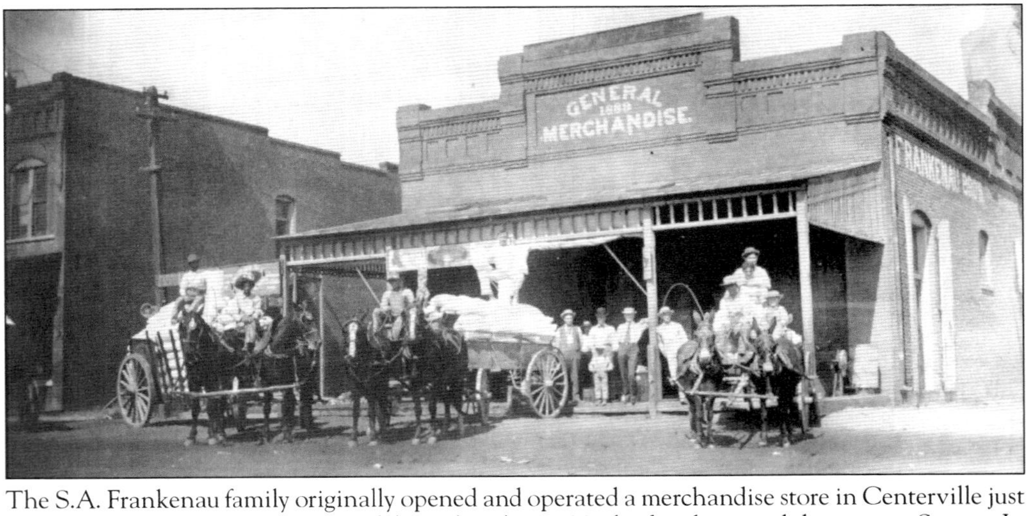

The S.A. Frankenau family originally opened and operated a merchandise store in Centerville just east of Sanger. With the building of the railroad in 1888, the family moved the store to Sanger. In 1889, it was located at Eighth and L Streets and provided the basic needs for the early pioneers.

Three

Early Pioneers

The growth of Sanger was due to the Southern Pacific line connecting Fresno to Porterville, along with the growing lumber and fruit industries, all of which needed workers. And the workers came. The original pioneers, the cattle and sheep ranchers, the grain farmers, and the river-bottom farmers were soon joined by others seeking opportunities to begin new lives.

Many Italian families discovered the Sanger area in the early 1900s. At first, many settled in the wine area near Asti, California. Work was hard to find there, but word spread that laborers were needed near Minkler, just east of Sanger. They worked on ranches there or in the booming lumber industry. Once settled, many of them sent for relatives in Italy. As their population increased, businesses in Sanger began catering to the needs and tastes of the growing Italian American community.

Mexican families came to California to work on the railroads. It was easy to cross the border at El Paso, Texas, and there were rail lines being built all over the area. The Southern Pacific rail spur from Fresno to Porterville, built in 1888, attracted many workers to the area. The development of irrigation and the growing fruit industry attracted many who had worked the same crops in Mexico, but at much lower wages. Also, the persecution of Catholics in Mexico in 1928–1929 caused many to flee to families already living in the Sanger area.

The Japanese were late arrivals to the area. Most of them settled in other parts of California before relocating to the Centerville area. These Japanese, mostly single men, were called "fruit tramps," because they followed the harvests. Some owned property, but, because of the Asian Exclusion Acts, they often did so in someone else's name. In 1924, the deed to the Domoto family's ranch in Centerville could not be in their name because they were Japanese. They had left Japan, but they brought their culture with them. Their children went to school to learn Japanese and attended a Buddhist temple to maintain their religion. They were taught the importance of respect for the Japanese way of life. Other families living in the area included Ihara, Mayeda, Watahira, Nishina, Nishioki, Matsumoto, and Ohama. Many of these families felt they were accepted as equals in the community.

These immigrants, along with growth in the area, made possible Sanger's booming economy. Land prices went up as fast as buildings were erected. Sanger was incorporated, had a fire department, schools, churches, infrastructure, electricity, constables, and a bright future.

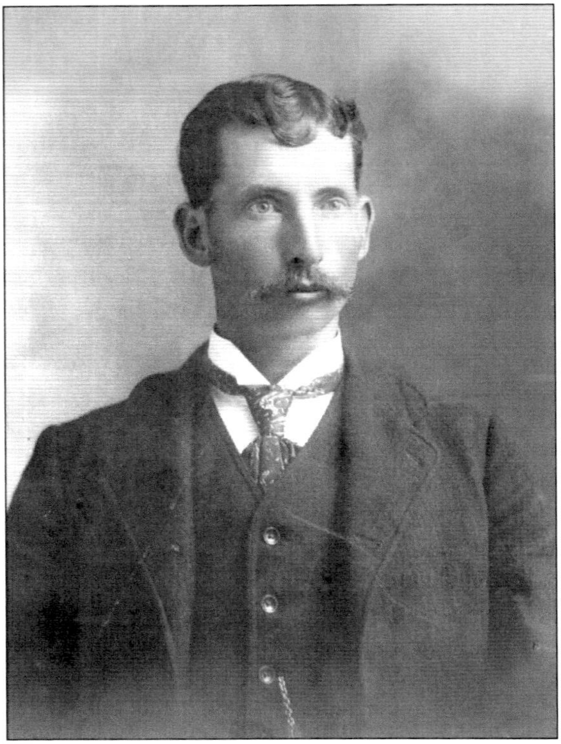

Leon Akers (left) was born in Centerville in 1896. He was a cattleman for more than 92 years. During World War I, he served on a warship called the S.A. *Frankenau*. The Frankenau family opened a grocery store in Sanger. Leon and his wife horse-packed materials to the men building the John Muir Trail. One of the earliest pioneers in the area was Mrs. Alexander Cameron (below). In 1852, after a long and dangerous covered-wagon trek, she arrived in the Sanger area and settled there. The Camerons raised a large family, and many of her descendents still live in the Sanger area. (Left, courtesy of the John and Bonnie Krum family.)

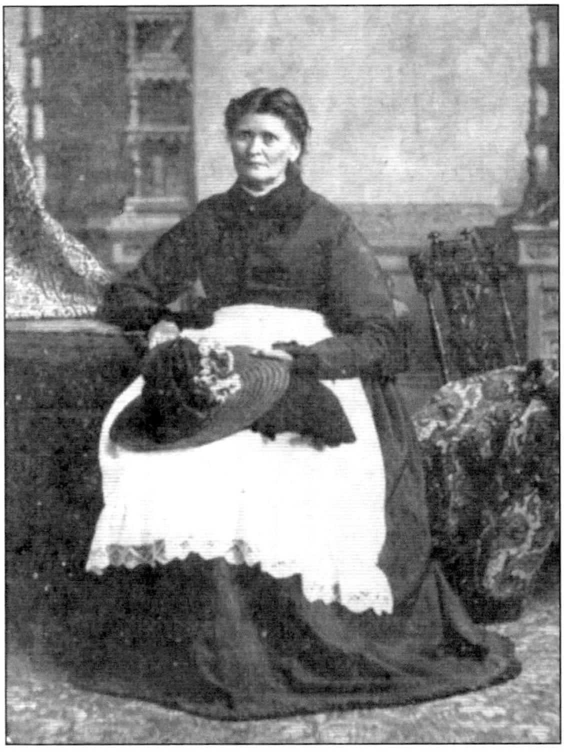

Joseph P. Sanger was the secretary and treasurer of the Railroad Yardmaster's Association. At the group's 1887 meeting, the members informed him that Southern Pacific Railroad was surveying for a new "junction" in Fresno County. They were going to name it the Sanger Depot in honor of him. Over the years, Sanger never had the opportunity to visit the area, but his name remains.

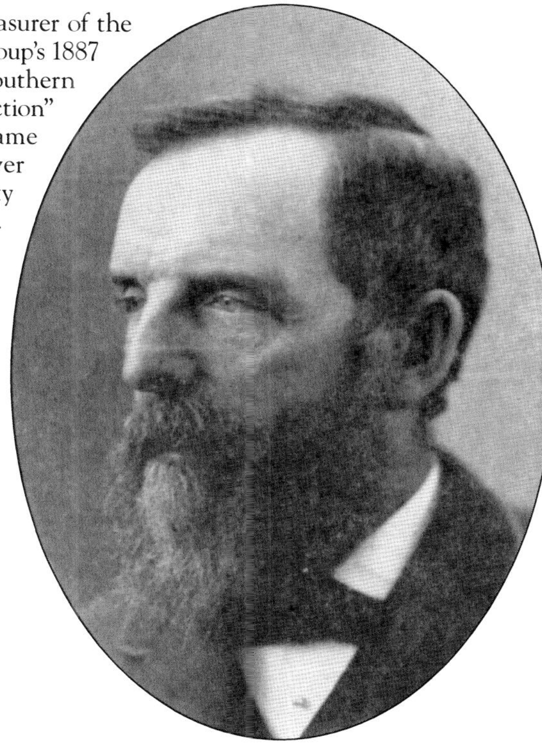

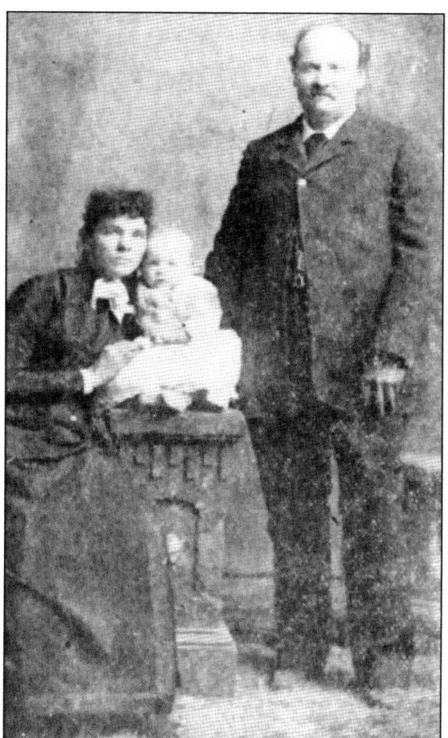

Mrs. Felix Hill is shown holding in her arms the first baby born in Sanger. The baby, born in December 1887, was named Eliza, but was always called "Sis." Sanger would not become a city until 1888. Fortunately, the Hills had a choice of five doctors at that time.

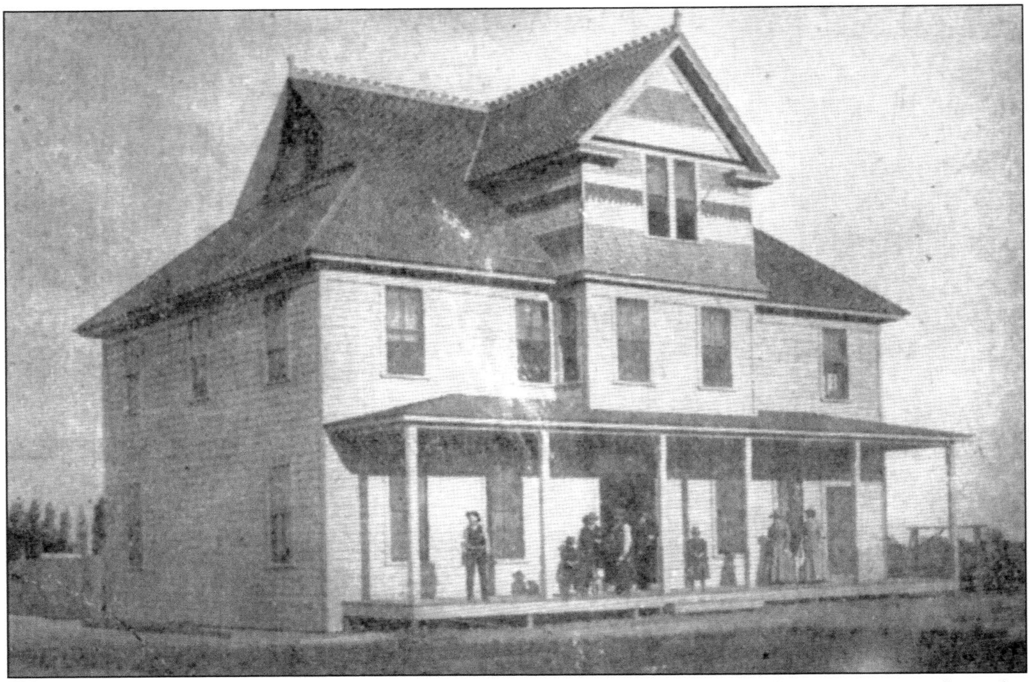

In 1890, this three-story hotel was one of the most popular lodgings in the area. Located on the east side of the Southern Pacific Railroad tracks, it housed long-term residents and overnight guests. The owner-operators were the Belvins family.

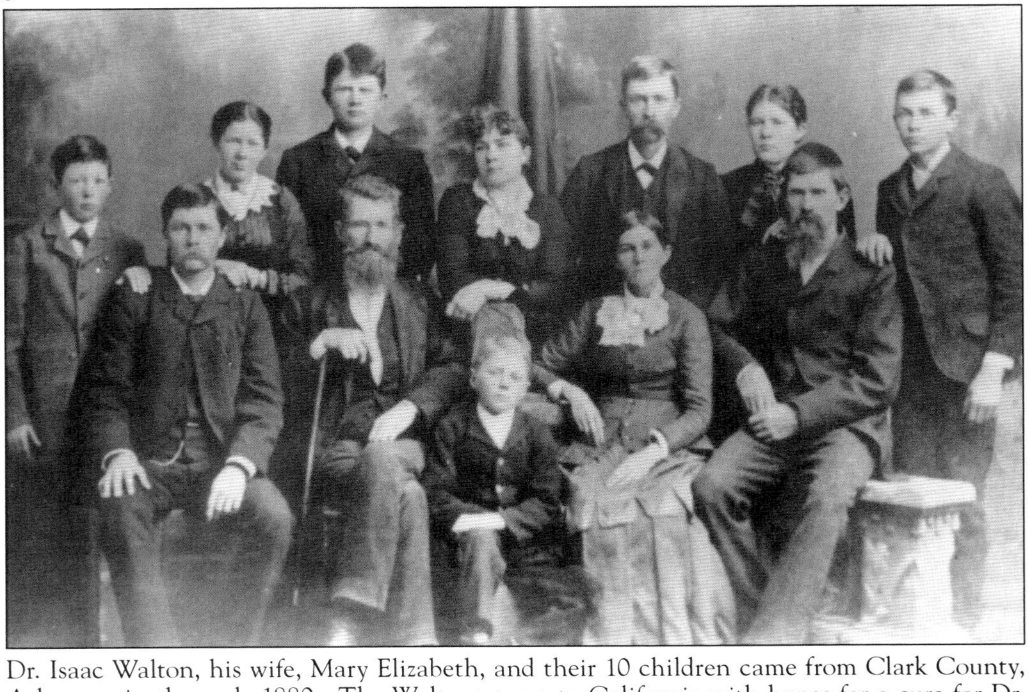

Dr. Isaac Walton, his wife, Mary Elizabeth, and their 10 children came from Clark County, Arkansas, in the early 1880s. The Waltons came to California with hopes for a cure for Dr. Walton's asthma, as well as to obtain some "homestead" land.

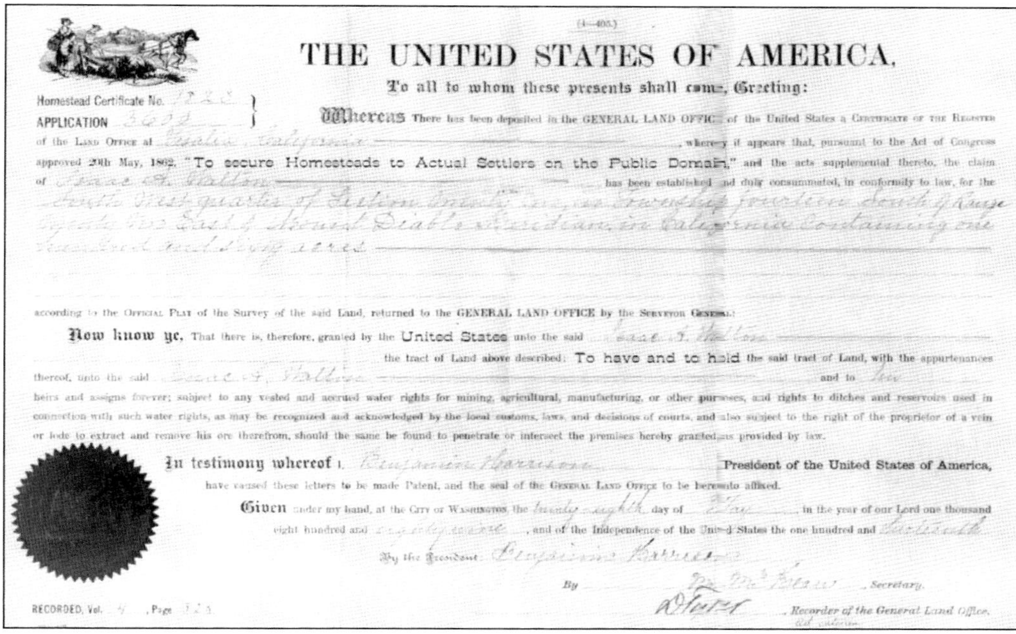

(4—405.)

THE UNITED STATES OF AMERICA,

To all to whom these presents shall come, Greeting:

Homestead Certificate No.

APPLICATION

Whereas There has been deposited in the GENERAL LAND OFFICE of the United States a Certificate of the Register of the Land Office at , whereby it appears that, pursuant to the Act of Congress approved 20th May, 1862, "To secure Homesteads to Actual Settlers on the Public Domain," and the acts supplemental thereto, the claim of has been established and duly consummated, in conformity to law, for the

according to the Official Plat of the Survey of the said Land, returned to the GENERAL LAND OFFICE by the Surveyor General:

Now know ye, That there is, therefore, granted by the United States unto the said the tract of Land above described: To have and to hold the said tract of Land, with the appurtenances thereof, unto the said and to heirs and assigns forever; subject to any vested and accrued water rights for mining, agricultural, manufacturing, or other purposes, and rights to ditches and reservoirs used in connection with such water rights, as may be recognized and acknowledged by the local customs, laws, and decisions of courts, and also subject to the right of the proprietor of a vein or lode to extract and remove his ore therefrom, should the same be found to penetrate or intersect the premises hereby granted, as provided by law.

In testimony whereof I, President of the United States of America, have caused these letters to be made Patent, and the seal of the General Land Office to be hereunto affixed.

Given under my hand, at the City of Washington, the day of , in the year of our Lord one thousand eight hundred and , and of the Independence of the United States the one hundred and

By the President:

By , Secretary.

RECORDED, Vol. , Page , Recorder of the General Land Office.

Isaac A. Walton and his family came to California with the intent to obtain homestead land. On May 28, 1889, their dream came true. This homestead grant was signed by Pres. Benjamin Harrison. The Waltons now had 160 acres of land. This area would later become the Walton Colony subdivision in Sanger. (Courtesy of James Walton.)

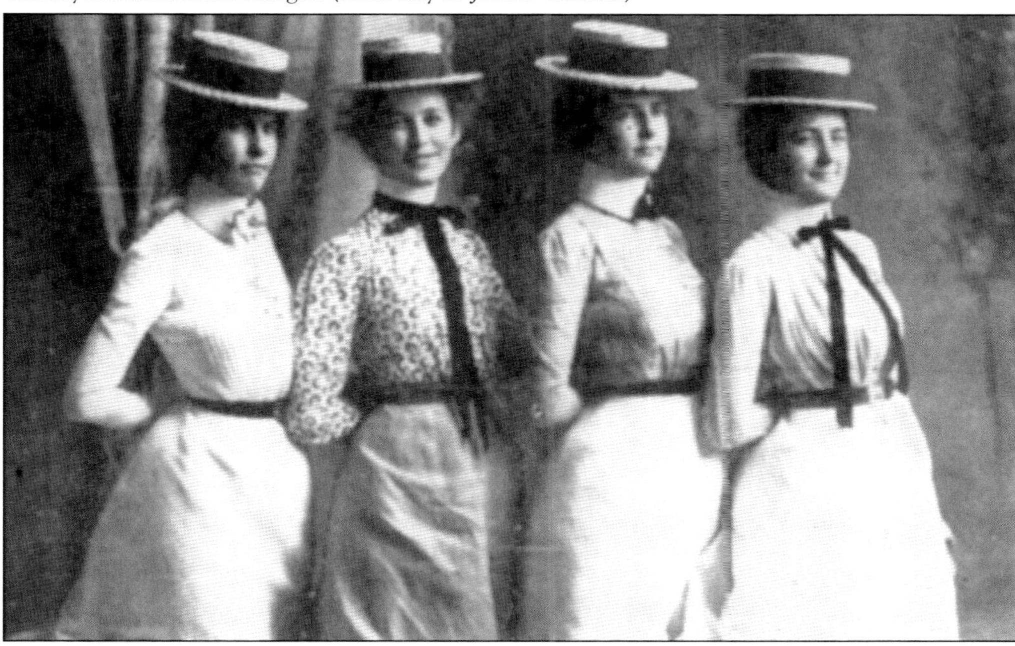

These dressed-up young ladies are being photographed wearing new straw hats. Shown here are, from left to right, Blanche Schaeffer, Annie Overholt, Maud Schaeffer, and Dollie Jack. Sanger's rapidly growing business segment had a variety of stores in which these young ladies could find the latest fashions.

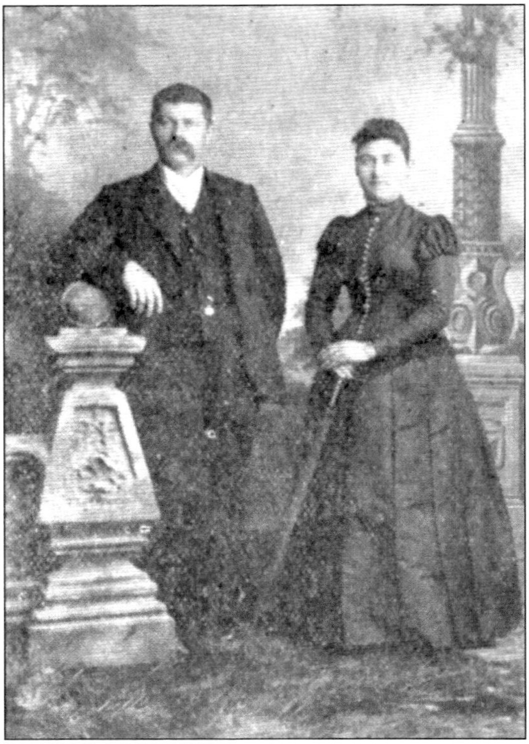

The photograph to the left shows the 1890 wedding portrait of John Thomas Walton and Augusta Hudspeth. They were the first couple to be married in the city of Sanger. Augusta was the daughter of Dr. J.D. Hudspeth, a Virginian. Walton was born in Clarksville, Arkansas, in 1880, the son of Isaac Walton. The family moved to Fresno County in 1880. He resided until his death on a ranch in the Walton Colony in the Sanger area. John is credited with being the first Sanger School trustee, first insurance agent, first real estate agent, first justice of the peace, first restaurant owner, and the first subscriber to the *Sanger Herald*. He had the first telephone installed in Sanger. He was also the first man to be married in Sanger. He and Augusta had six children who would carry on the Walton legacy, making important contributions to the community. The below photograph shows the couple on their 60th wedding anniversary.

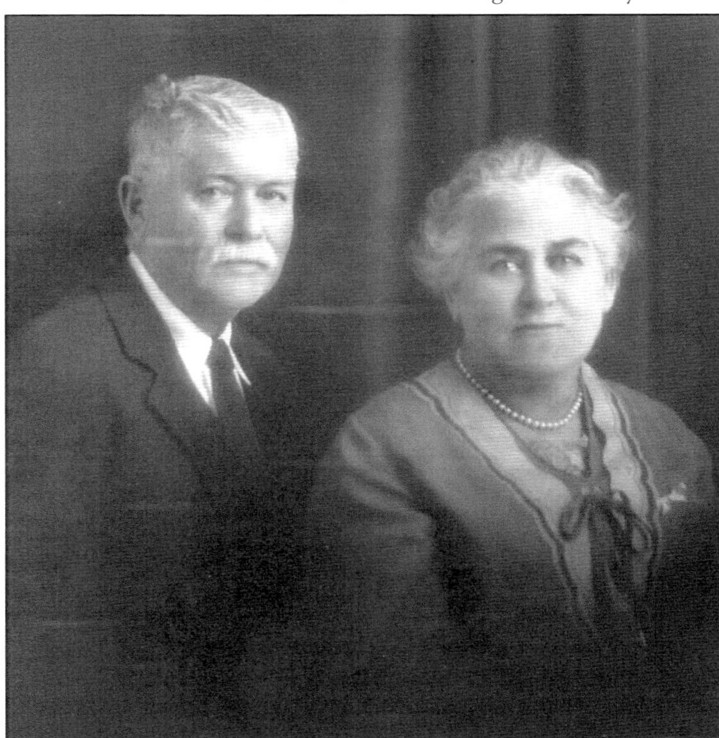

William Hazelton (right) was one of the powerful cattlemen of the pioneer days. In 1853, he invested in bottomland about four miles northeast of Centerville. Along with other cattlemen such as the Akers and the Mchaleys, he prospered on this "open land" grazing. Mary Akers (below) came from Arkansas with her parents, Henry and Delilah Akers, along with 11 brothers and sisters. The Akers settled in Centerville. With Mary's marriage to William, two major cattle families were joined. In 1866, on one of his many trips to Mexico for cattle, William Hazelton brought oranges back home, and his wife planted the seeds. From these seeds would come the orange industry in California. Two of the original trees were still standing and producing in 1963.

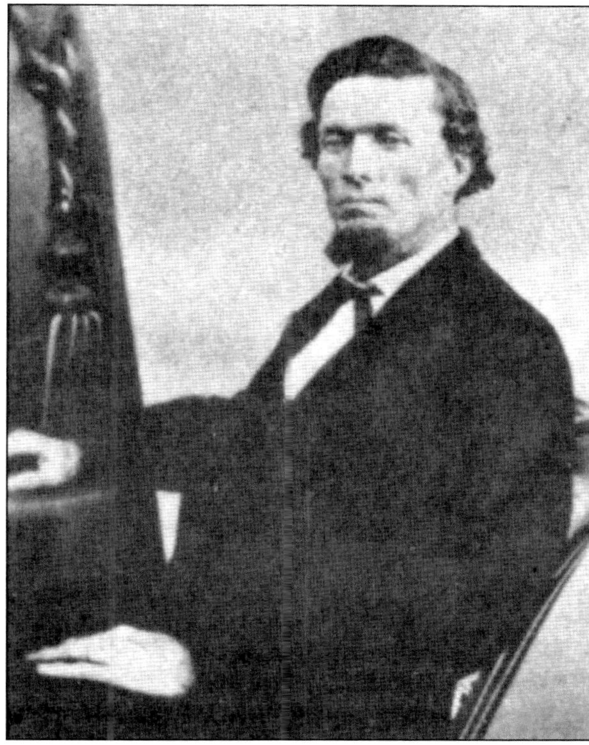

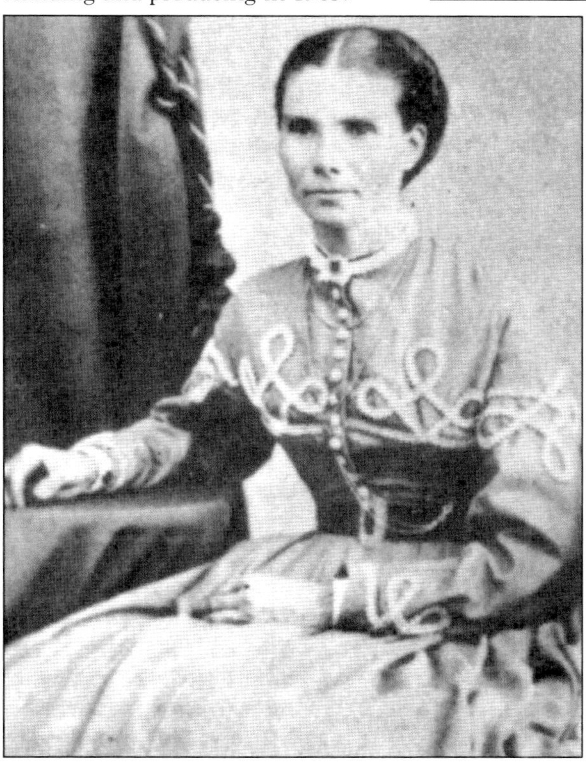

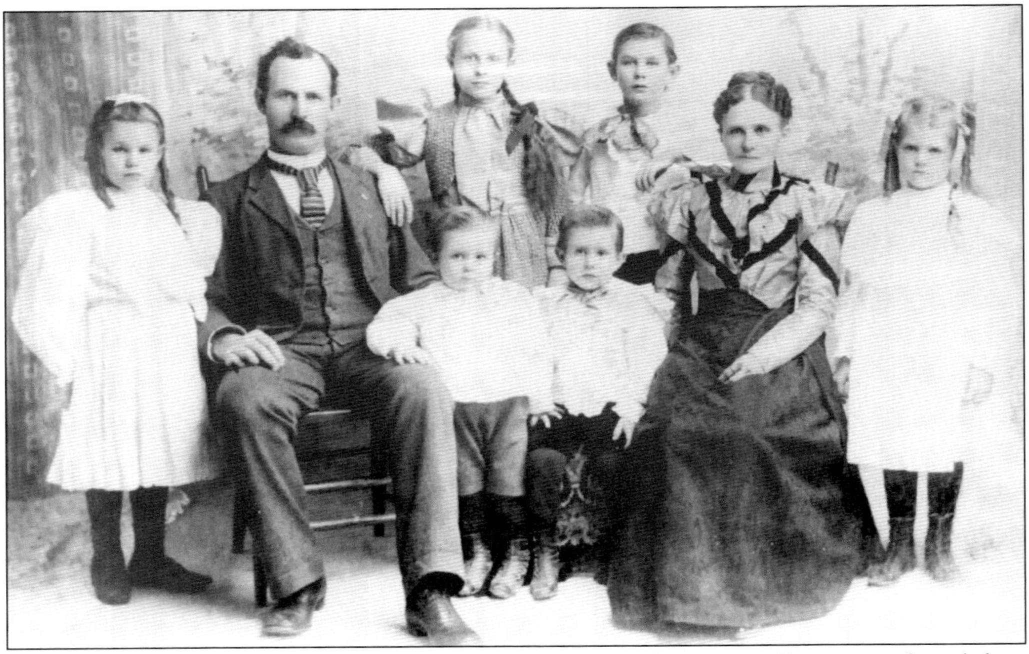

The William M. Barr family is seen in the above photograph in 1898. Shown are, from left to right, (seated) William, Edwin "Ted", Milton, and Janice C.; (standing) Mary Rob, Carrie, Jim, and Alice. William was born in Fayette County, Illinois, in 1857. He arrived in Sanger in October 1888. His first work was in the lumber and grain business. He went on to be very prosperous. The below photograph shows the Odd Fellows picnic held in April 1898. The Mistletoe Orchestra, in the front row, provided entertainment. The orchestra members are, from left to right, Mittie Rogers, Fred Rogers, George Wood, Annie Overholt, Pearl Friend, Bill Bailey, and Hattie Harrison. Other persons in the photograph are Billy Jackson, John McHaley, William Radley, Henry Rodgers, Dick McHaley, Ethel Ackers Craghead Mary Douglas Jackson, W.D. Mitchel, Wilber Grimes, Dollie Jack Ambrose, Will Douglas, Mrs. J.P. Nelson, Frank Lindsey, and A.H. Powers.

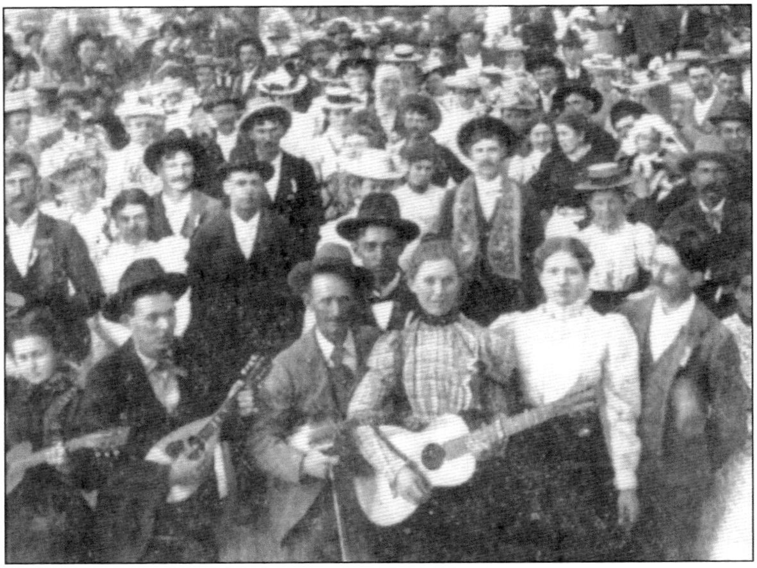

Al Elmore (pictured at right) and his brother Dick moved to Sanger in late 1888. At that time, the population was about 1,000 residents. The Elmores established the first drugstore in the same year. The store was located on the north side of Seventh Street between M and N Streets. H.F. Messer bought Elmore's Drug Store in 1900. In 1909, it was sold to Oscar A. Brehler.

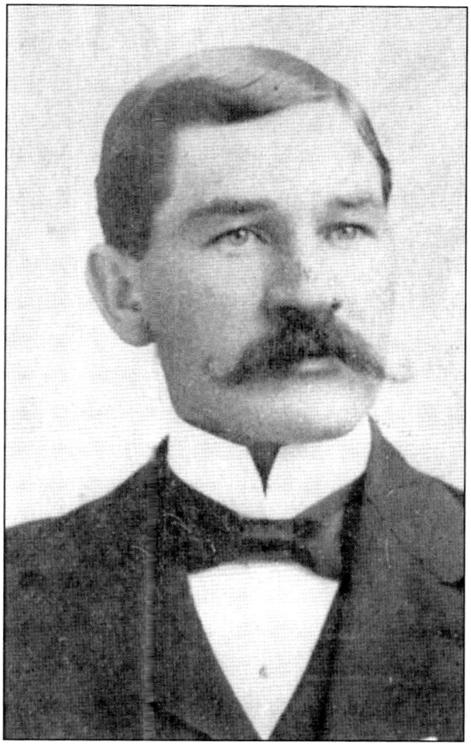

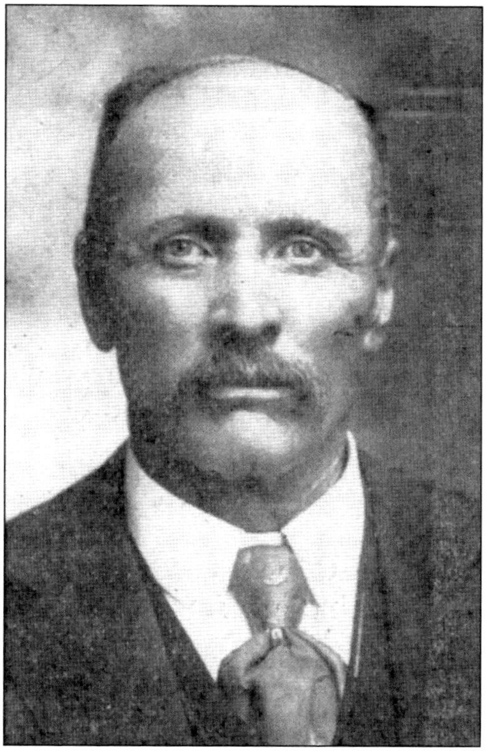

This 1901 photograph is of Warren Hill, one of the first constables in the Sanger area. He was known for his participation in the investigation of the infamous Sontag and Evans Southern Pacific train robberies, which took place between 1889 and 1892. Ironically, it was John Sontag's brother George who told the authorities that Sontag and Evans had committed the robberies.

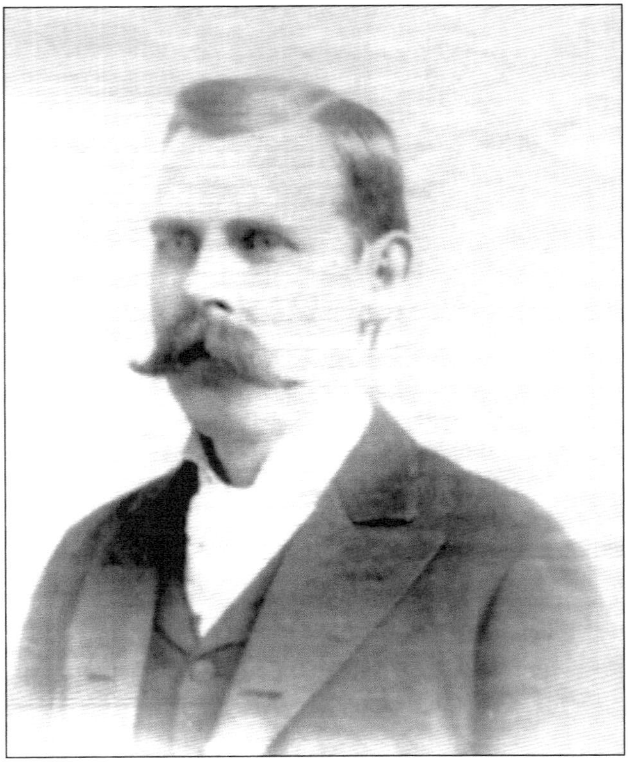

Dr. E.E. Baird was named the first mayor of Sanger. At the time, the town's population was 2,967 residents. One of the first items on the agenda was a motion to close all saloons. After a bitter and intense struggle, they were closed in 1911. Dr. Baird should also be credited with bringing a Carnegie library to Sanger.

Born in April 1872, Yasumatsu Domoto poses with his family in 1936. He and his wife, Koto, were born in Nagata Mura (Village), Naga Gun (District), Wakayama Ken (Prefecture), Japan. Yasumatsu arrived in the United States in 1899, followed by Koto in 1907. Living in Centerville, they boarded workers and grew vegetables for sale. Shown here are, from left to right, (first row) Lena, Yasumatsu, Koto, and Rebecca (wife of George); (second row) Lyman, Shig, and George.

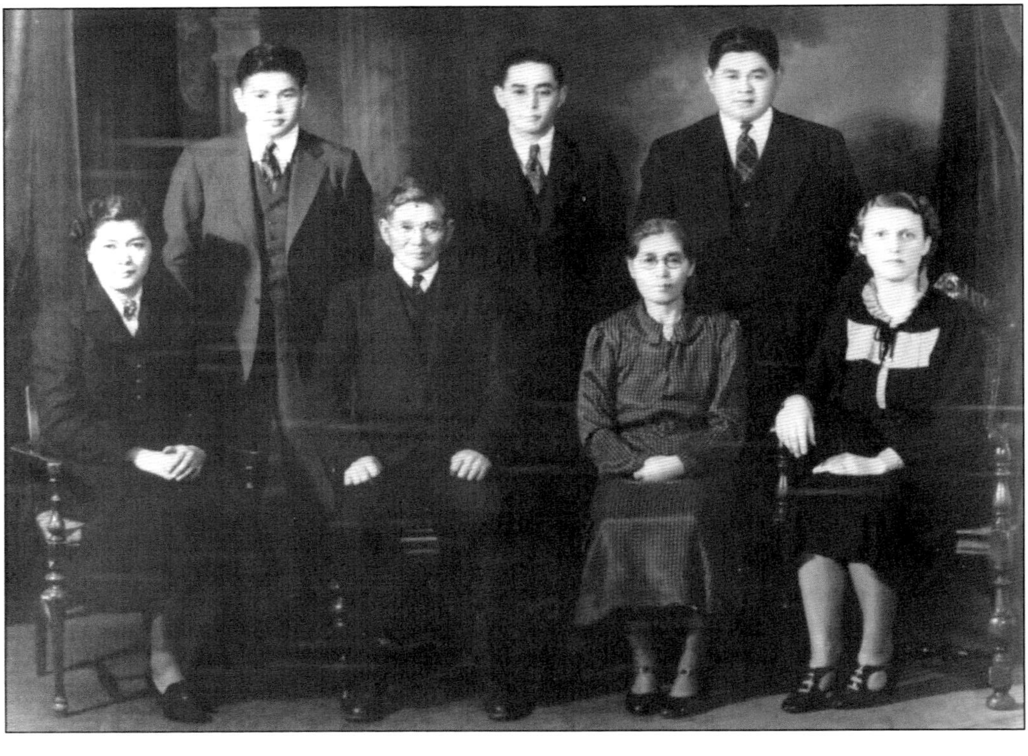

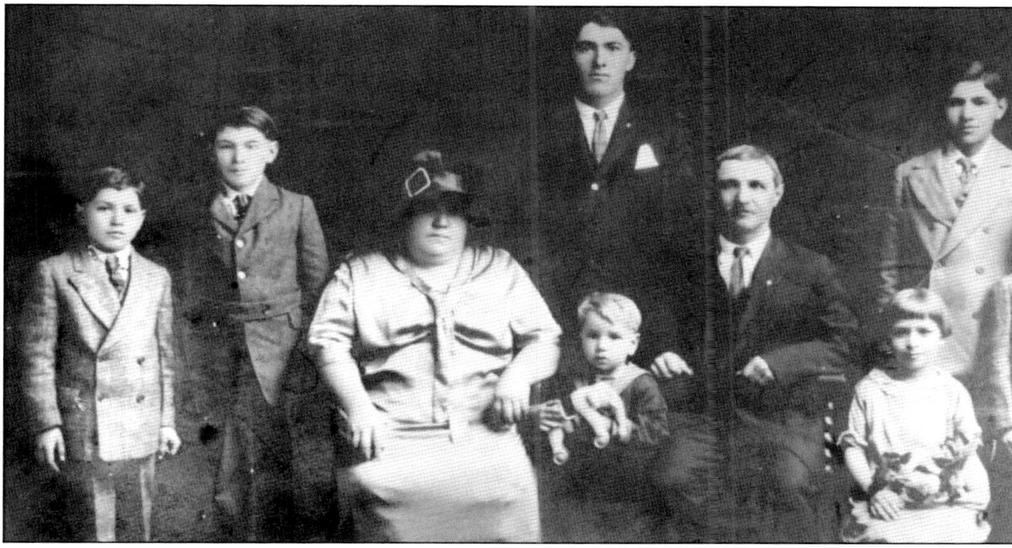

Sebastiano Merlo was born in Italy in 1877 and eventually migrated to Minkler, just east of Sanger. In 1906, he worked many years at the Louis Rusconi Ranch. He returned to Italy and married his sister-in-law Caterina and brought her and her children to Minkler. In 1923, they settled on 30 acres that Rusconi gave them on Indianola Avenue. Shown in the above photograph are, from left to right, Peter, Frank, Caterina, Lodovico (holding toy), Joseph, Sebastiano, Mary Teresa, Aldo, and Quinto (only right arm and shoulder visible). The Napoleon Moglia family also migrated from Italy and was successful in the Sanger area. Below, posing in 1915 are, from left to right, (first row) Jess, Agnes, Mabel, Jeanie, Dee, and Victor; (second row) Richard, Angelina, Neil, Napoleon, Louise, and John.

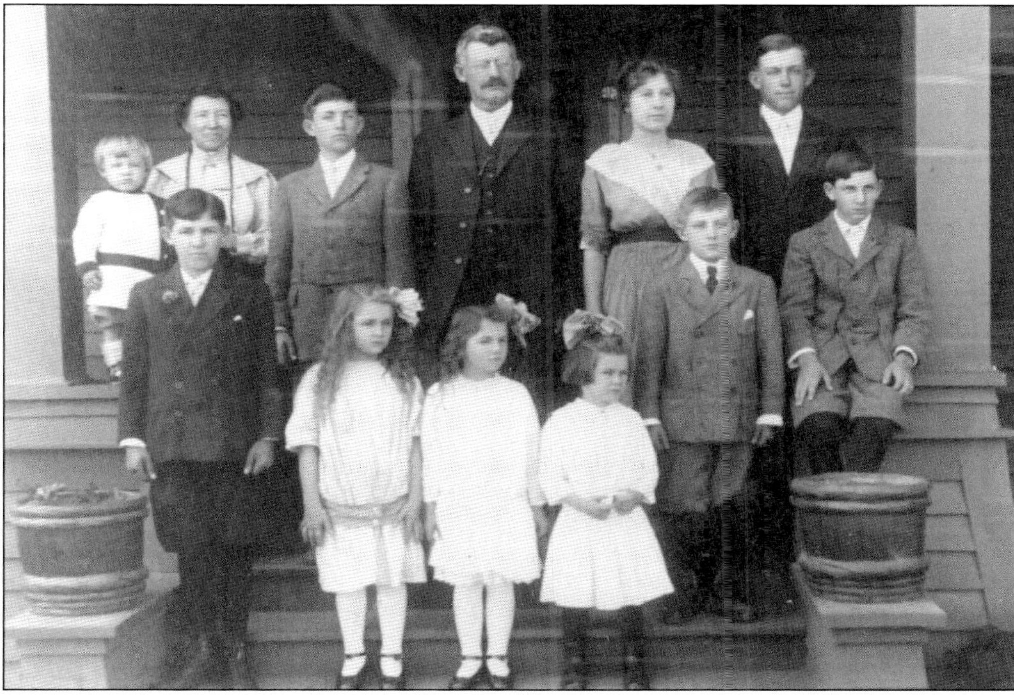

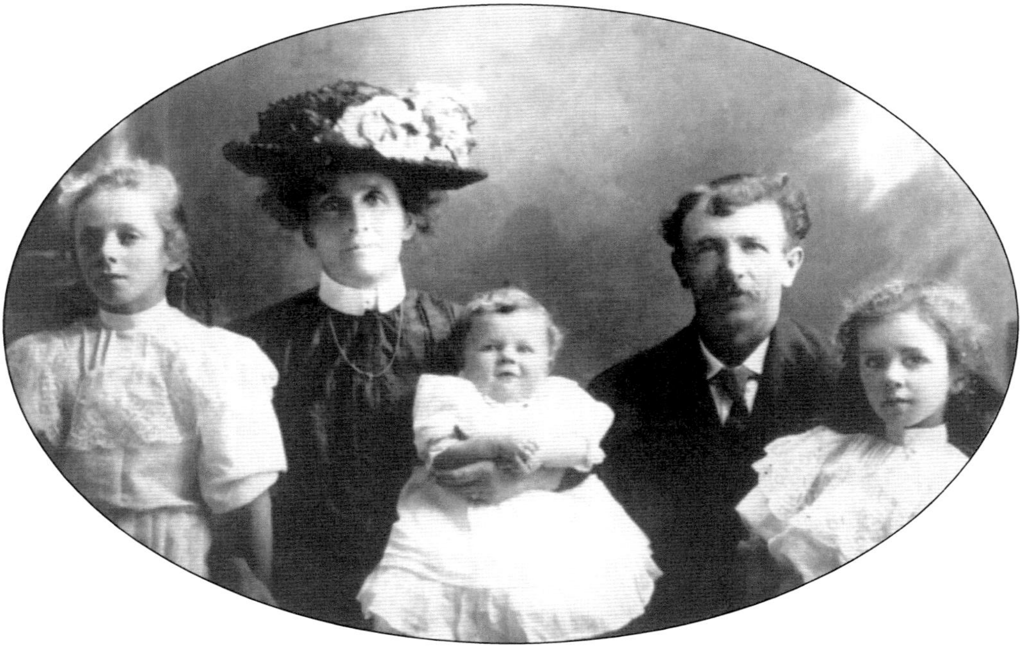

This is a 1911 photograph of the Colombero family. Pietro "Peter" and his family migrated to Sanger in 1909, and he found work with the Hume Bennett Lumber Company. The family settled on 20 acres they bought at Academy and Butler Avenues. Shown here are, from left to right, Margaret Andreis, Jennie (wife), Jennie Sassano, Pietro, and Katherine Imperatrice.

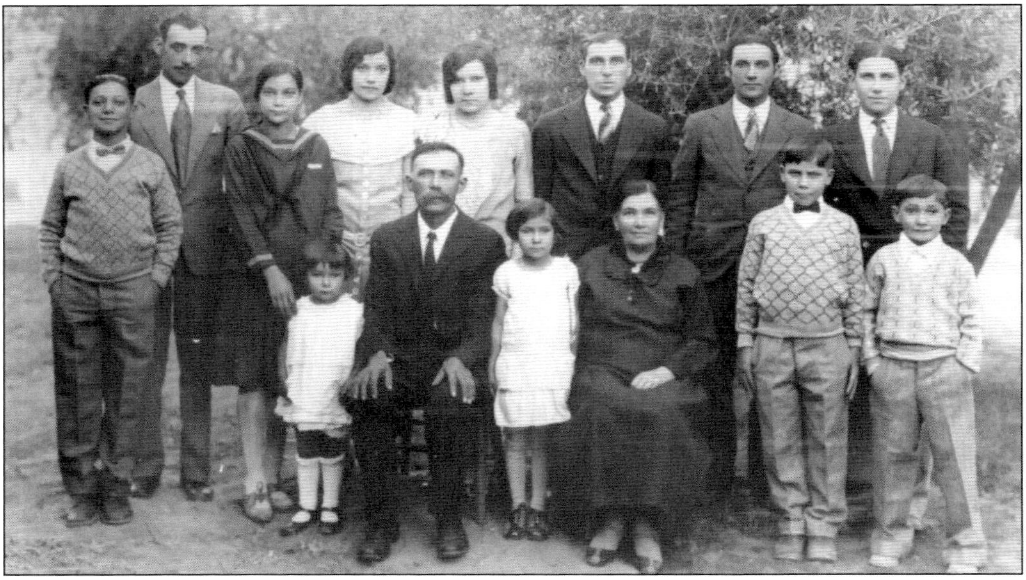

Joseph Villalobos was born in 1879 and entered California in 1899 with his wife, Frances, who was born in 1881. They arrived in Sanger in 1918. The family made a living by leasing farmland and having the whole family provide the labor. In this family photograph are, from left to right, (first row) Joseph Jr., Ruth (with bow), Lupe, Joseph Sr., Victoria, Frances, Tony, and Frank; (second row) John, Jennie, Mary, Angelo, Lawrence, and Nieve.

Four

The Lumber Era

Prior to 1888, the area that would become known as Sanger had a population of about 250 individuals, who were growing grain and raising cattle. In July 1888, the Southern Pacific Railroad built its Porterville branch along the eastern side of the San Joaquin Valley. In the 1860s, logging of the redwoods, sugar pine, yellow pine, and cedar began in the Sierras. Several mills, including the Smith Comstock Mill (1883–1889), near present-day Big Stump, were built. Due to the rough terrain, primitive lumbering methods, and lack of roads, lumbering was an extremely expensive endeavor for the small companies. The growing demand for lumber and the construction of the Southern Pacific's Porterville branch were both to have a major influence on the small community that was to become Sanger. Realizing that the California "timber belt" was virtually untouched and still in the public domain, lumber barons wasted no time in acquiring as much timberland as they could, by any means they could.

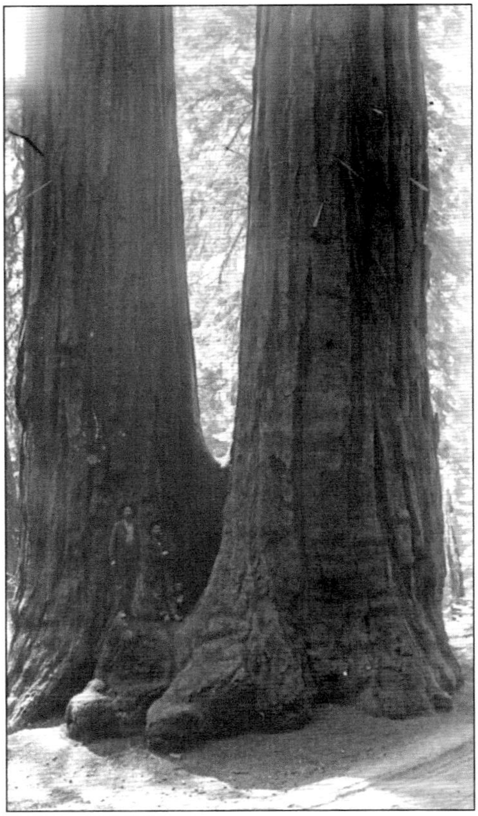

When Hiram C. Smith and Austin D. Moore saw photographs similar to this one (left), they saw potential for the large profits that could be made if these giants were felled and made into lumber. It is alleged that "representatives" of Smith and Moore canvassed the San Francisco area as well as any small towns they passed, looking for men to file claims. These men were hired to visit the area and then go to the land office to file claims. They would receive payment of between $100 to $600, depending on the quality of the timber on the particular claim. In some cases, deeds were signed over for as little as a bottle of whiskey. Shortly after the transaction, the men would then sign over the deed to Smith and Moore's representative, collect their money, and most of them would never be seen again (below).

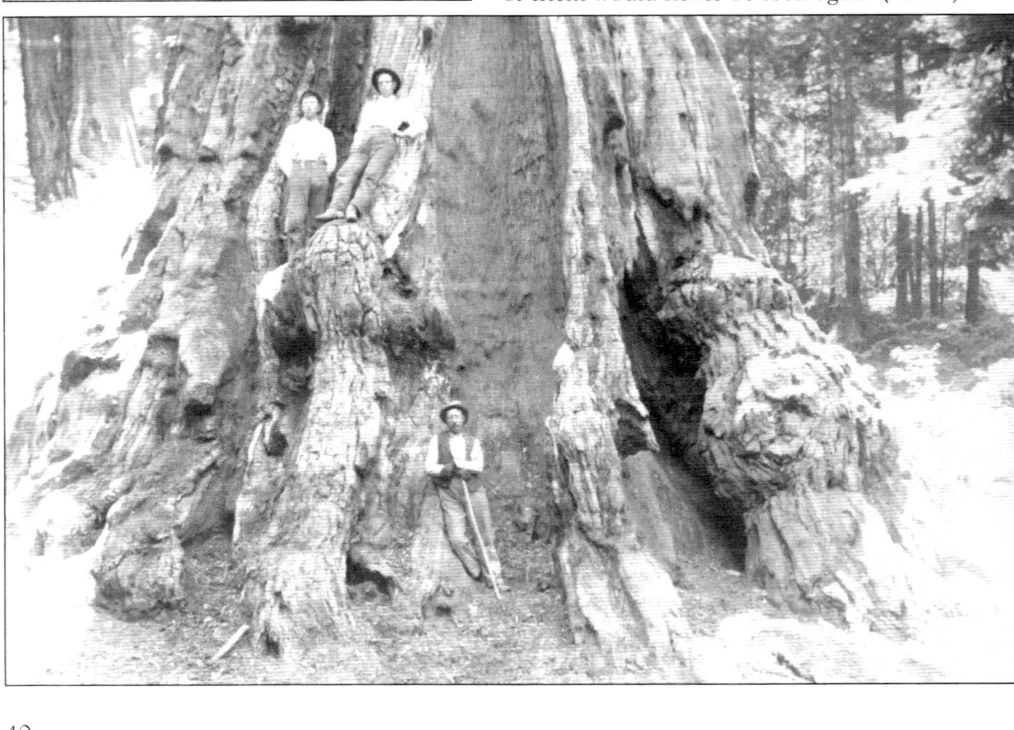

In April 1888, Smith and Moore incorporated the Kings River Lumber Company. Smith, chosen as the general manager, had planned on building a standard-gauge rail line up the Kings River Canyon to the mill site. Due to the extremely high cost of building a rail line through such rough terrain (as evident in this photograph), his plan was abandoned. Instead, it was decided that the most cost-effective method was to build a lumber flume down the canyon to the San Joaquin Valley floor.

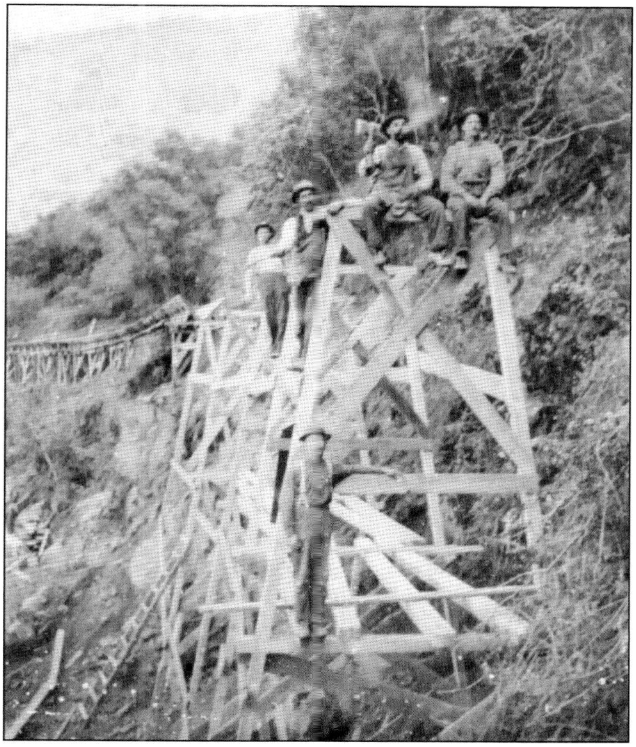

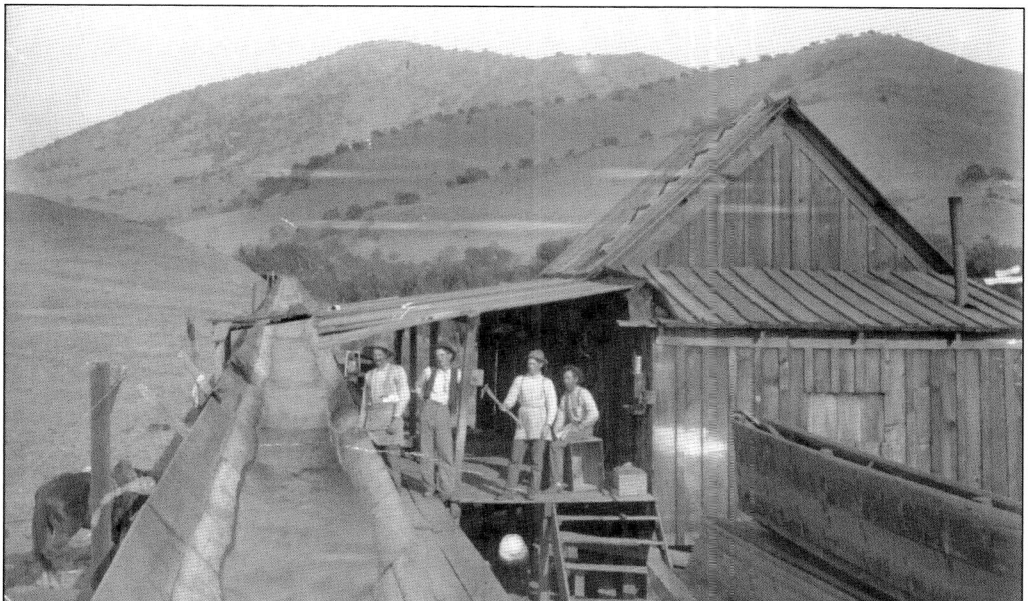

At least 11 "flume houses" were built along the original 54-mile stretch of flume. Workers known as "flume herders" lived in the houses. Using their axe-shaped picaroon tool, they walked along the flume's narrow catwalk, eliminating jams and reporting any breaks. Shown here is flume station No. 10, just down river from Piedra and across the river from present-day Avocado Lake.

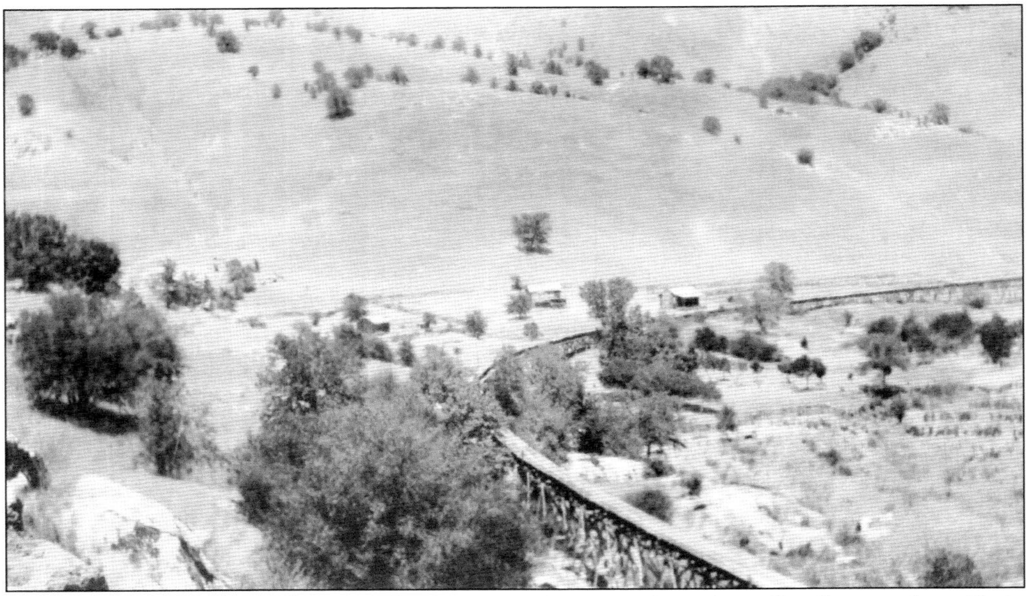

The flume ran parallel to the Kings River as it made its way from the valley floor to the mills in the forest. Homesteads and ranches were situated seen along the flume route. Most of the foothill route that the flume traveled is now covered by Pine Flat Reservoir.

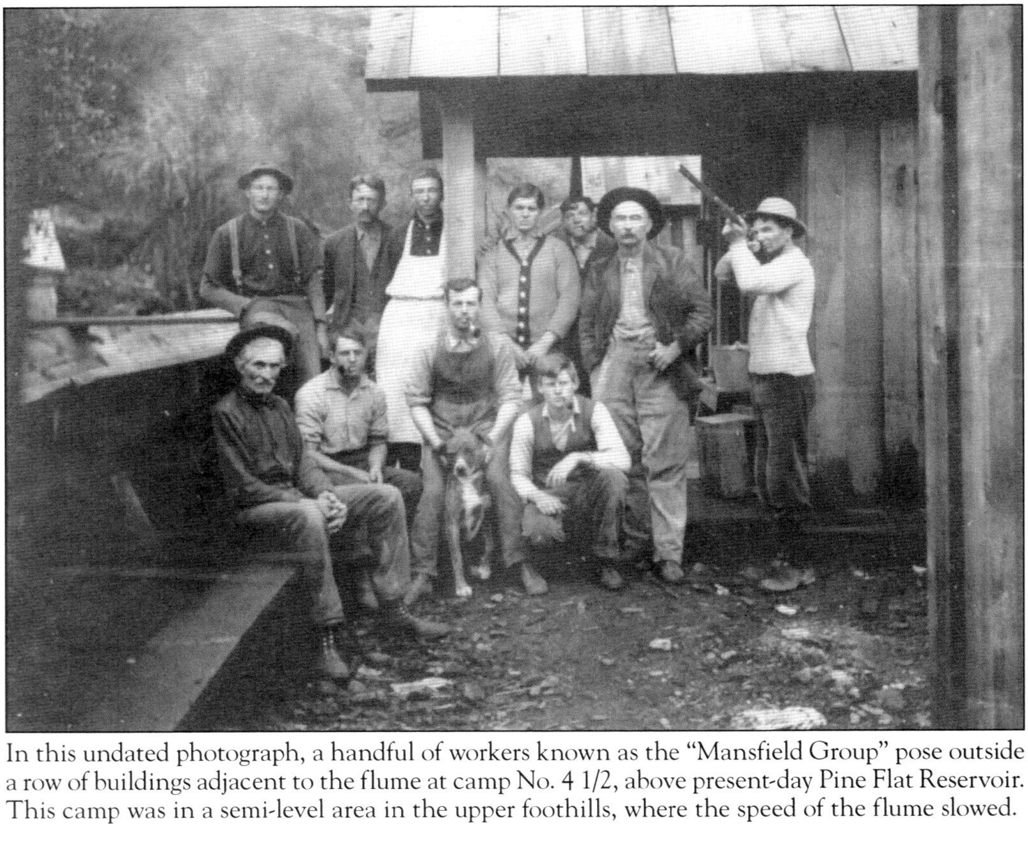

In this undated photograph, a handful of workers known as the "Mansfield Group" pose outside a row of buildings adjacent to the flume at camp No. 4 1/2, above present-day Pine Flat Reservoir. This camp was in a semi-level area in the upper foothills, where the speed of the flume slowed.

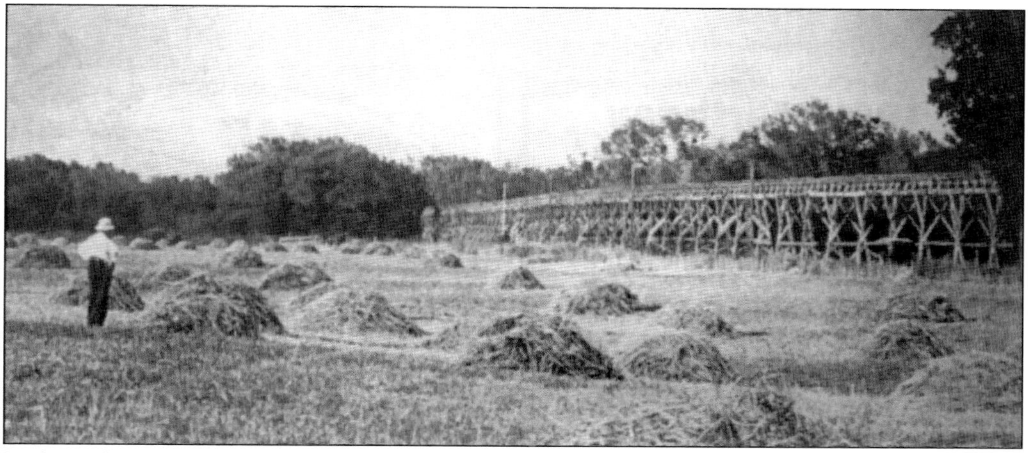

Early settlers to the Sanger area made their living raising cattle or growing wheat. A man can be seen here harvesting what appears to be a crop of wheat as the flume passes nearby on its way to the terminus in Sanger.

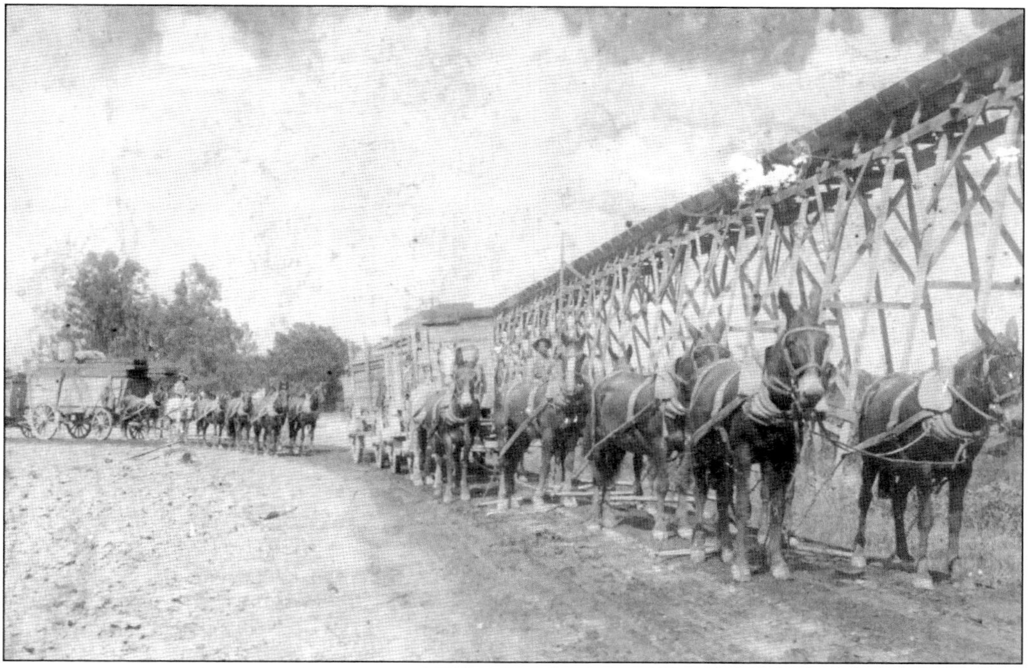

Teams of mules pull loads of lumber to the Sanger mill. The lumber that came to Sanger via the flume endured quite a beating during the long trip. Wood was cut oversized at the forest mill and then would be cut again into smaller dimensions in Sanger, hence the term "finishing mill." It was common for the finest lumber specimens to be transported to the Sanger mill by wagon.

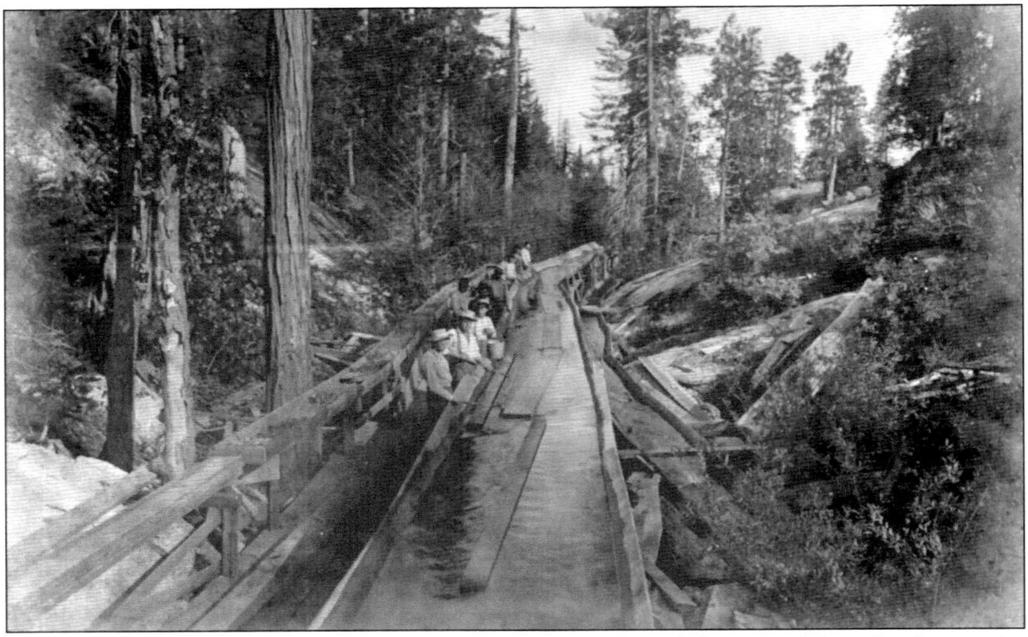

The Kings River Lumber Company chose to build a V-shaped flume to deliver lumber to the finishing mill in Sanger. This shape required much less water than the square box-style flume. If lumber started to jam up in the V-box flume, the water level would rise to the widest point of the flume, allowing the jam to clear itself in most cases.

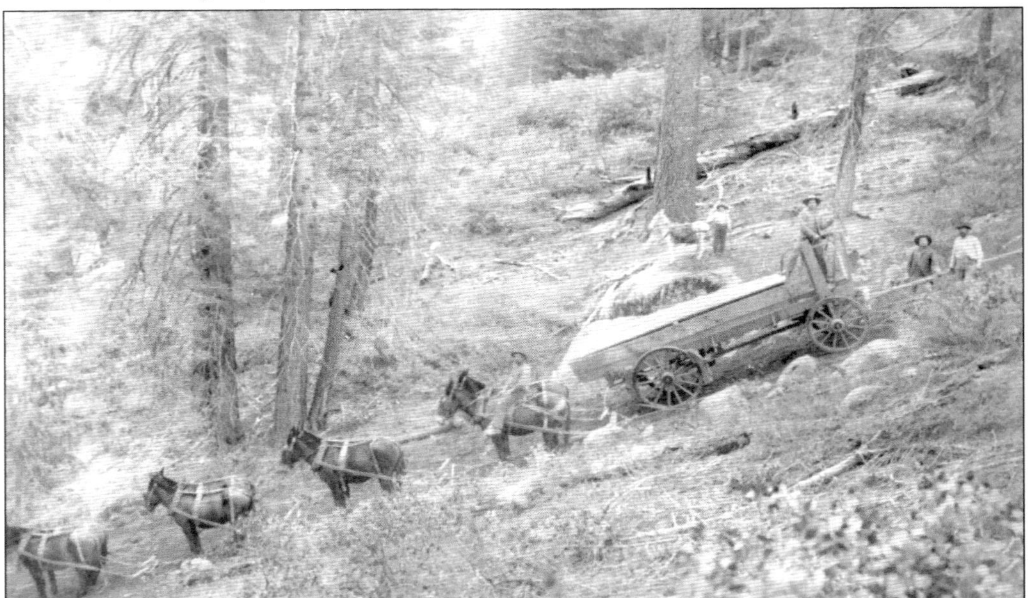

As previously stated, the rough terrain and lack of decent roads made it extremely difficult for the small lumber companies to be successful. In the early days, teams of oxen and mules were required to transport lumber supplies to the remote sites. The oxteams were also used to pull the cut logs to the mill.

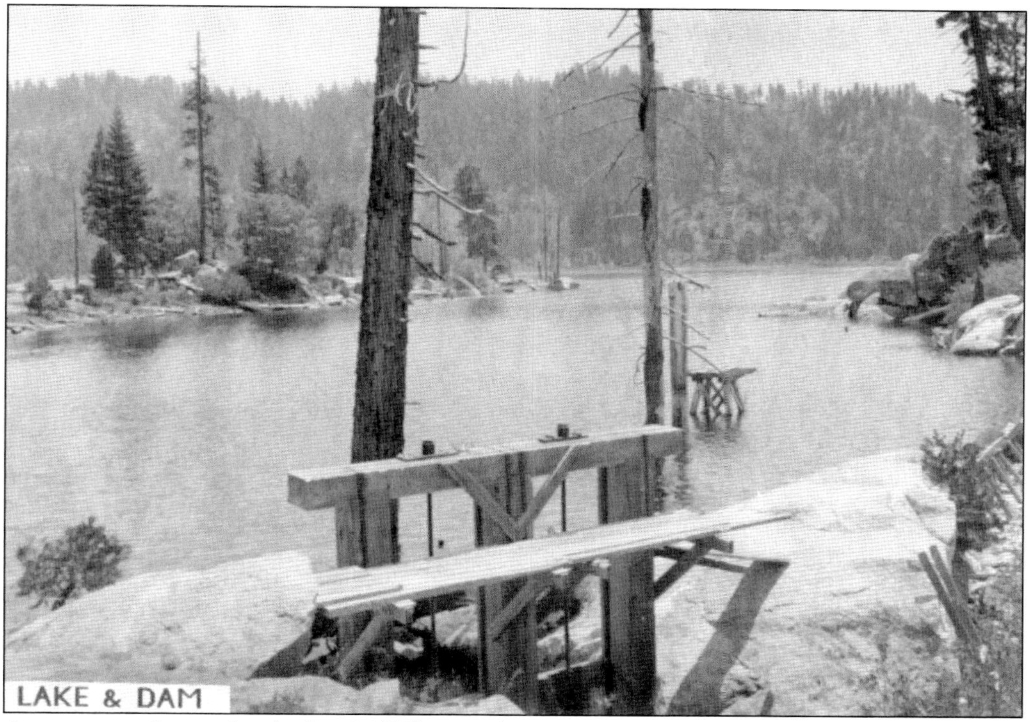

A concrete and stone dam built at Mill Flat Meadow provided water for the flume. Dam construction began in the summer of 1889, and it is said that the contractor utilized Chinese labor to complete the project. The water supply for the flume to Sanger was turned on as workers began their day, and then turned off at the end of the shift.

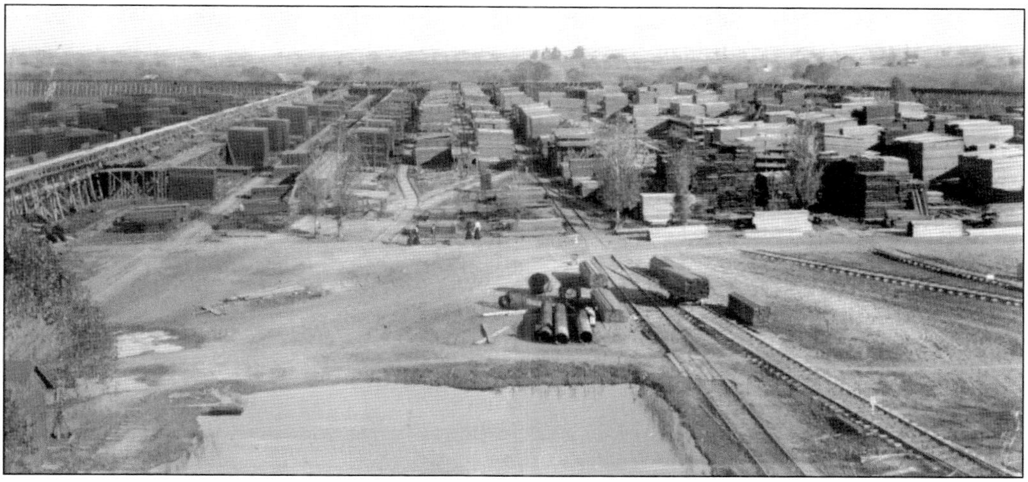

Sanger was selected mainly because it offered 65 acres of land and all the right-of-ways needed to build the terminus and associated mill. On August 29, 1889, Smith and Moore accepted Sanger's offer. The lumber company immediately began constructing the terminus buildings. The mill was just below the pond, near the drying yard shown here. All rough-cut lumber was finished for retail sale in a series of buildings located at the mill.

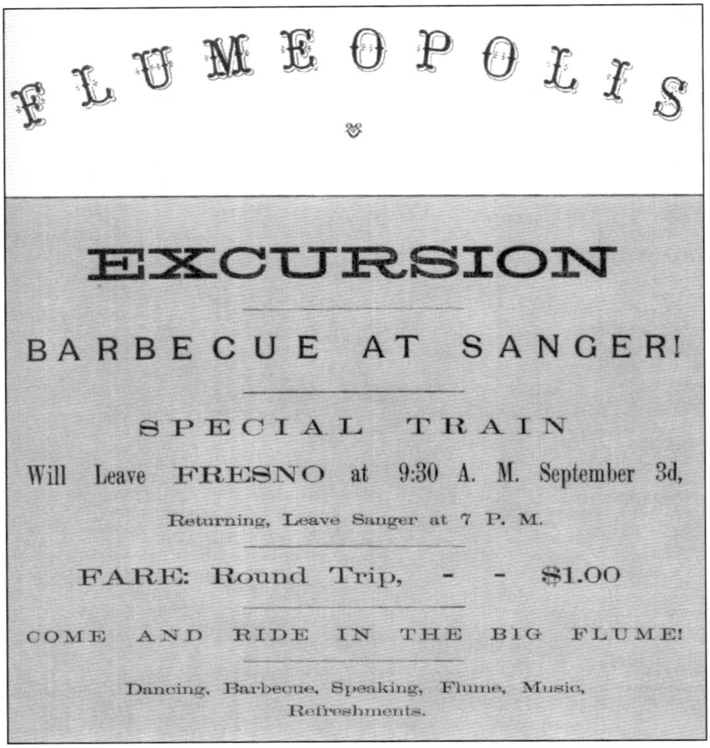

FLUMEOPOLIS

EXCURSION

BARBECUE AT SANGER!

SPECIAL TRAIN

Will Leave FRESNO at 9:30 A. M. September 3d,

Returning, Leave Sanger at 7 P. M.

FARE: Round Trip, - - $1.00

COME AND RIDE IN THE BIG FLUME!

Dancing, Barbecue, Speaking, Flume, Music, Refreshments.

Construction of the flume was finished in plenty of time for the celebration on September 3, 1890, recognizing the completion of the initial 54 miles of the flume. "Flumeopolis" was a play on the word *metropolis*. It is as if the planners knew that a city would arise at the end of the flume. And so it did!

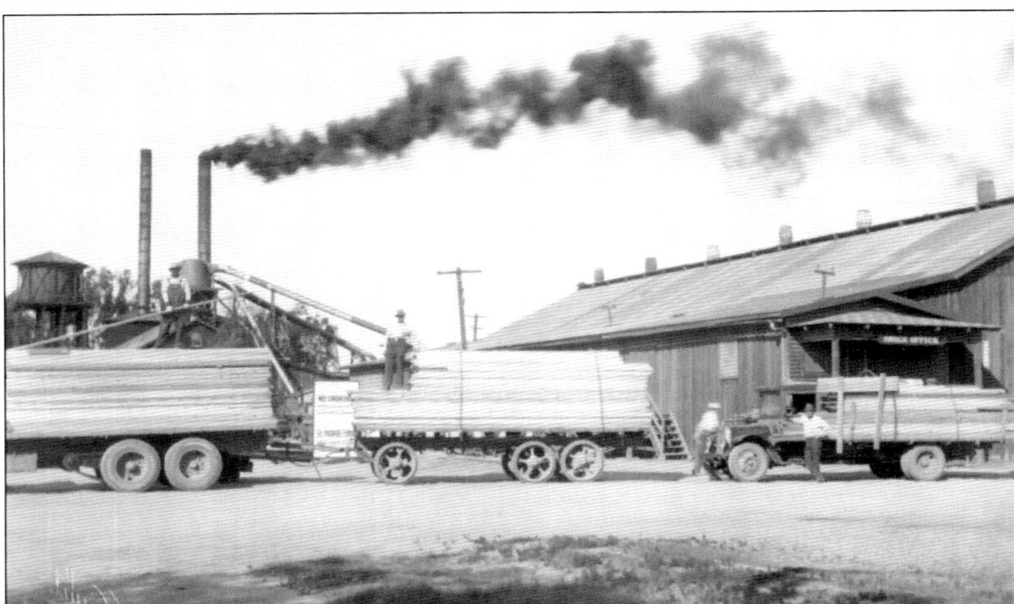

A load of lumber is seen here near the shook office. Shook was a set of parts for assembling barrels or packing boxes. Note the barrels on the roof. Great caution was used to maintain the safety of the lumber, evident by the sign between the truck and trailer on the left. It reads in both English and Spanish, "No Smoking—Violation of this rule will be grounds for dismissal."

In order to maintain a constant rate of descent over extremely difficult terrain, trestles were needed to span the gorges and valleys. Here, a crew uses a crane to lower heavy beams to the workers below. It was difficult and hazardous work. During the rainy season, flash floods were known to wash away all of their hard work.

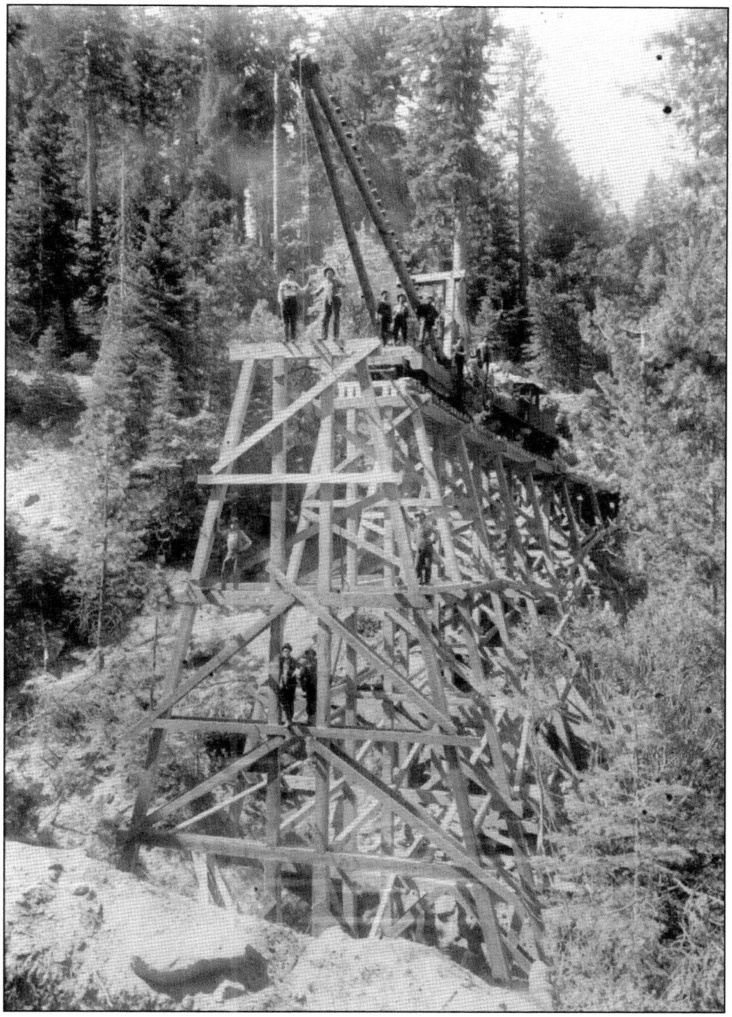

There was an immediate impact on the value of land in Sanger. Seemingly overnight, lots that had sold for $300 now sold for $4,000. The view in this 1890 photograph is looking east down Seventh Street. The four structures, beginning at left, are the J.S. Filloon residence, a blacksmith shop, the water tower, and a livery stable. The French Hotel is the building on the far right. (Courtesy of the *Sanger Herald*.)

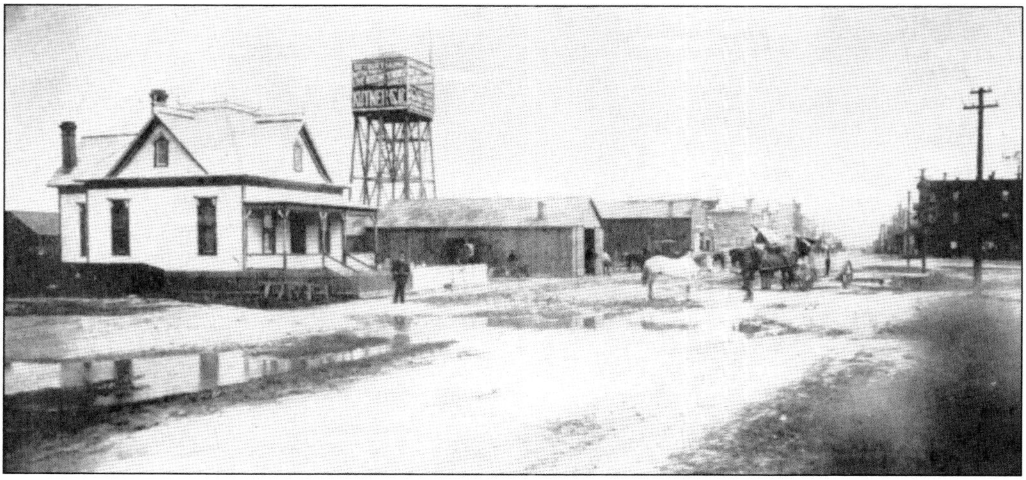

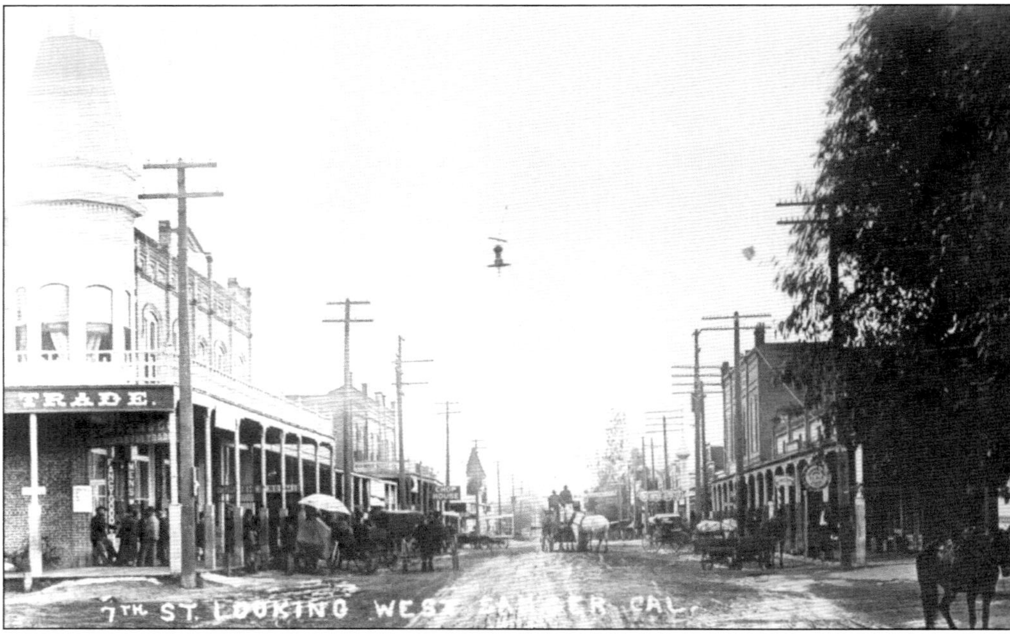

The population exploded, from 250 to 1,000 people. The railroad and lumber company were a boon to the community. This view is looking west down Seventh Street from N Street. Brehler Block can be seen on the right. The office of the *Sanger Herald* is located on the left, just west of the café sign.

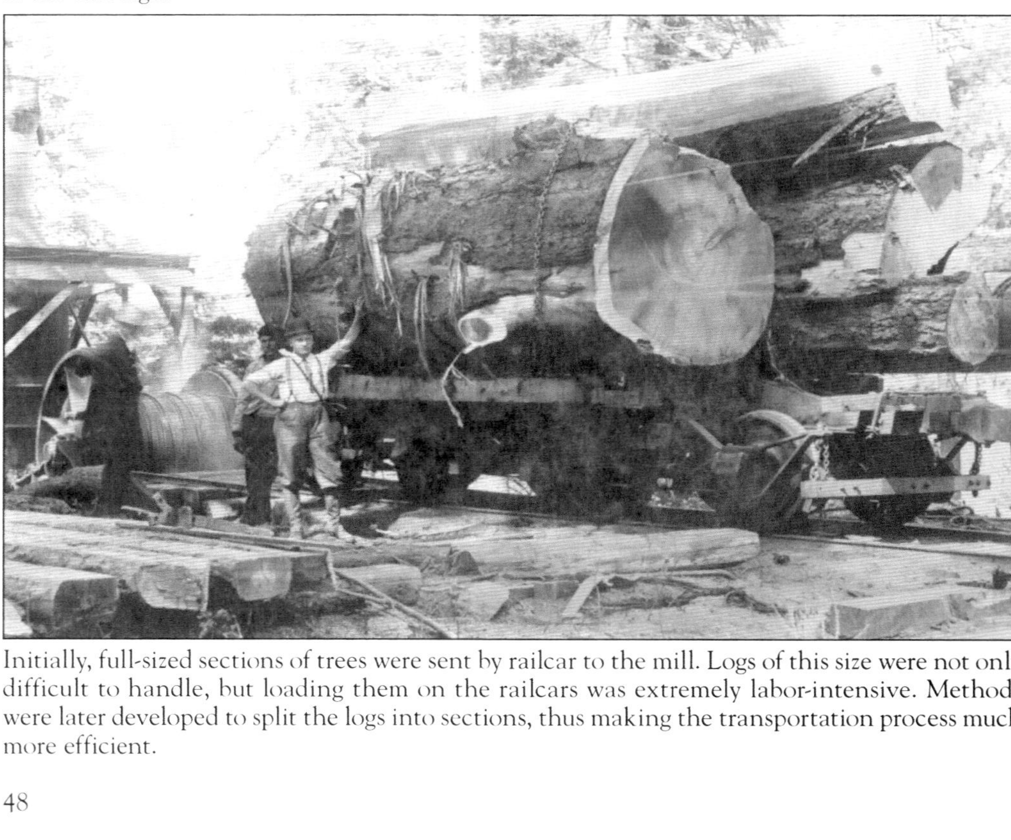

Initially, full-sized sections of trees were sent by railcar to the mill. Logs of this size were not only difficult to handle, but loading them on the railcars was extremely labor-intensive. Methods were later developed to split the logs into sections, thus making the transportation process much more efficient.

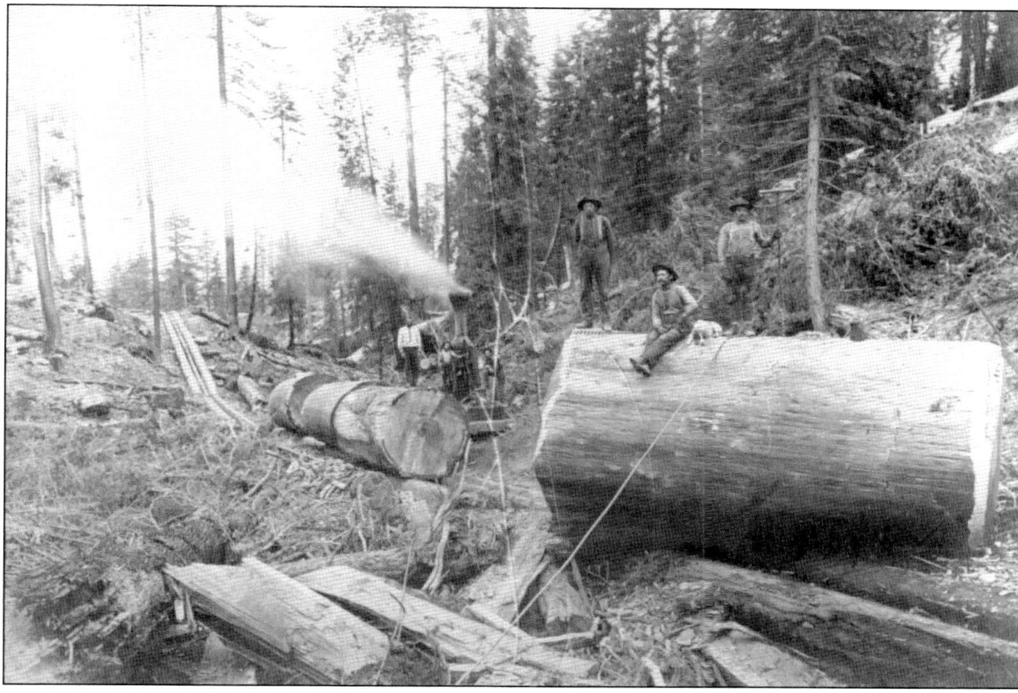

A crew is shown taking a break on a large redwood, near Millwood. Even after being cut into smaller sections, logs were often still too big to be moved by chutes or railcars. It was often necessary for the crews to drill strategically placed holes in the logs. The holes would then be filled with black powder, and the logs would be split into smaller sections after the blast.

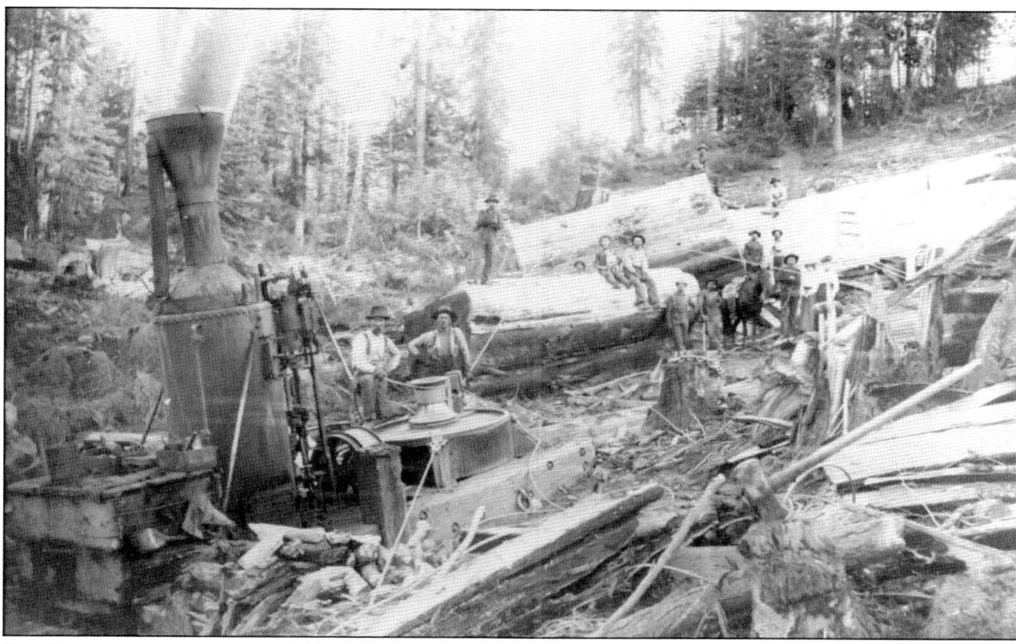

Donkey steam engines would be used to pull the sections of logs to the staging areas so they could be transported by chute or rail to the nearby mills.

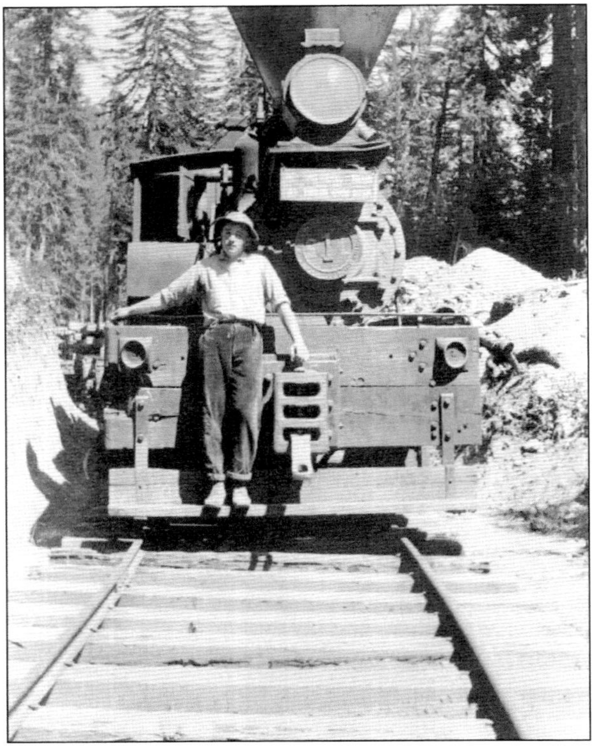

In the early days of logging, many attempts were made to replace animals with locomotives as a better way to haul logs. Unfortunately, existing locomotive models, not designed for logging, would lose traction on the slightest grades. However, upon introduction of the Shay engine in the 1870s, lumber crews finally had an engine that could handle the grades. Although very slow in speed, the Shay had tremendous pulling power and was geared to be used in logging. Rail spurs soon expanded throughout the forest terrain in order to bring lumber from distance locations. The first engine to be used in the Millwood area was called the *Sequoia*. It should be noted that, since no tracks ran from the valley to Millwood, all trains had to be completely dismantled and transported to the mountains by wagon, then reassembled.

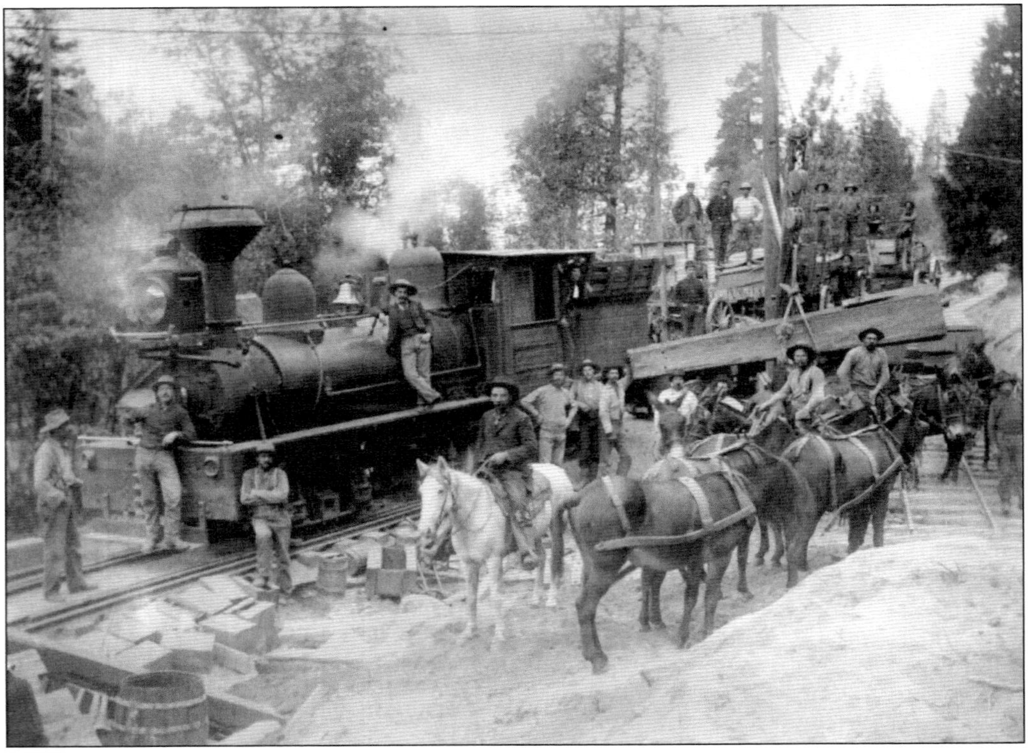

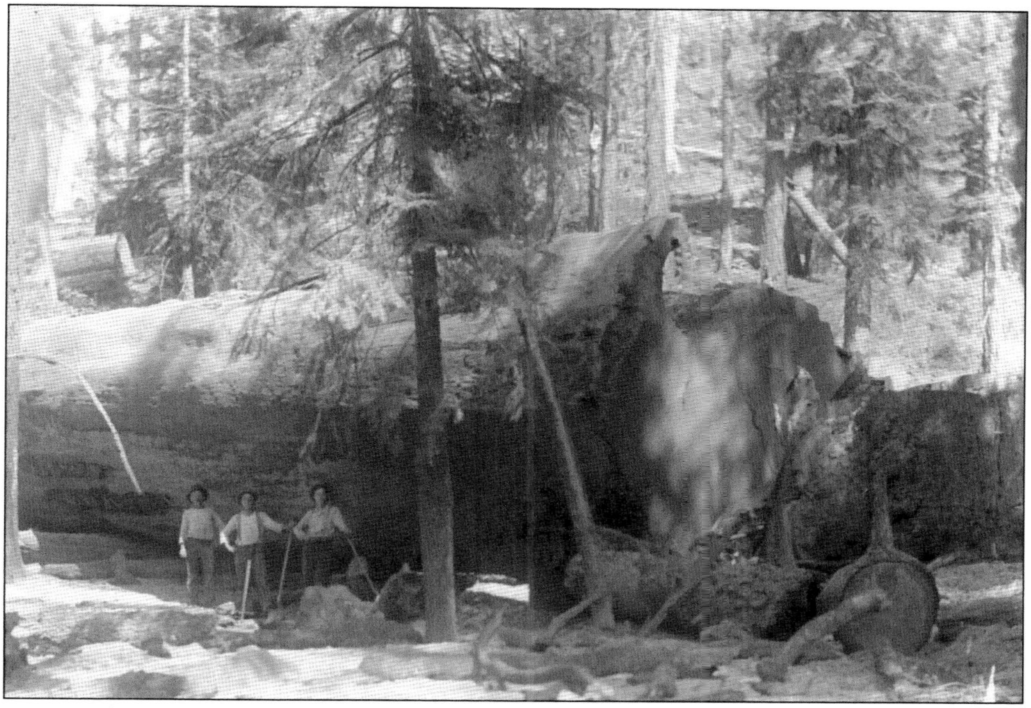

In 1884, the Kings River Lumber Company reorganized into the Sanger Lumber Company. It then shut down the Millwood operation in order to concentrate on logging the redwoods in the Converse Basin (above). The falling tree (right) is classified as a *Sequoiadendron giganteum*, the Sierra redwood or giant sequoia. They are the largest known living single organisms, and specimens can live up to 3,200 years or longer. Most of them live along a 260-mile stretch of the Sierra Nevada Mountains. They grow at elevations between 3,000 and 8,000 feet. They are easy to recognize because of their cinnamon-red bark. On older trees, this bark may be more than a foot thick. They have blue-green leaves and small yellowish pinecones measuring from one to three inches. Because of their girth and height, it was difficult and wasteful to cut these trees down.

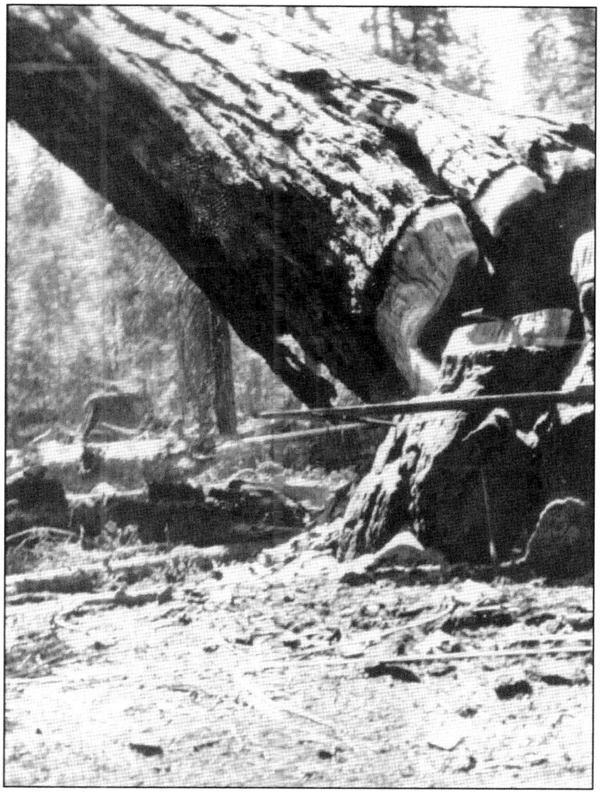

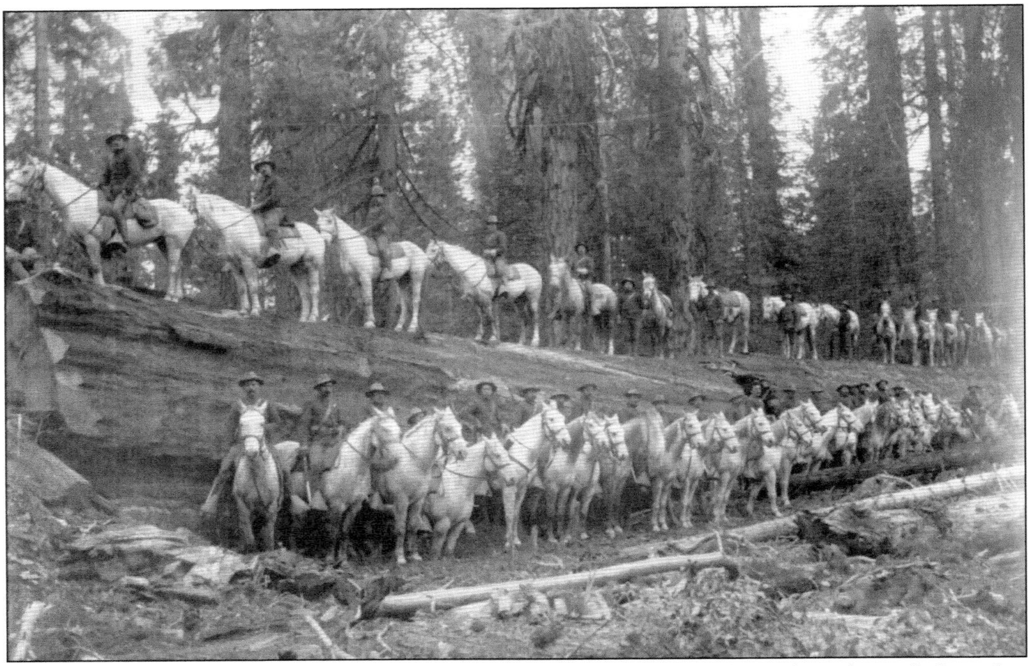

Many photographs were taken to demonstrate the massive size of the redwoods, including this 1895 photograph. Troop 1 of the 4th Calvary can be seen posing on a recently felled giant.

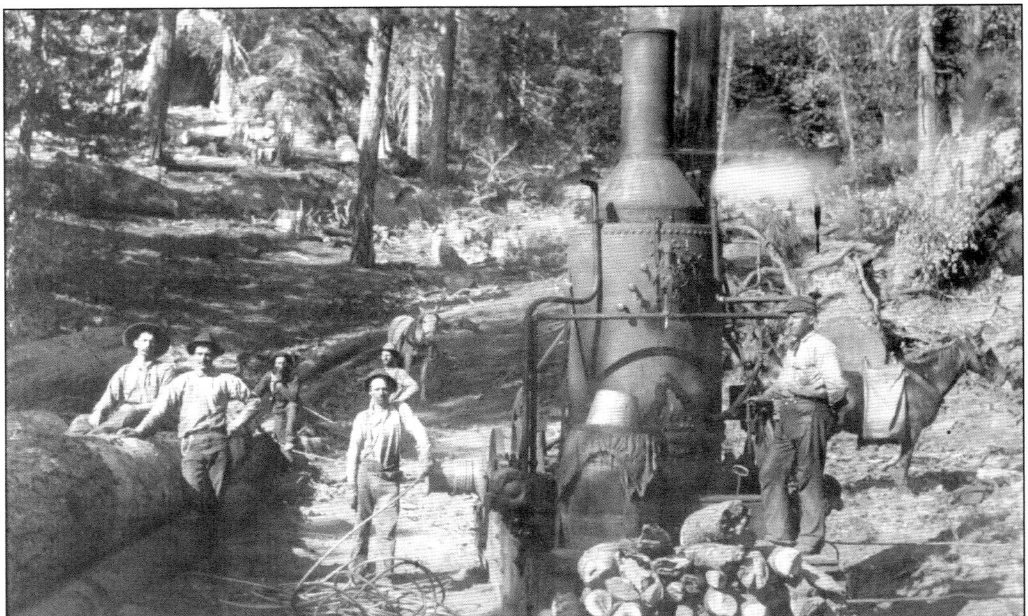

The donkey engine, invented by John Dolbeer, replaced the work of animal teams by 1890. The engine, powered by steam, would turn a drum upon which rope could be coiled. Soon, rope was replaced by cable, making it possible to pull logs and railcars from long distances. In order to be moved, the large donkey steam engines were mounted on skids. Leon Akers can be seen at left, sitting on the log.

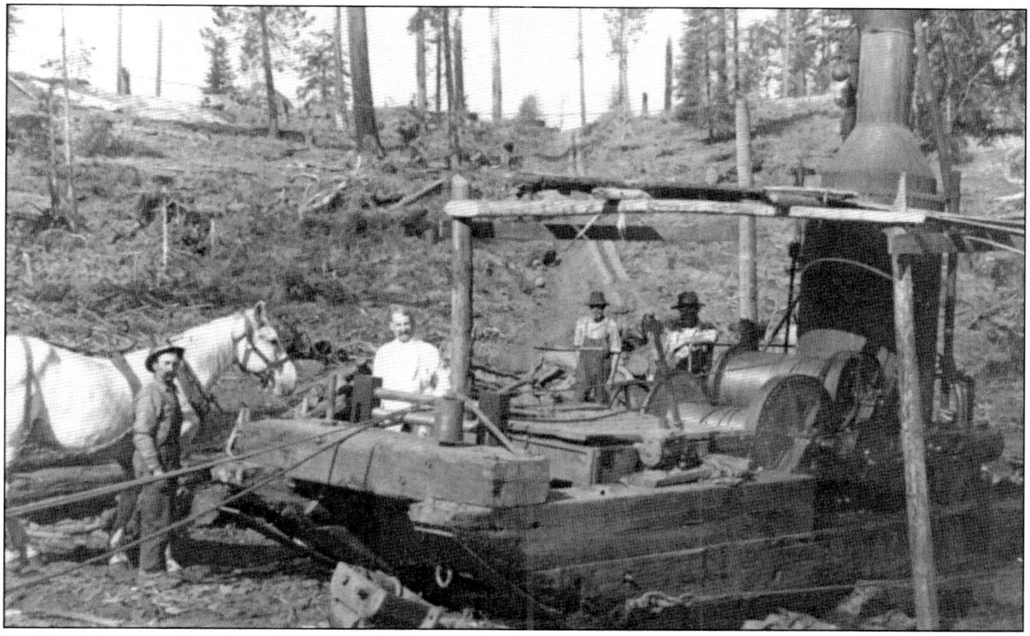

Cables were hooked onto distant trees, and the donkey would pull itself across the forest floor. Here, Leon Akers can be seen standing next to the white horse near the Millwood/Converse Basin area. In the background is a log chute, which allowed the donkey engine to move logs from one area to another.

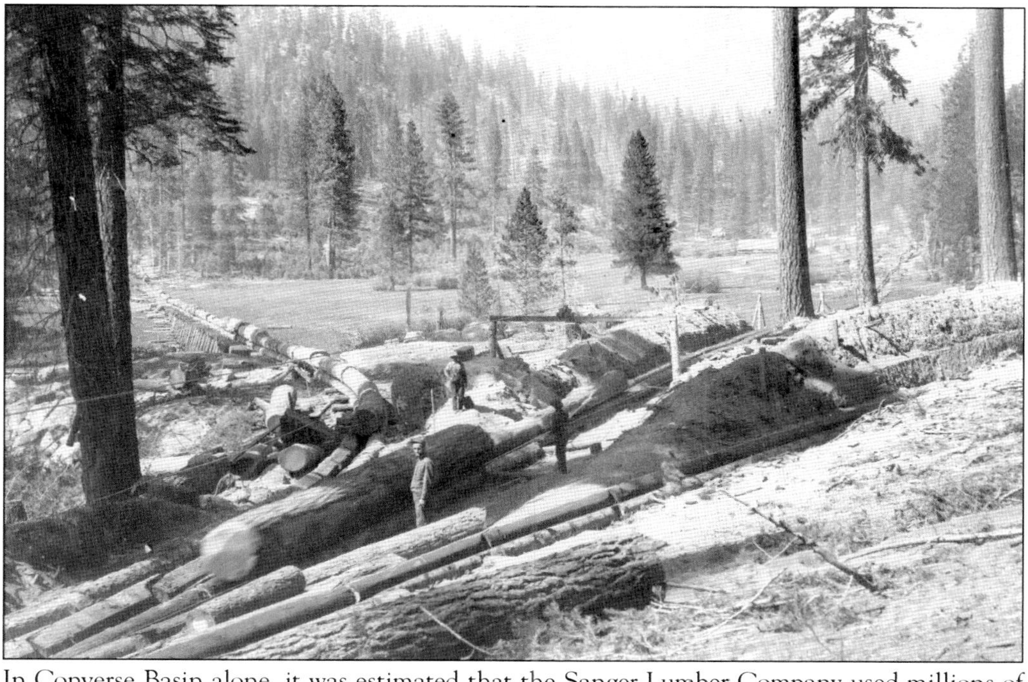

In Converse Basin alone, it was estimated that the Sanger Lumber Company used millions of board feet of lumber just to make the miles of chutes. One of the chutes in the Millwood area was a mile in length. In the firm's early days, the lumber company itself was its biggest customer.

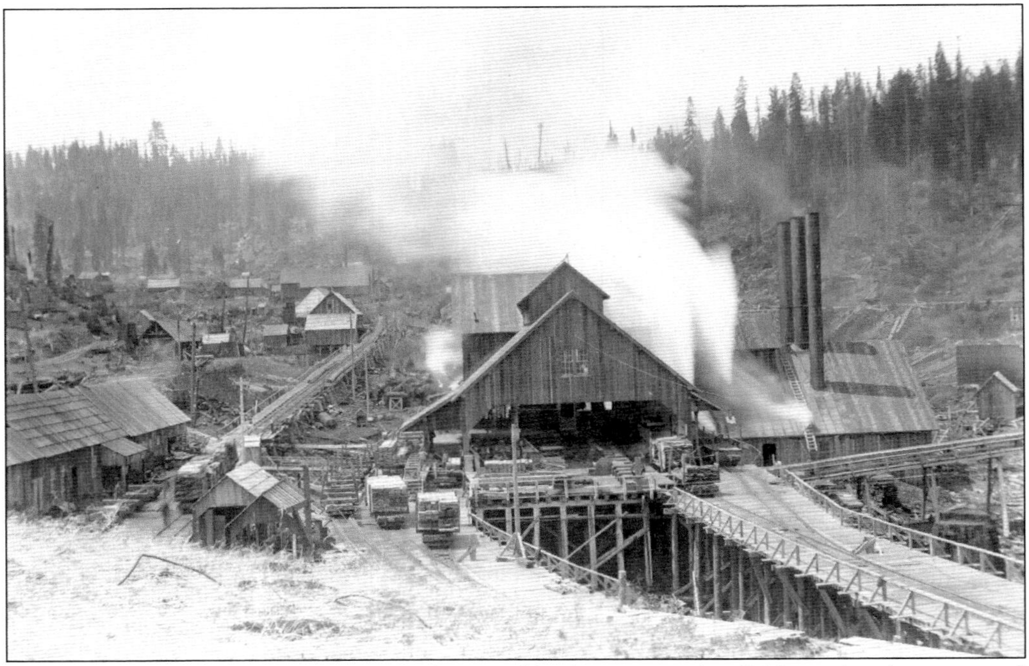

After the first Converse Basin mill was destroyed by fire, a second mill (shown here) was erected in early 1906. It featured a pair of 90-foot band saws, which gave the mill a daily output of 175,000 board feet. Workers can be seen loading railcars with rough-cut lumber and preparing loads to be sent to the flume staging area, where it would soon be sent down to Sanger.

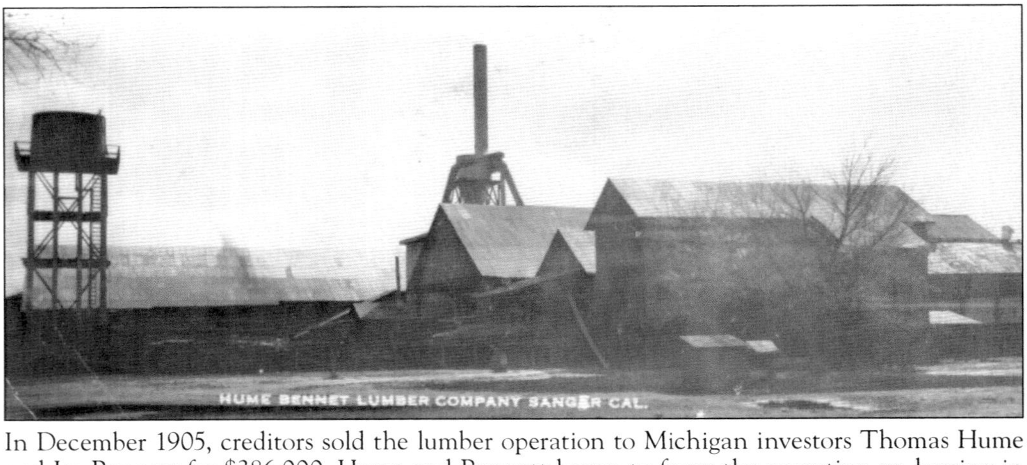

In December 1905, creditors sold the lumber operation to Michigan investors Thomas Hume and Ira Bennett for $386,000. Hume and Bennett began to focus the operation on logging in Indian Basin and then, in 1908, the Long Meadow area. The company continued to cut the giant redwood trees until only a select few remained in the area.

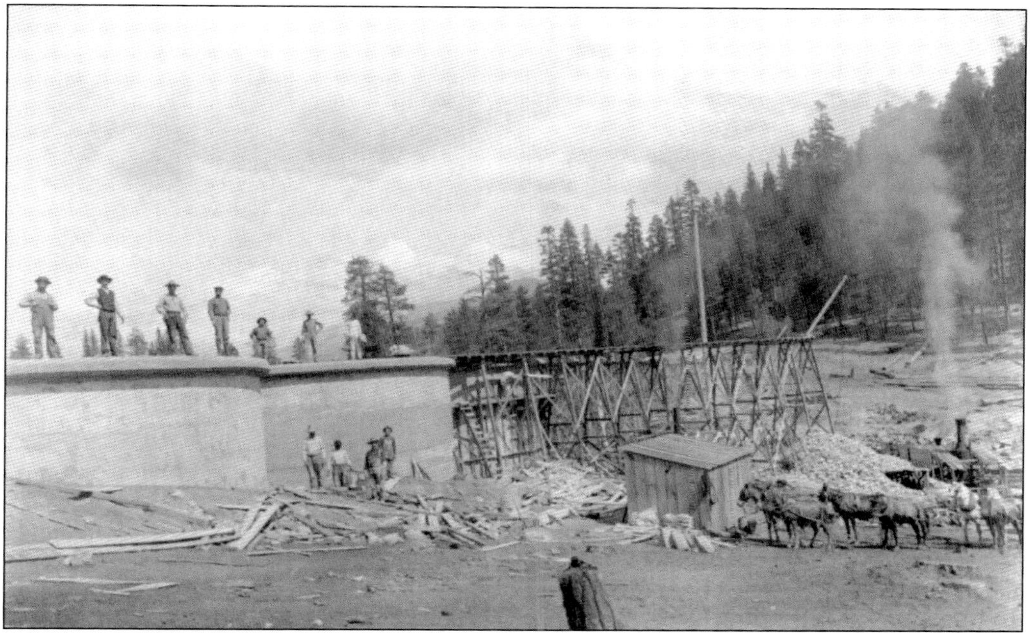

Hume hired engineer John Eastwood to design and construct a dam, which would create Hume Lake. Eastwood developed an innovative multiple-arch design for the project. The design proved not only to be very strong, but it used much less concrete than traditional designs. Engineers from all over the world came to copy Eastwood's techniques. The original dam is still in use today.

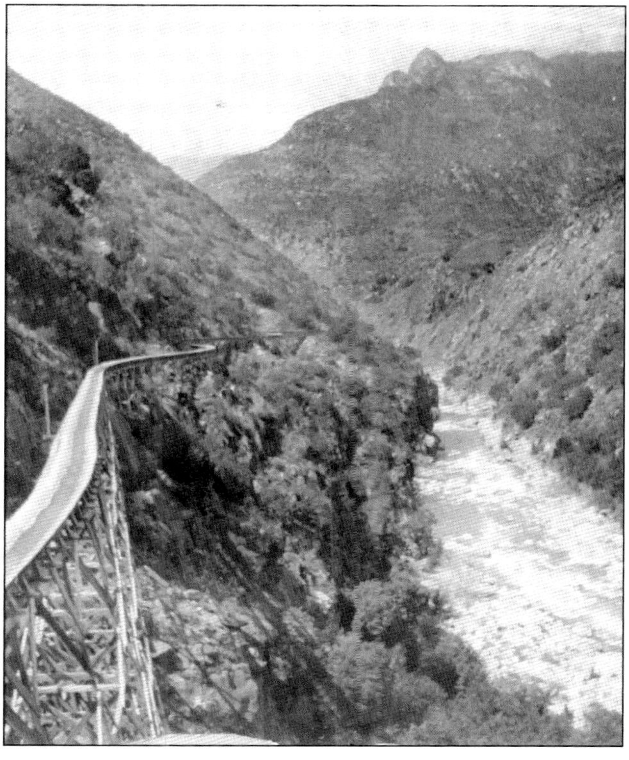

The flume is shown high on its perch above the rushing Kings River. This stretch of canyon, below the confluence of Ten Mile Creek and the Kings, proved to be steep and narrow. Not only did workers have to deal with the steep terrain, they also encountered poison oak and rattlesnakes. Due to the remote canyon location, building supplies were floated down the completed portion of the flume. Crews assembled the flume in sections as they worked their way down the river.

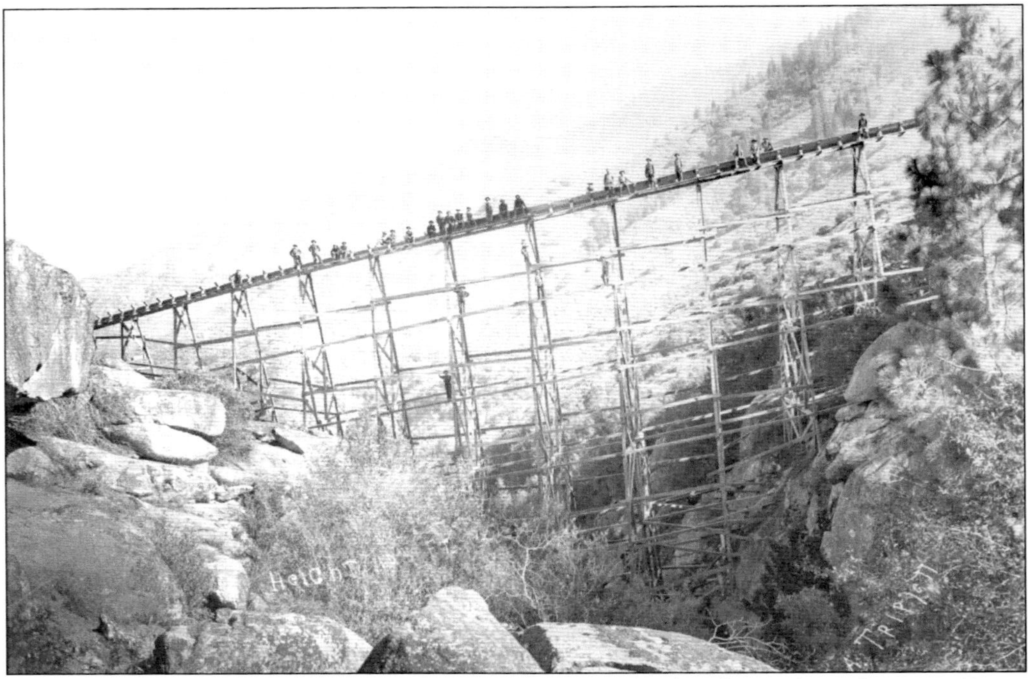

Hume and Bennett would also build an extension to the lumber flume, from the Kings River, up Ten Mile Creek, to the newly constructed mill that sat below the dam. The extension of the flume to Hume Lake increased its length to 62 miles, making it the longest in the world.

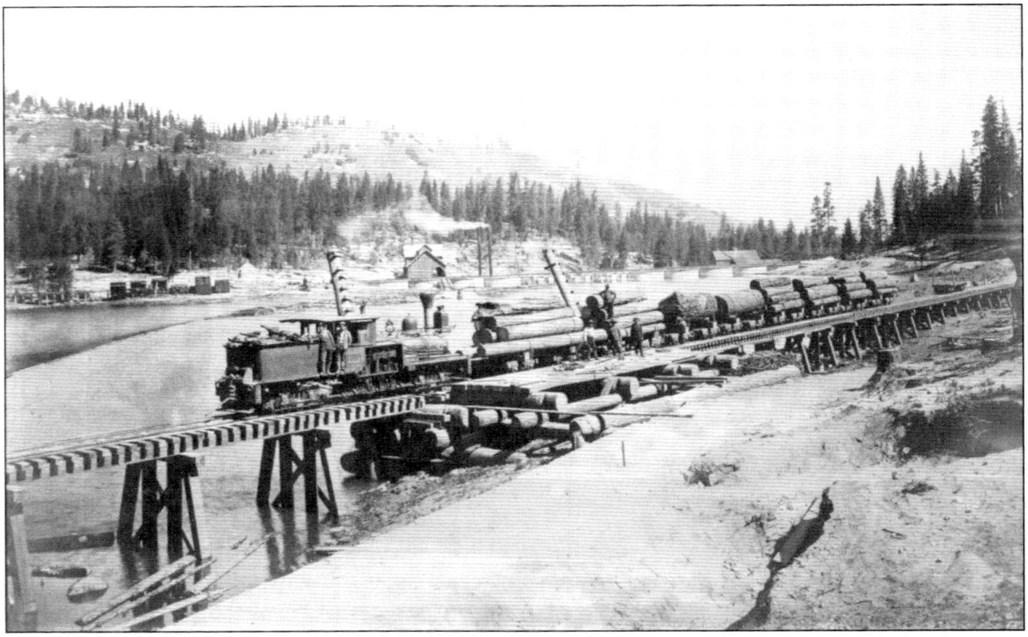

A fresh-cut load of logs is shown at the log-dump area located along Hume Lake's eastern shore. Hume would build many branches of his expanded rail line deep into the forest above the lake.

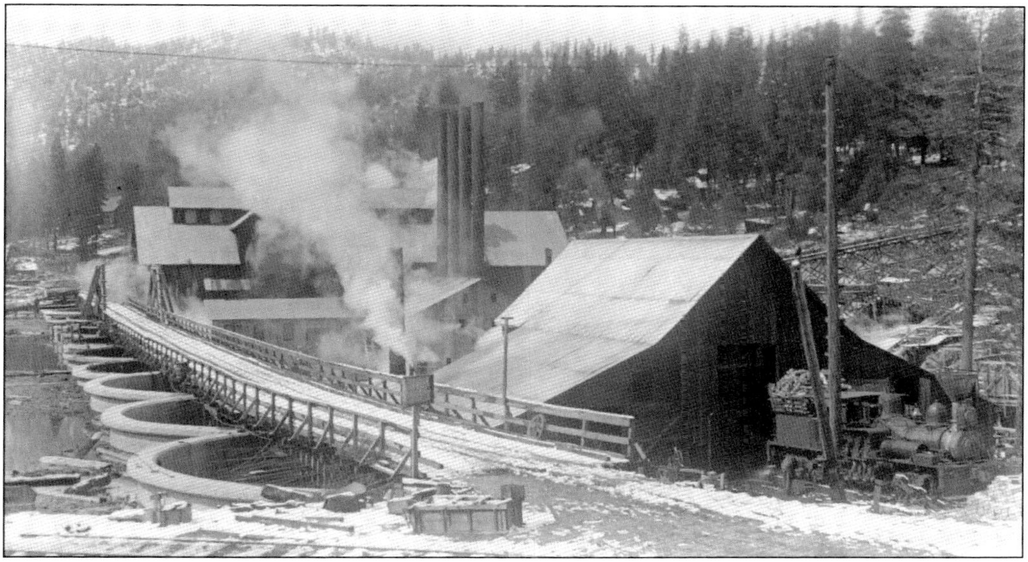

In this photograph, a Shay engine is visible in front of the machine and foundry shop. Eastwood's innovative multiple-arch design is also clearly seen here, as is the mill just below the dam. Smoke can be seen billowing from the various smokestacks of the mill. An unexpected snow may have caught the lumber crew off guard, as the operation was normally shut down in winter months.

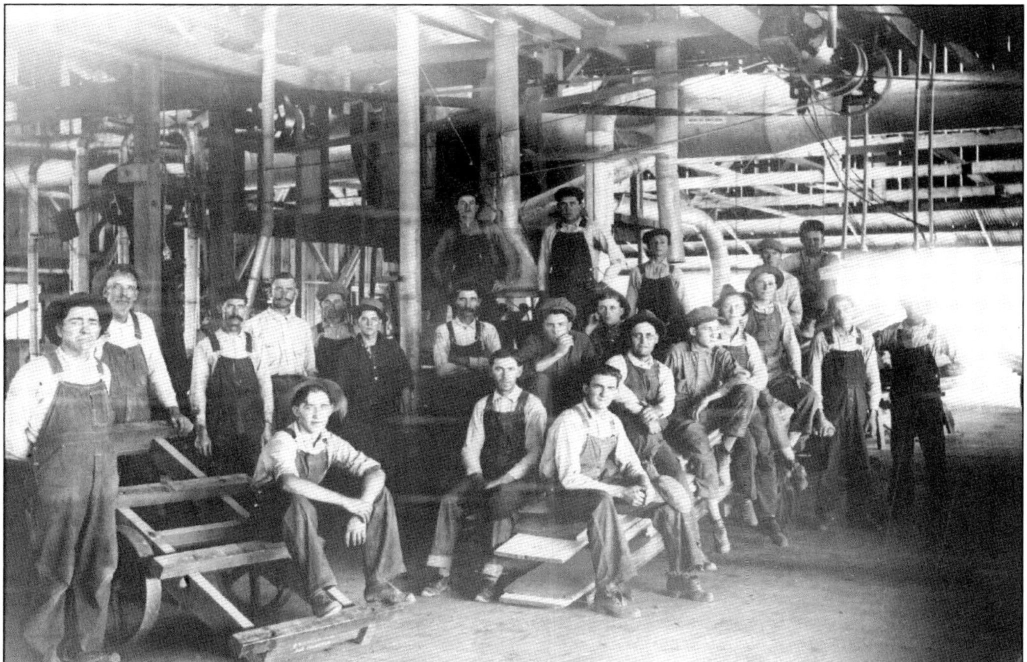

Hume Bennett Lumber Company Mill and Box Factory is shown in this 1912 photograph. The partial list of timber crew includes the following: Mr. Carlisle, Mr. Kelley, Tommie Zinn, Claude Buffalo, Dick Carlisle, Claude Houdashell, Mr. Vance, Bill Bender, Max Peterson, Lawrence Peterson, John Maxwell, B. Thurman, and W. Lust. Max Peterson is the young man with a hat shown seated on the cart in the left foreground.

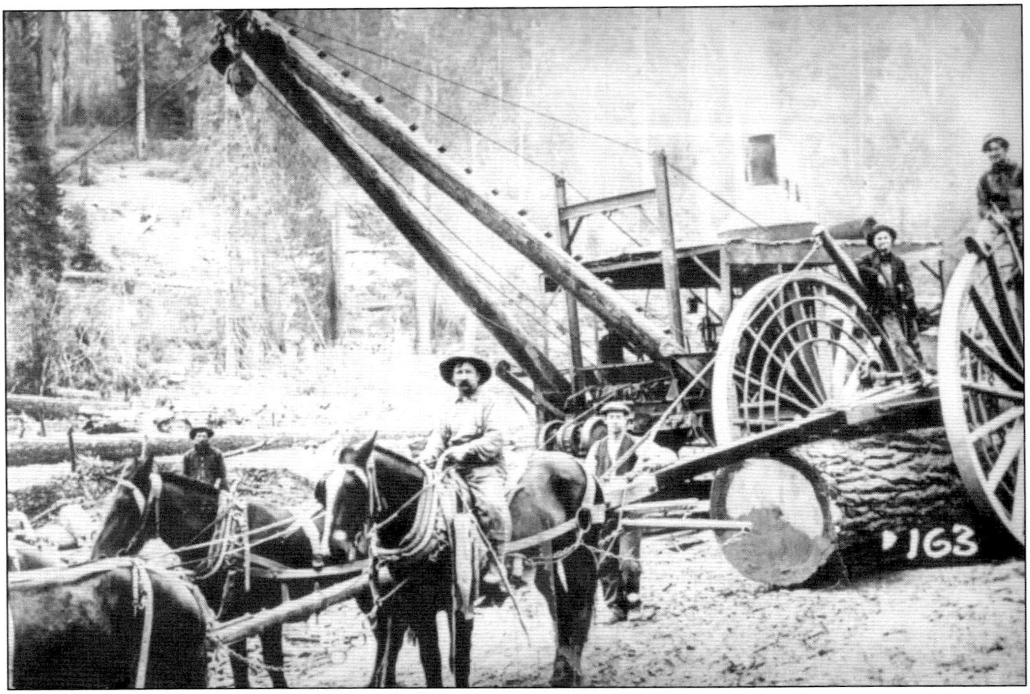

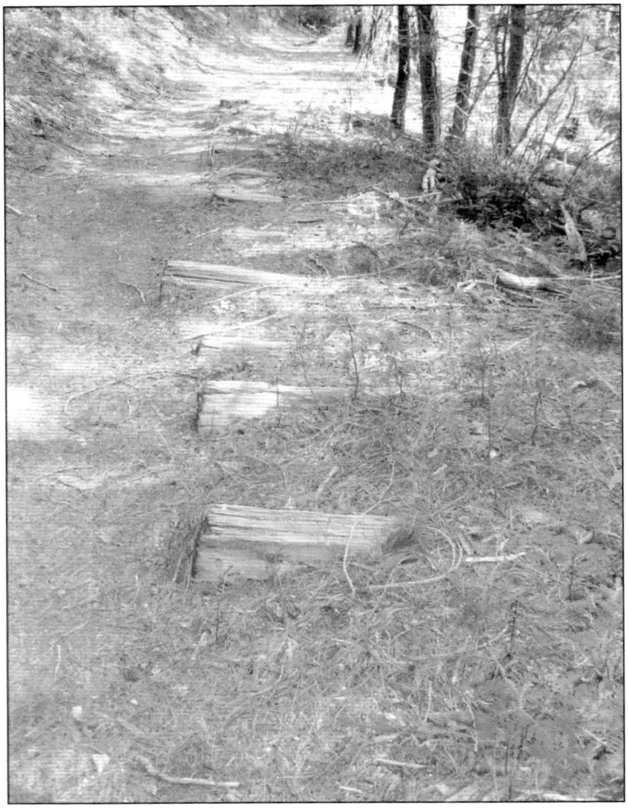

Bennett was forced out of the operation in 1912 and replaced by Thomas Hume's son, George. He was responsible for expanding rail service and adding new engines and equipment to the operation, such as the Big Wheel shown here. However, despite his best efforts, the lumber operation was still not making a profit.

None of the lumber barons ever made a profit. Other than the dam at Hume Lake, a few building foundations, and trace remnants scattered across the forest, little remains of the giant lumber operation. In this photograph, partially exposed railroad ties are visible on an old railbed hidden deep in the forest. (Scott Haugland collection.)

Five

Agriculture and Packinghouses

In the summer of 1846, Gen. John C. Fremont explored the Central Valley. He wrote that "there is not, and never will be anything there. It is barren and worthless." How wrong he was.

In 1895, Fresno County was shipping 30 boxcars of citrus. By 1898, that number had increased to 300 carloads of oranges and 6,000 boxes of lemons. The first citrus was packed by the Early Fruit Company and Farmers Warehouse of Sanger. With the high return on citrus, more acres were planted and harvested. This created the need for more packing companies. Sanger, with its railroad, became the hub of the growing packing industry.

The packing operations were a boon to Sanger. Names and brands like Chooljian, Ballantine, Bianco, Blue Goose, and others would locate their operations along the Southern Pacific tracks parallel to Academy Avenue. Citrus was not the only valuable crop packed in Sanger. In 1918, the Sanger Fruit Growers, a cooperative packing company, was formed. In that year, it shipped 86 carloads of grapes to markets across the country.

In 1920, the Tracy Waldron Fruit Company was formed. Waldron was a lettuce grower and packer in Salinas. The Sanger branch company shipped wine grapes all over the country for domestic wine producers. In 1938, he sold the business to Estey Walton and C.B. Jensen. Walton and Jensen expanded the packing operation to include fresh grapes and peaches.

To pack and preserve the fruit during shipment, ice was needed. Charles Gabriel had the idea of opening the Mountain Water Ice Company. He and his new operating partner, Ted Blue, changed the name to Sanger Ice and Cold Storage. The business expanded rapidly with the growing need for ice and cold-storage facilities for the fresh fruit.

With the rise of the trucking industry, packing plants were no longer tied to the railroad. Refrigerated trucks could get fresh fruit to market faster than trains could. To cut costs, many farmers packed their own fruit, known as field packing. In this way, the farmers bypassed the packinghouses in Sanger altogether. Some of the larger farmers opened their own packinghouses, where they packed fruit for themselves and nearby farms.

By the 1970s, an industry that had given employment to thousands for half a century was dying out. Today, a drive down Academy Avenue gives no hint of this once thriving industry. Most of the old packinghouses have been torn down and replaced by small strip malls. Today, the operation worthy of the name is packing garbanzo beans in a portion of the old Barr Packing Company.

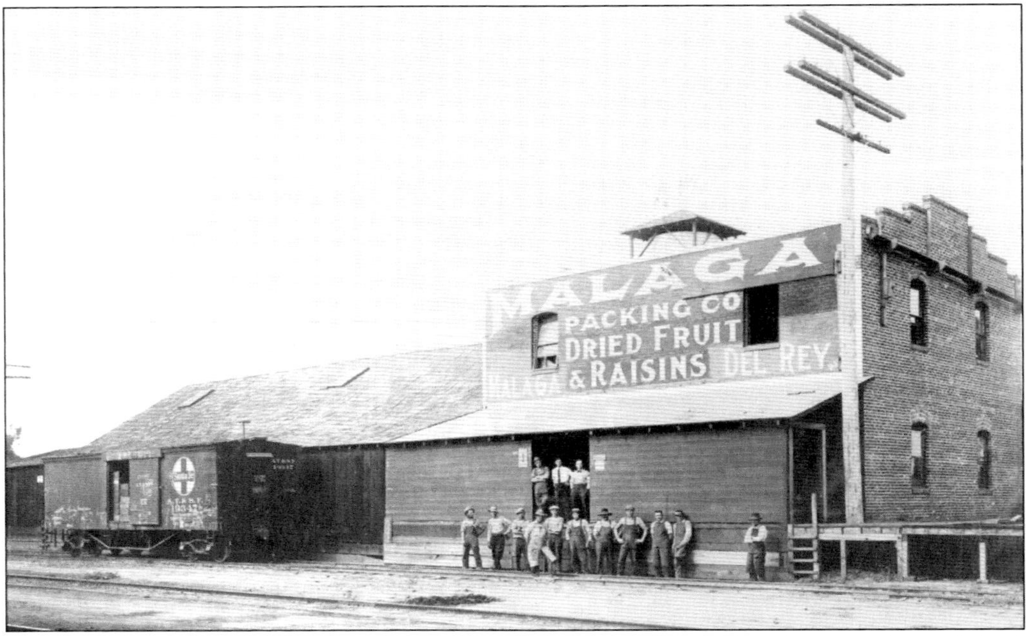

The Malaga Packing Co., seen here in 1905, was one of the first in the Del Rey area. Around 1884, a trading center called Clifton was started in the area. In 1896, the Santa Fe Railway constructed a branch line to Clifton and built a station, Del Rey. The name derived from the nearby Del Rio Rey Raisin & Fig Company property. Clifton's name became Del Rey.

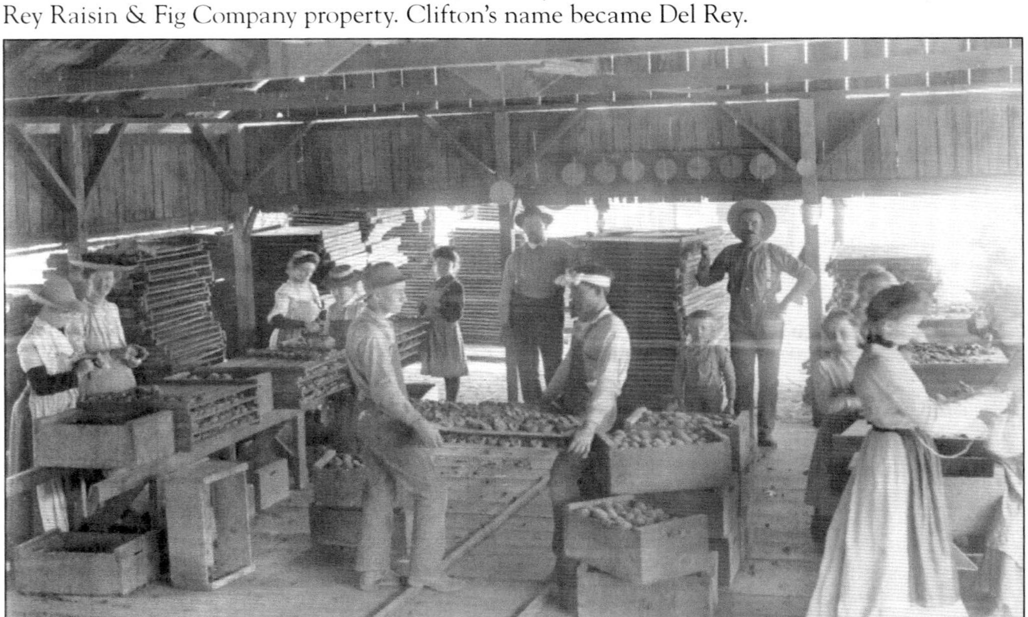

George Dockery's cutting shed is seen here in 1904. Among those shown are Eliza M. Hanke (far right), George Dockery Jr. (boy right of center), and George Dockery (rear right). To the left of the trays in the rear is George Rodgers and, next to him, Muriel Dockery. The women on the right are cutting peaches to put on the wood drying trays.

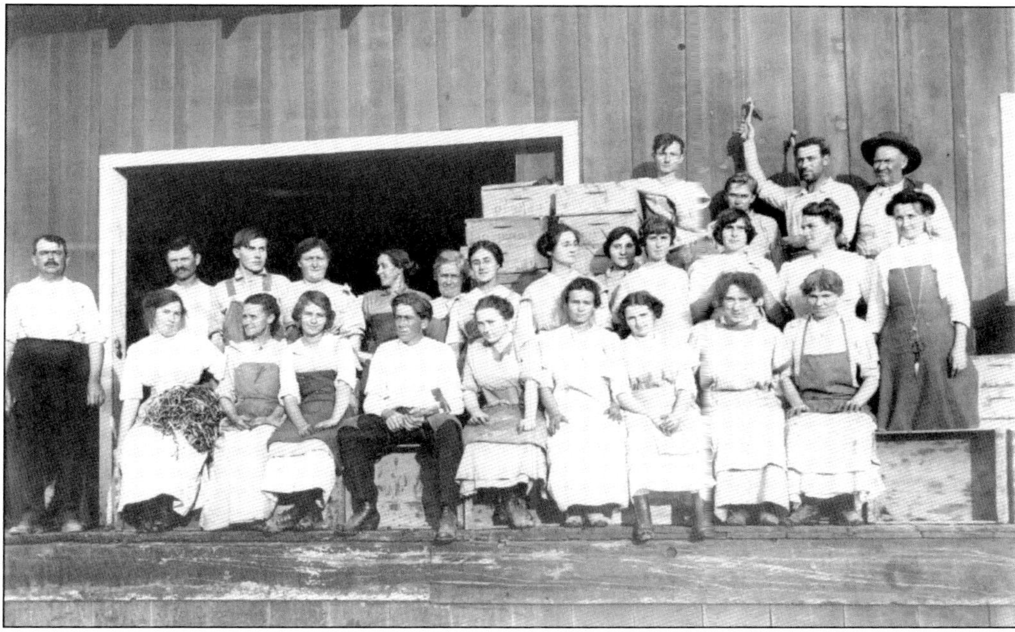

Employees of the Friedheim Co. pose outside of the grape-packing shed in 1913. Charlie Hall, the manager, is standing on the far left. When Charlie began his own company, this crew went to work for him. Ida Picchi (first row, third from left) stayed with the new company for 49 years. During most of those years, her position was "floor lady."

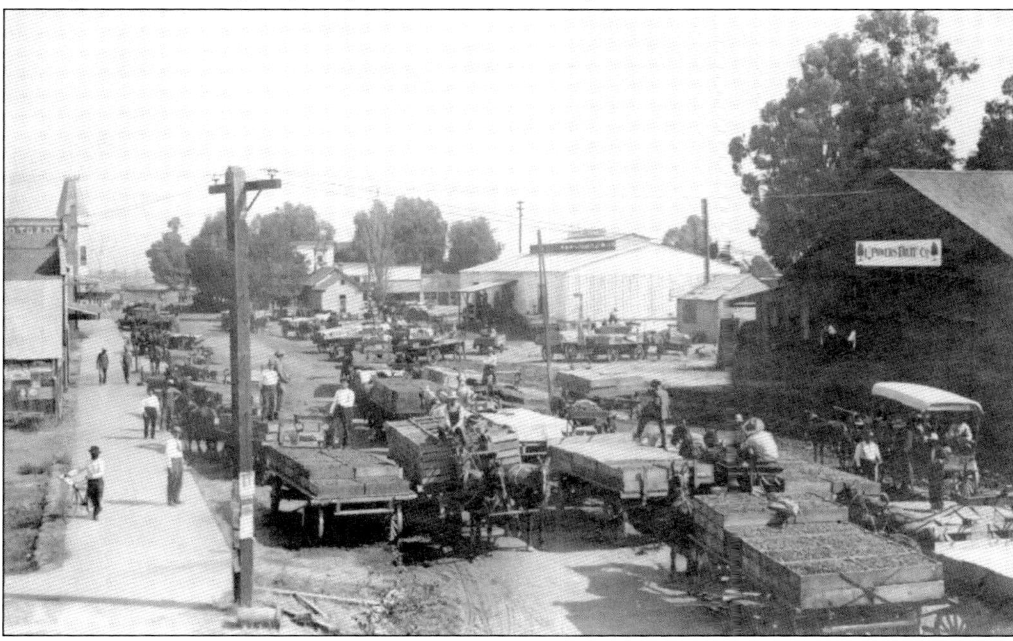

This 1913 photograph shows a view looking north along Academy Avenue. It is September, and the growers are bringing their dried fruit to J.K. Armsby's shed (the large white building near the center). In the background is the fire station on Seventh Street with its bell in the belfry. At right in the foreground is one of the L. Powers Fruit Co. sheds.

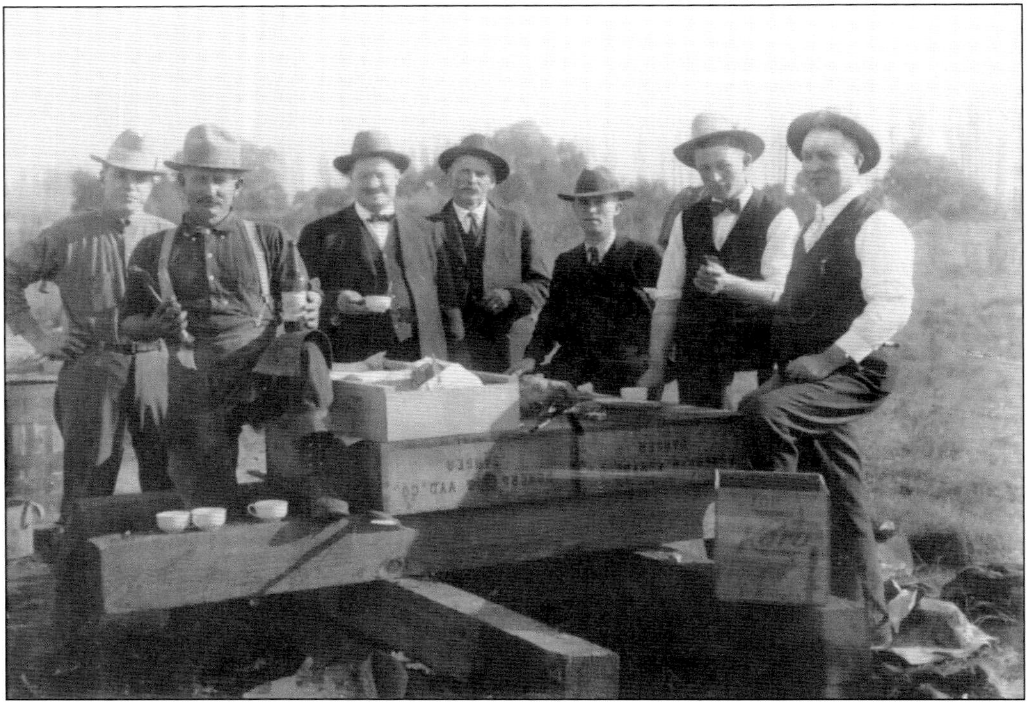

Charles Hall (third from left, holding a wine cup) is among those celebrating the season in this photograph. In 1910, Hall arrived in Sanger to manage the Friedheim Packing Company. In 1914, Hall, Max Flato, and A.M. Setback formed the Alamo Packing Company. Hall and his son Edward took control of Alamo in 1927, and the Hall Packing Company was formed. Hall's success spawned the growth of Sanger's packing industry. By 1923, the United Packing Company was operating.

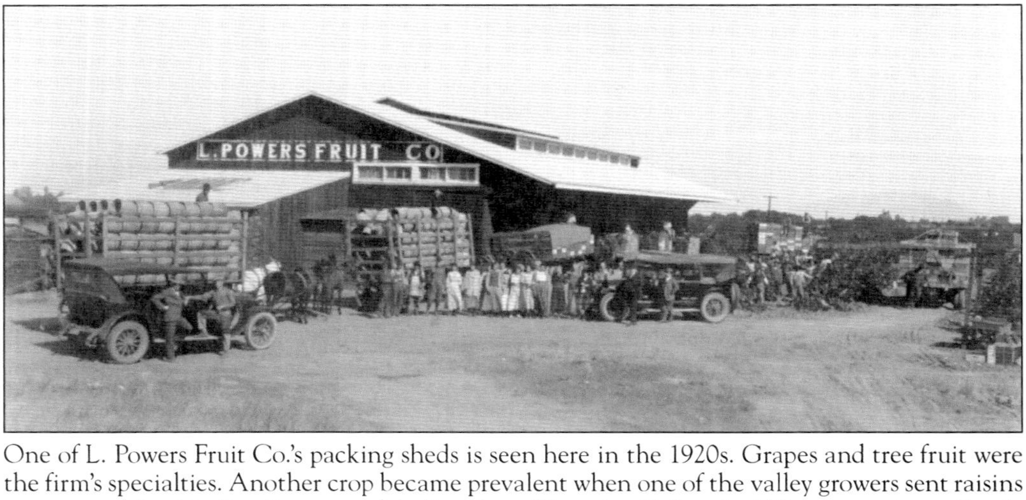

One of L. Powers Fruit Co.'s packing sheds is seen here in the 1920s. Grapes and tree fruit were the firm's specialties. Another crop became prevalent when one of the valley growers sent raisins to a grocer friend in San Francisco, labeling them "Peruvian Delicacies." The grocer immediately sold out. The grape growers had found a new market.

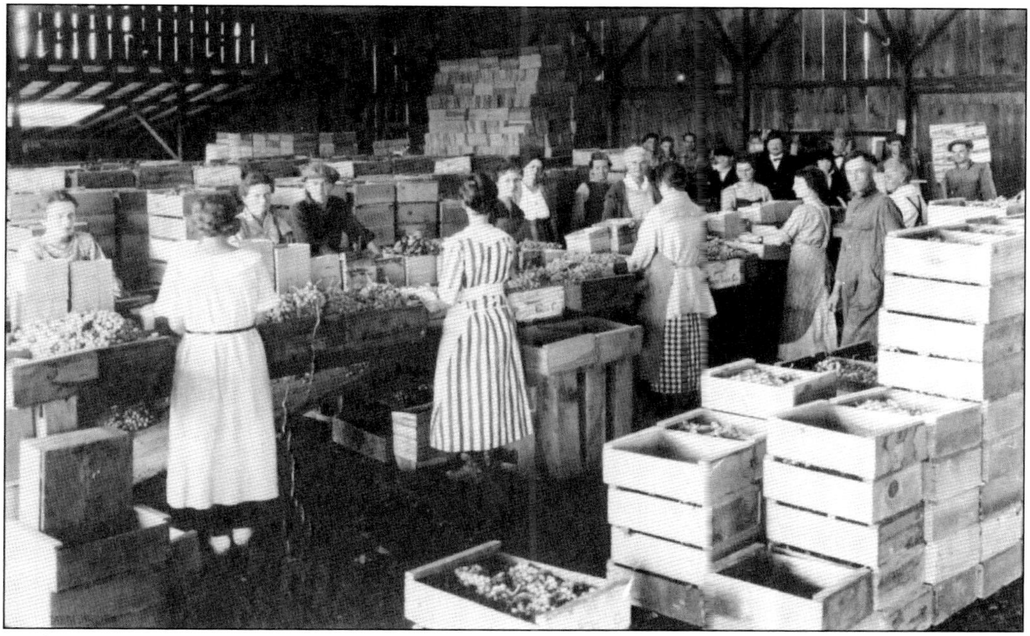

In this L. Powers packing shed, men have already brought in field boxes (the dark ones) of grapes to the women at the sorting tables. The women sort and pack the grapes, and the men then nail the lids on the boxes and stack them for shipment. These grapes are not packed for shipping long distances.

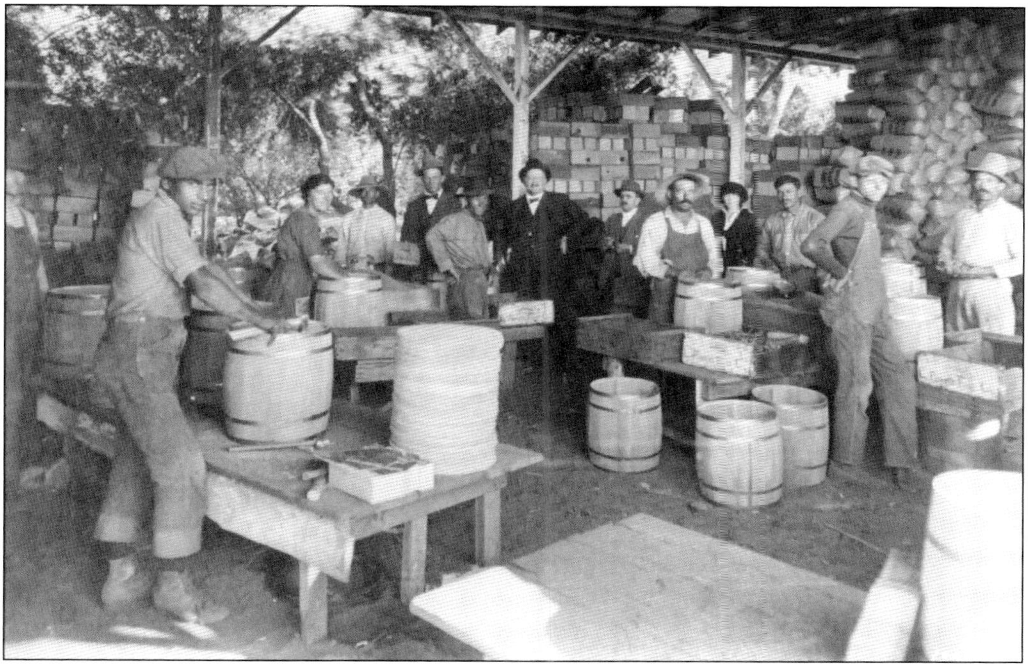

Another one of the Powers Fruit Co.'s packing sheds is shown here. In this shed, workers are packing the fruit for long-distance shipping throughout the nation and overseas. The young man on the left is not making the barrels, or kegs; he is putting the lids on after they are packed.

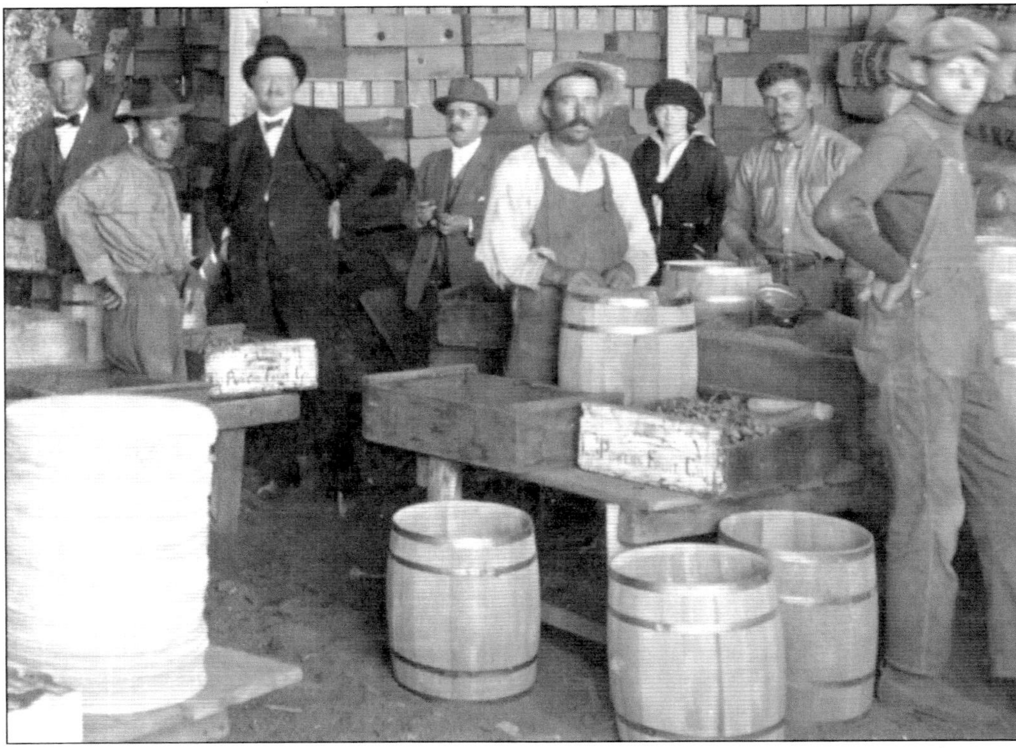

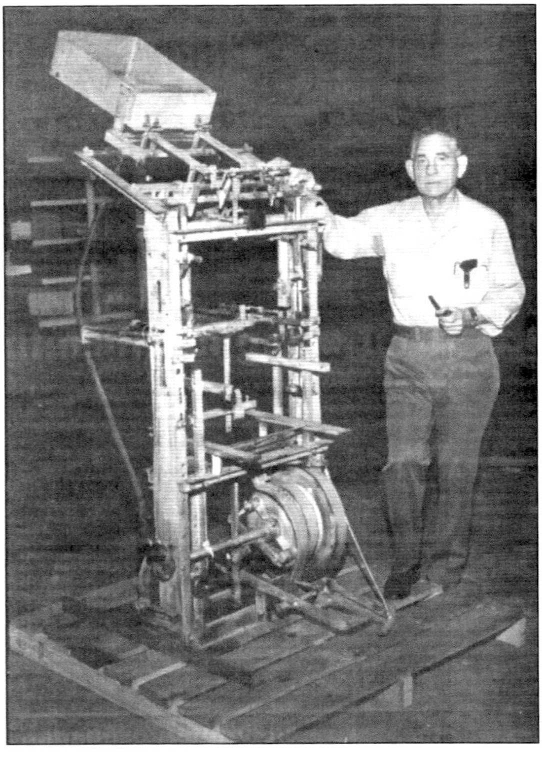

Emperor grapes arrive in "swamp" boxes straight from the fields. The grapes were not washed, but leaves, bad grapes, and debris were removed, and the grapes were placed in the barrels along with sawdust. L. Powers (third from left) and his staff are keeping a close eye on the procedure.

Fruit was packed and shipped in wooden boxes, which were assembled by hand. But in 1921, the Paxton brothers, Gerald (shown here) and Hale, patented the Paxton Nailing Machine, which put the boxes together. Their small Sanger company was soon selling machines all over the world.

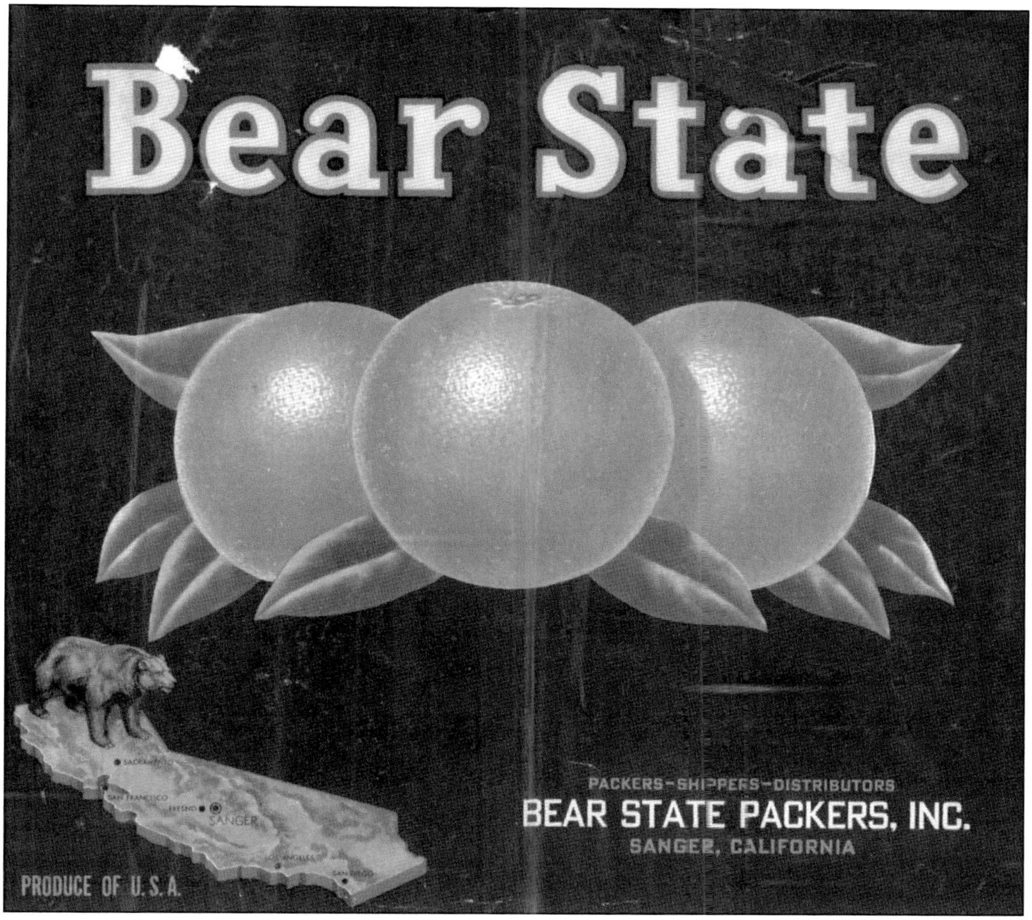

As the lumber industry faded away, Sanger's main business became a thriving and bountiful agriculture industry. Dozens of packinghouses dotted the town's landscape. Fruit crate labels often consisted of beautiful artwork with catchy names related to the region. The Bear State brand (above) honored the official state animal, the California grizzly. Among the many brands packaged by Bear State Packers, Inc. were Sunny Bear, Sweet Sue, and The Wonder Valley (below). The Blue Goose Growers, Inc. purchased Bear State Packers in 1961. Blue Goose Growers, Inc. was located at 1305 Tenth Street. (Both, courtesy of the Henry J. Provost family collection.)

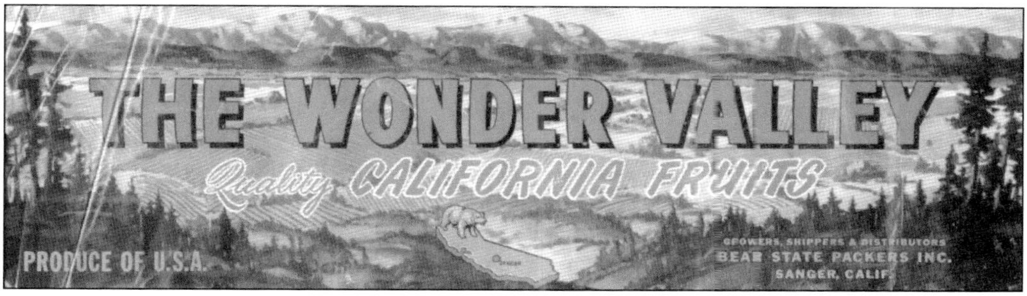

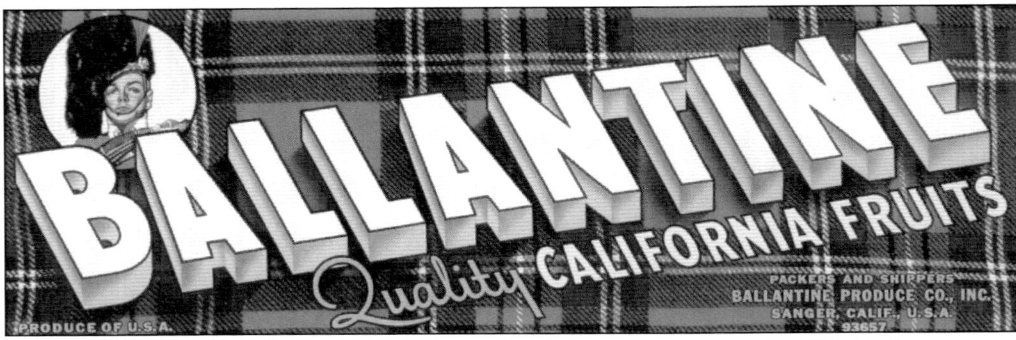

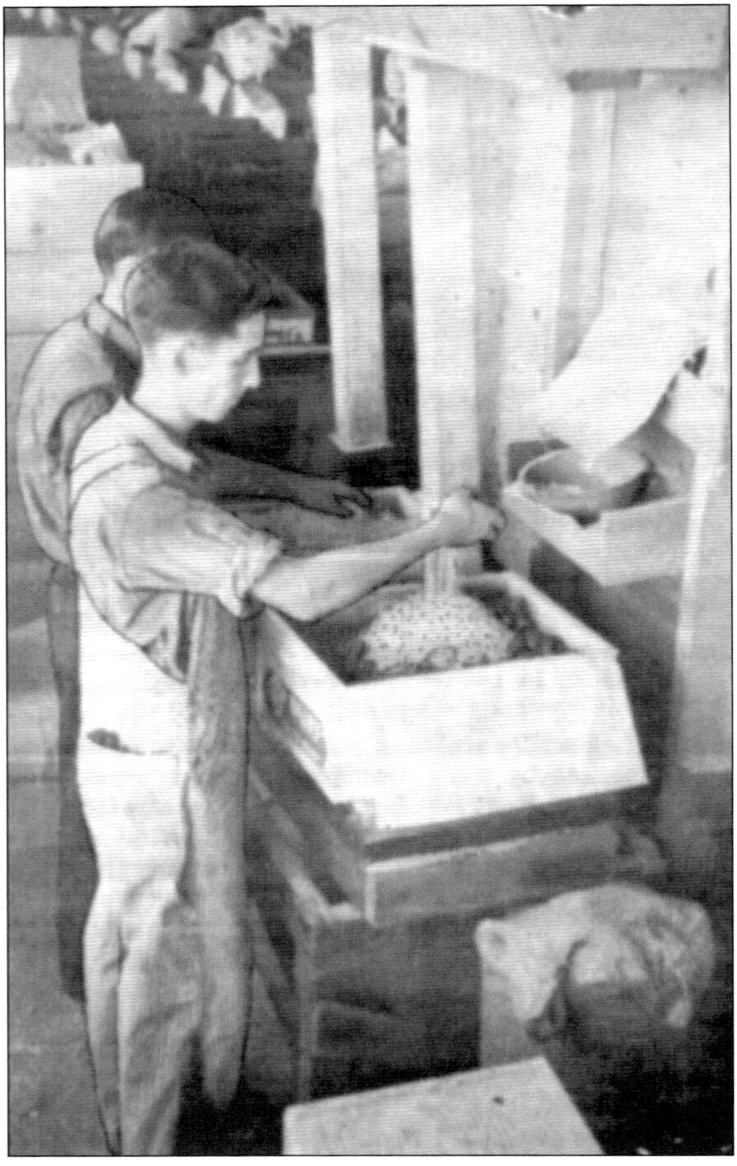

In 1938, Ballantine Produce Company, Inc., opened a small packing shed at Seventh Street and Academy Avenue. It later built a more modern operation on Academy, just south of Church Avenue. Ballantine shipped a wide variety of fruit, including plums, peaches, nectarines, and a wide variety of grapes. Ballantine packed fruit under various labels, including Ballantine, Barile, Dutch Boy, and Redwood Farms. Ballantine and Barr Packing were the last two operating packinghouses along Academy Avenue in Sanger. Both facilities remain as a constant reminder of Sanger's heyday.

This is an assembly line for packing grapes for shipment by railroad. In the background are the women on the assembly line sorting and packing the grapes. The young men at the end of the line are pouring sawdust on the grapes to keep them fresh until they reach the market.

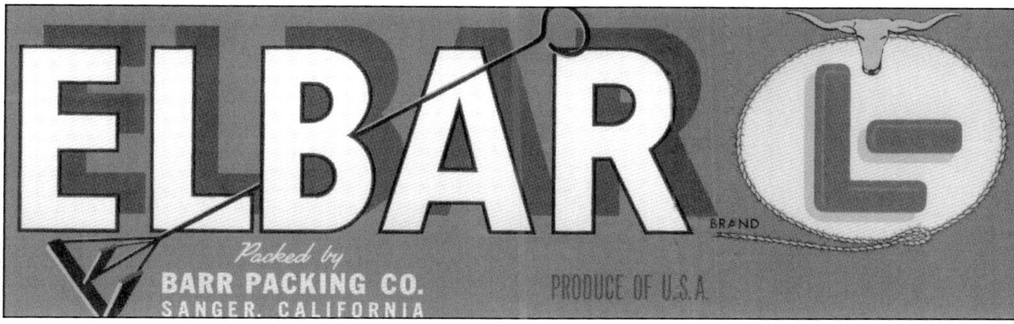

Barr packing brand labels were well known throughout the fruit industry. Tree fruit was packaged by Barr under the Swan, Daisy, and Elbar labels. Grapes were packaged under the Daisy, Swan, Elbar and Halloween labels. By the 1960s, the Barr Packing Company was shipping approximately 1,100 railcar loads of product a year.

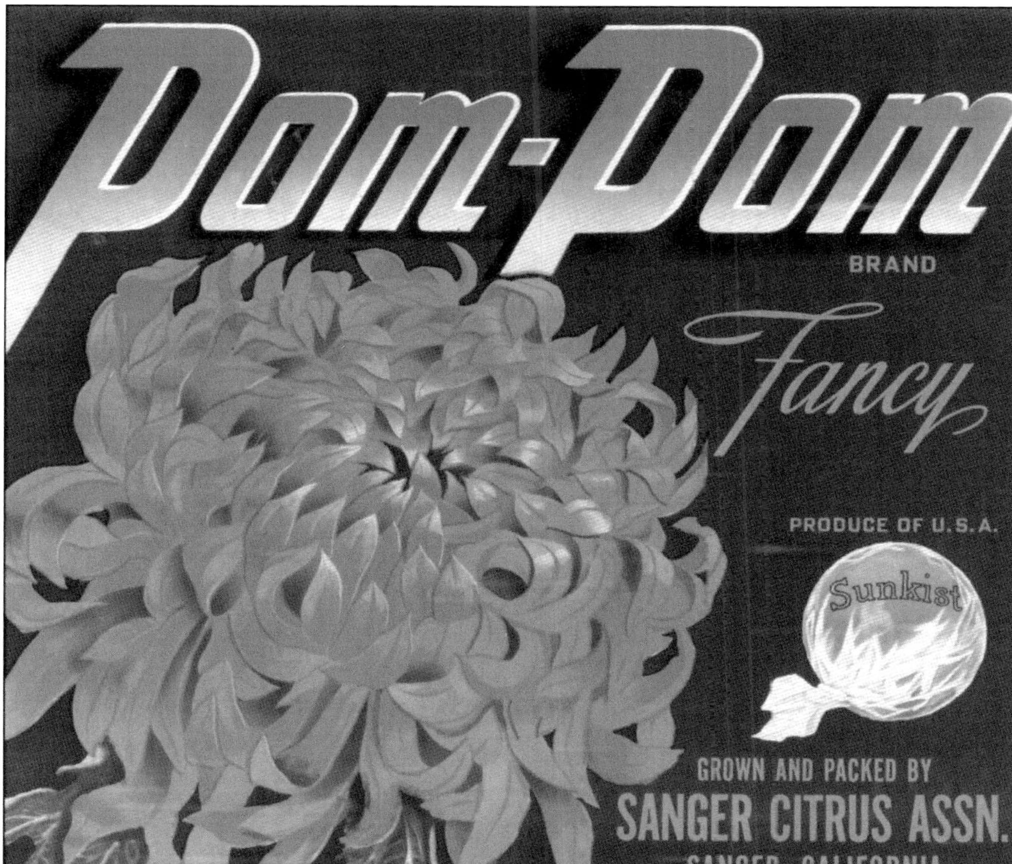

The Sanger Citrus Association, founded in 1920, was owned and operated by the growers themselves. Starting with 52 members, the association grew to over 300 members. The association was well known both domestically and around the world for high-quality products. Among the brands packed by the Association were Pom-Pom (shown here), Four Square, Order, and Sanger Gold. (Courtesy of the Barbara Haugland collection.)

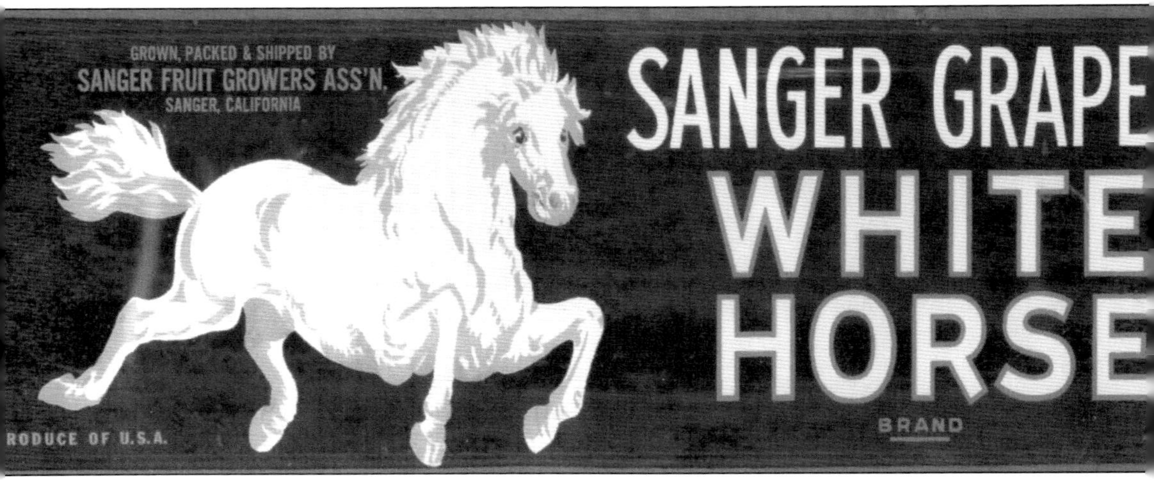

The Sanger Fruit Growers Association established itself in 1919 as a grower cooperative packing company. Brands packaged by the association included White Horse (shown here), Red Crown, and Rose. Longtime Sanger residents may remember the overhead conveyer that crossed Eleventh Street, just east of Academy Avenue, connecting the packing operation to the cold-storage plant.

Six

Early Sanger

In 1888, the area that was to become Sanger consisted of grain fields and was populated by grazing cattle and sheep. By 1889, the population was about 250 inhabitants. Major events would soon change the area. The first was the Southern Pacific Railroad's construction of a line between Fresno and Porterville. Along the line was a junction where a depot would be built. The railroad named it the Sanger Depot, and the area around it became the town of Sanger.

The second major event was the decision by two San Francisco lumbermen, Hiram C. Smith and Austin D. Moore, to lumber the vast virgin forests of fir, cedar, pine, and, later, redwood trees in the forests east and southeast of Sanger. Small independent sawmills were already operating in the area, but their output of lumber was minimal. The terrain was difficult to operate in, the roads were hard to traverse, the distance to market was long, and operations depended on horse-drawn equipment. Smith and Moore had the capital to buy large tracts of timber, to build sawmills and housing for the loggers, and to solve the transport problem. They decided that a flume was the most cost-effective means of moving the cut lumber to the San Joaquin Valley. In 1888, they surveyed a route for a 54-mile flume. It was finished in September 1889, and its terminus was a lumber company in Sanger, including a planing mill, box factory, and engine house.

These two events—the building of the railroad and the growth of the lumber industry—brought hundreds of workers to Sanger and to the forests in the area. Many of these workers also brought their families to the area. When the winter snows ended the logging season in the Sierras, many of these workers stayed in Sanger until the next season.

The building of a dam in Mill Valley to provide water for the flume and to create Sequoia Lake spurred a major summer tourist industry. Many visitors who came each summer passed through Sanger, buying their supplies in Sanger stores and using Sanger coaches and wagons to travel to Sequoia Lake, where hotel accommodations allowed them to spend the long hot summers in relative comfort.

Economically, Sanger soon became a boomtown. By 1890, it had grown to 500 inhabitants, and that number soon reached 1,000. Property prices soared, business was booming, and churches, homes, and schools were being built. Then, in 1911, Sanger was incorporated as a city with its own government.

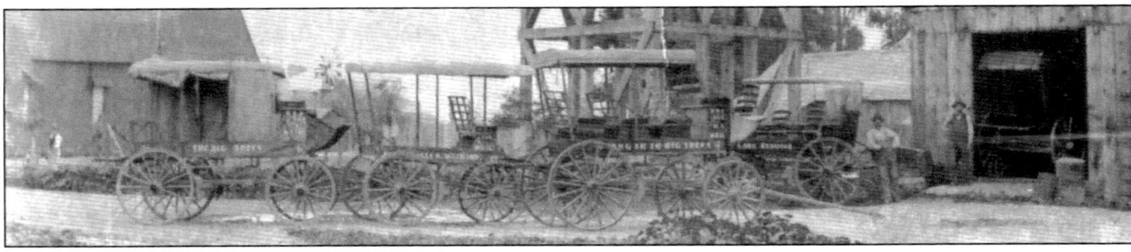

Located at the base of Sanger's water tower was a coach service, one of the earlier businesses in the area. Coach rides were available to the Big Trees, Millwood, and Sequoia Lake. In the summer tourist season, this was a long, dusty ride over dirt roads. On the weekends, many of the lumberjacks used the coaches to return to Sanger for a break from a long week of working. This photograph was taken in 1894.

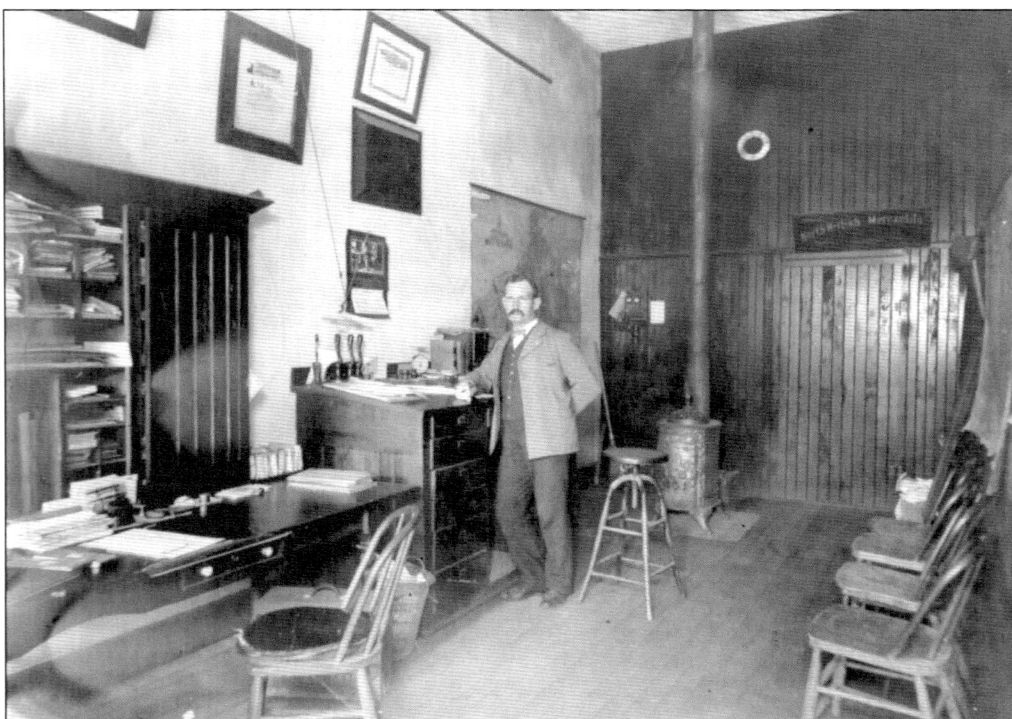

W.M. Barr is shown here in his Seventh Street office in 1894. Barr was the father-in-law of A.B. Olson and great-grandfather of John A. Olson, who began an insurance and real estate business in Sanger in 1889. The present-day office is occupied by Frederick McNairy, CPA.

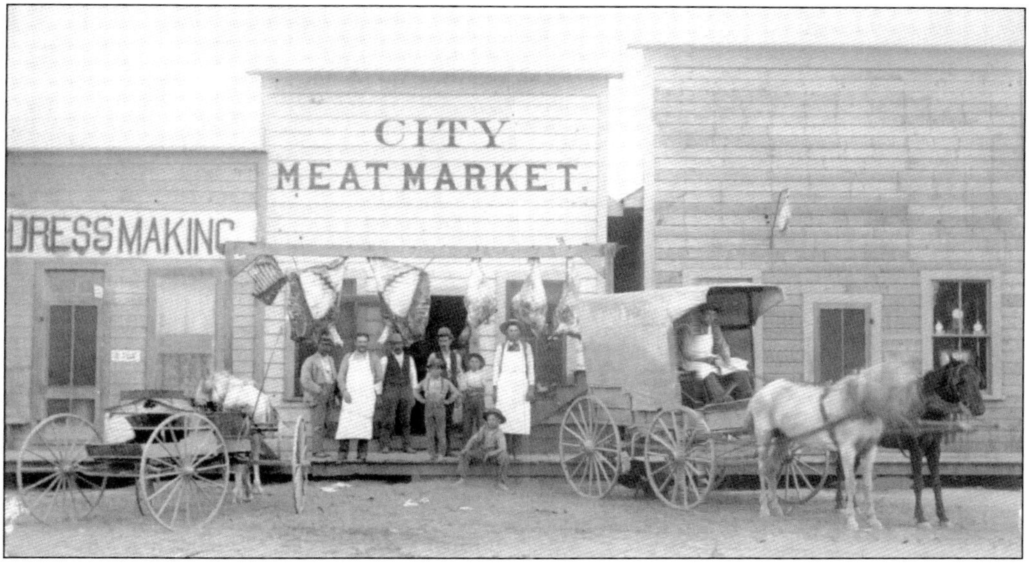

Shown here in 1890, the City Meat Market was a major source of meat for local residents. Bill Swaggert (second from left) was head butcher. Also shown here are H.G. Friend (in apron on the right), Ralph Friend (in wagon), and William P. Friend, the owner (not identified specifically). To the left of the store is Baby Sisters' Dressmaking Shop.

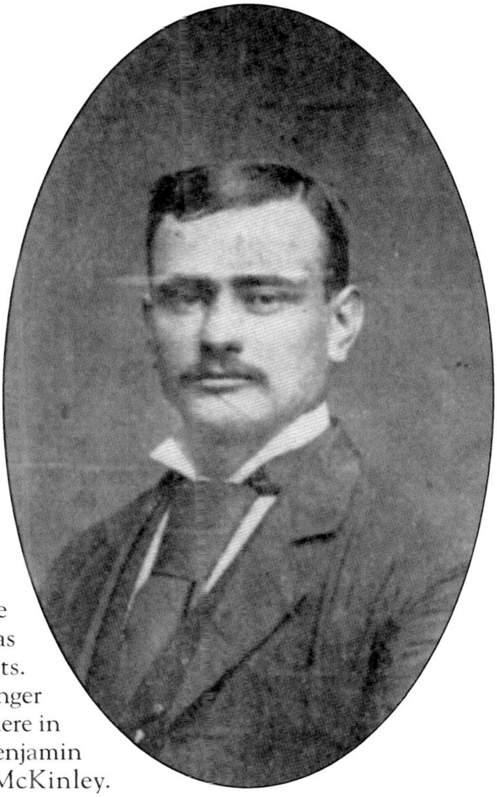

Sanger's first postmaster was Lee McLaughlin, one of the town's earliest settlers. The post office was located on the corner of Seventh and M Streets. Until McLaughlin's commission was approved, Sanger had an unofficial postmistress. McLaughlin, seen here in 1889, was postmaster under three presidents—Benjamin Harrison, Grover Cleveland, and William McKinley.

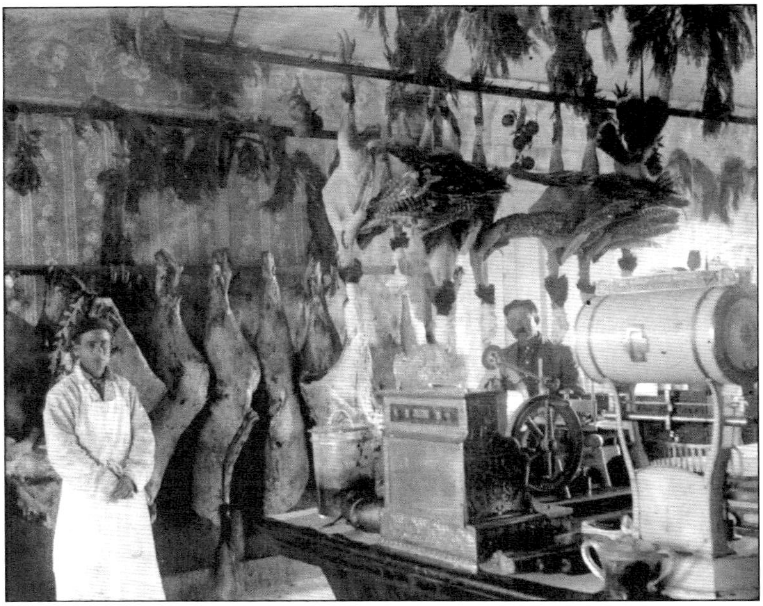

In the 1890s, butcher shops did not have ice or other means to keep their merchandise fresh. In order to help keep the products cool, the butcher would hang them outside on cool nights, and then bring them inside as the day warmed. The shops had no problem with theft on those cool nights, but, at times, dogs would try to get the meat. Note the various types of fowl and other meat hanging in this store.

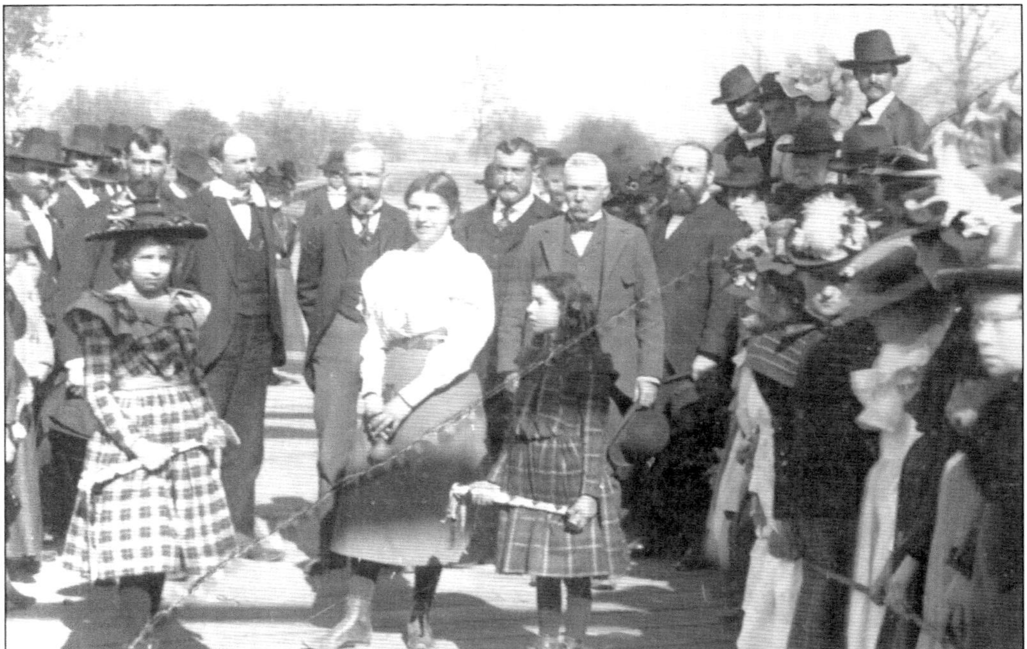

A "golden spike" was driven at this ceremony commemorating the completion of the bridge across the Kings River. This was an important occasion, as evident by the apparel worn by those in attendance, many of who seem to be of importance. This new bridge connected Sanger with communities to the east and to the lumber industry in the Sierras.

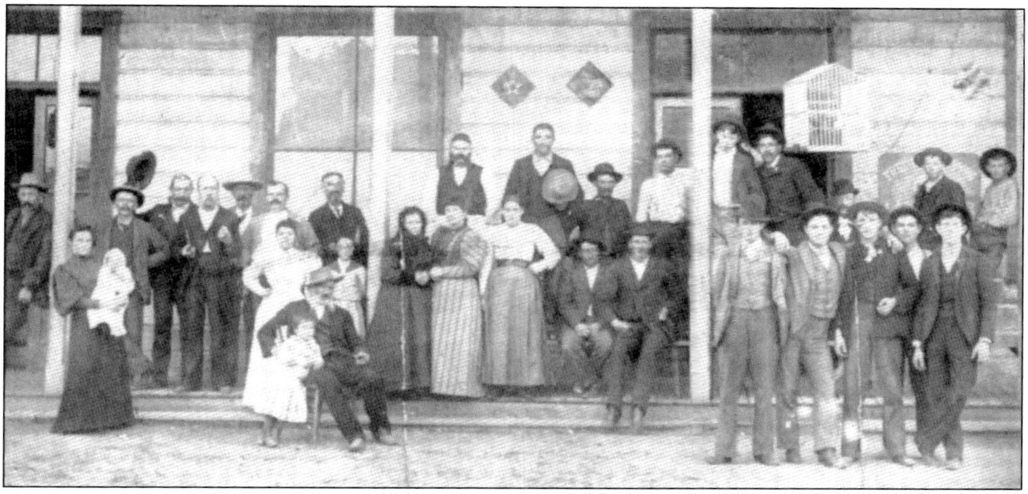

The French Hotel, seen here in 1894, was managed and operated by the Rogallo family. Located at N and Seventh Streets, it was a favorite of lumberjacks when they could no longer work in the high country. A son, Francis Rogallo, was the inventor of the Rogallo wing, still used for ultralight aircraft.

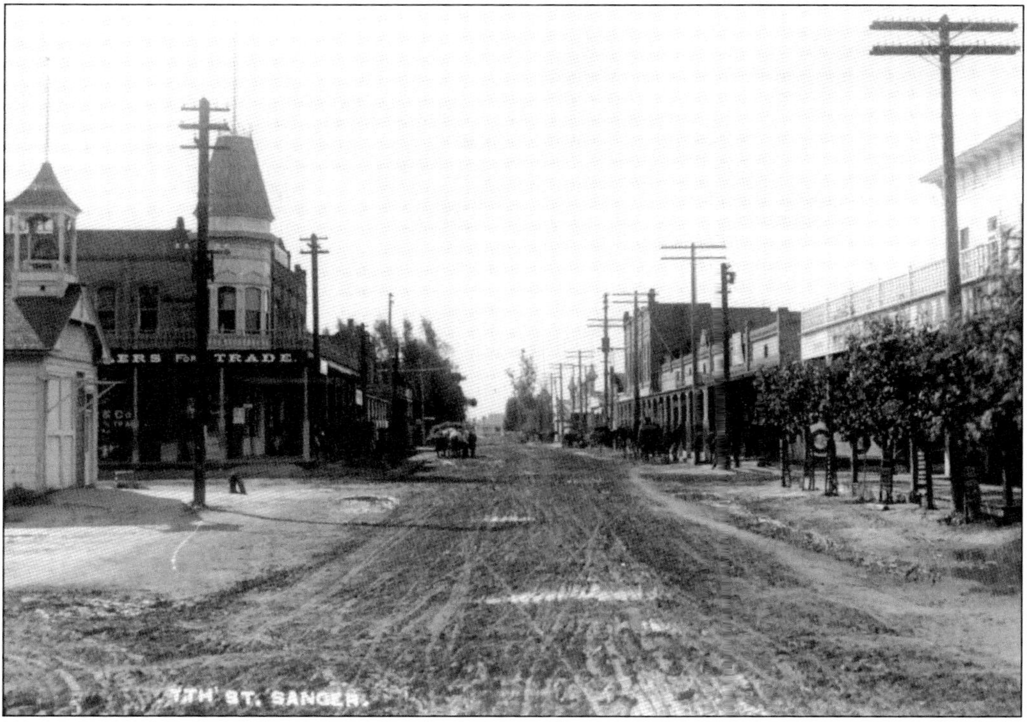

The view in this photograph from the early 1890s shows the intersection of Academy Avenue and Seventh Street, looking west. The little building with the bell tower on the far left is Sanger's firehouse. A 1921 photograph of this location can be found on page 81, showing Sanger's new motorized fire truck and its volunteer crew.

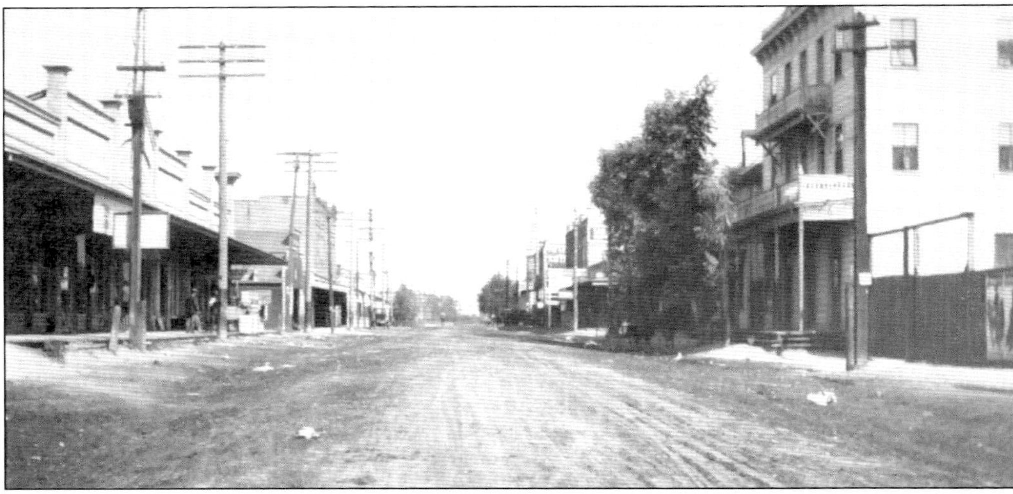

The view in this photograph from the turn of the 20th century is looking east on Seventh Street. The most common form of transportation in Sanger at the time was the horse. Automobiles were a curiosity, and the car in this photograph was one of Sanger's first. Electric power had just been introduced, as evident by the power lines. The wooden walkways and dirt roads were still the norm.

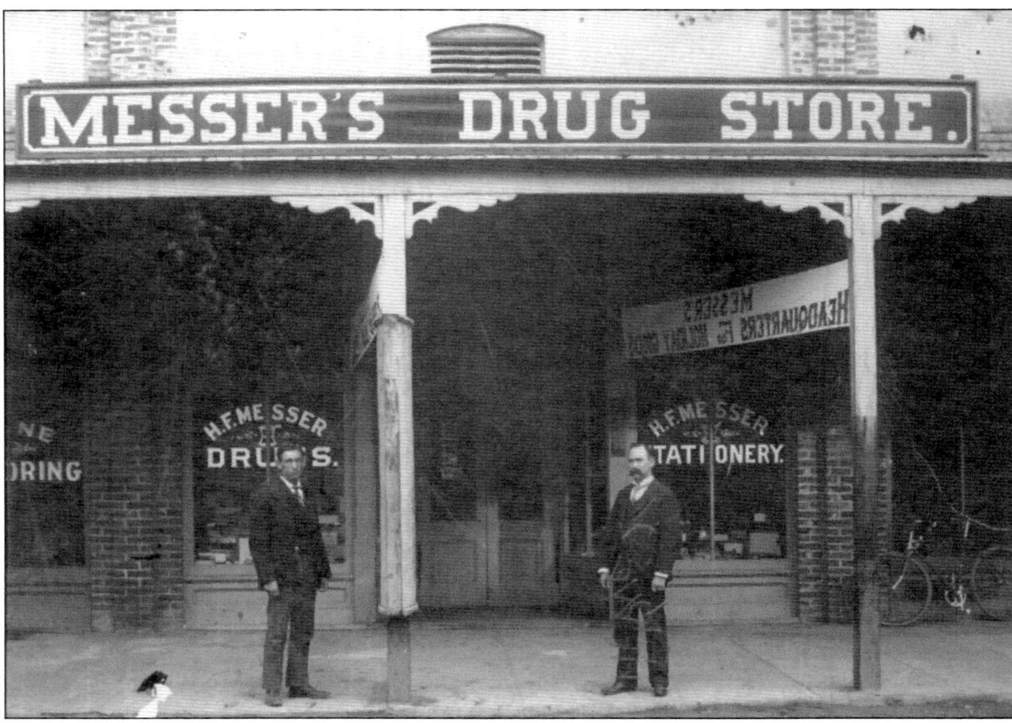

The first drugstore in Sanger was established in 1888 by Dick and Al Elmore. It was located on Seventh Street between Academy Avenue and N Street. In 1900, it was bought by H.F. Messer. The store was sold in 1909 to Oscar A. Brehler, who operated the business under the name of Brehler Drug Store. Later in 1909, it was relocated to the Rogallo building, on the corner of Seventh and N Streets.

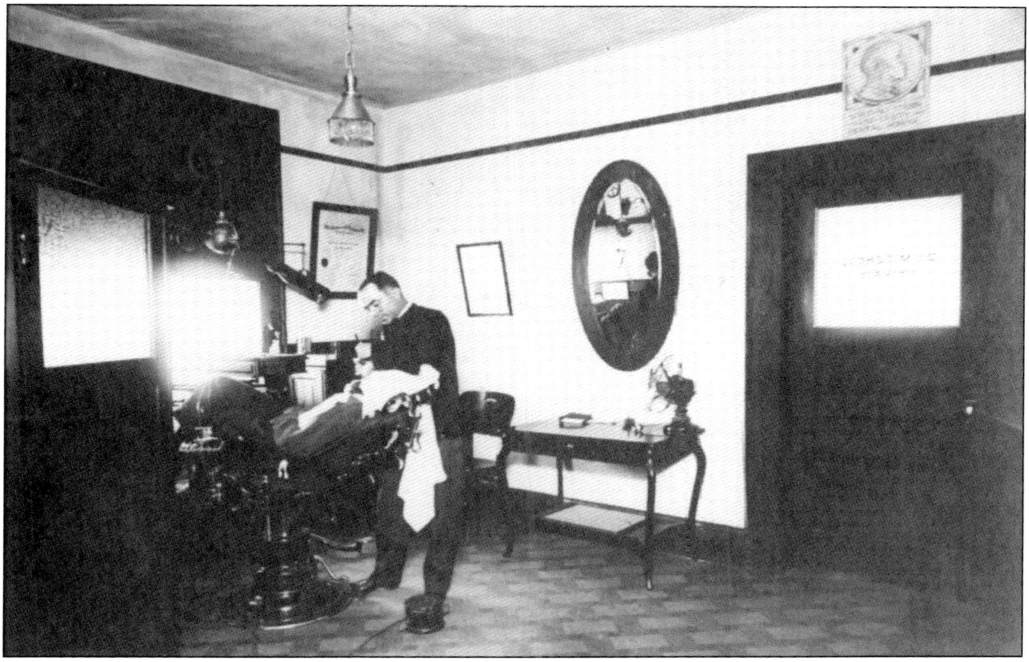

A Mr. Mitchell was one of Sanger's early dentists. His office was in the Rogallo block above Brehler's Drug Store and shared a reception room with Dr. L.P. Fleming. A trip to the dentist's office at the turn of the 20th century usually meant the patient was having a tooth pulled.

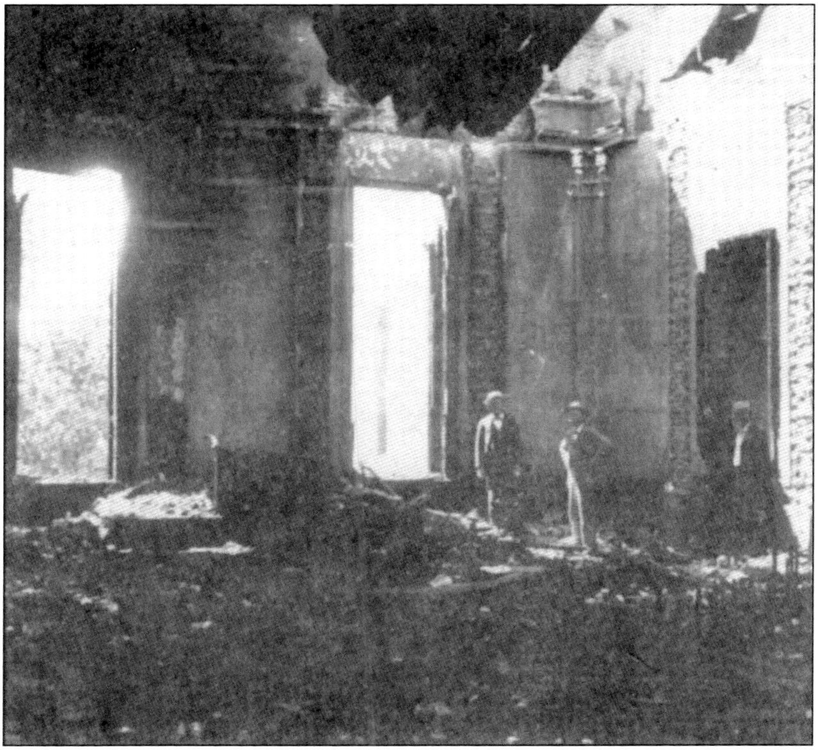

The "Old Opera House" was located on N Street near the site of the post office. In 1903, a fire destroyed the structure. Standing in the ruins are, in no particular order, Henry Rodgers, Frank Lindsey, and Jeff Davis. Memories of the first high school on the second floor, the "best" dance floor in all of Fresno County, and the many social activities all went up with the fire.

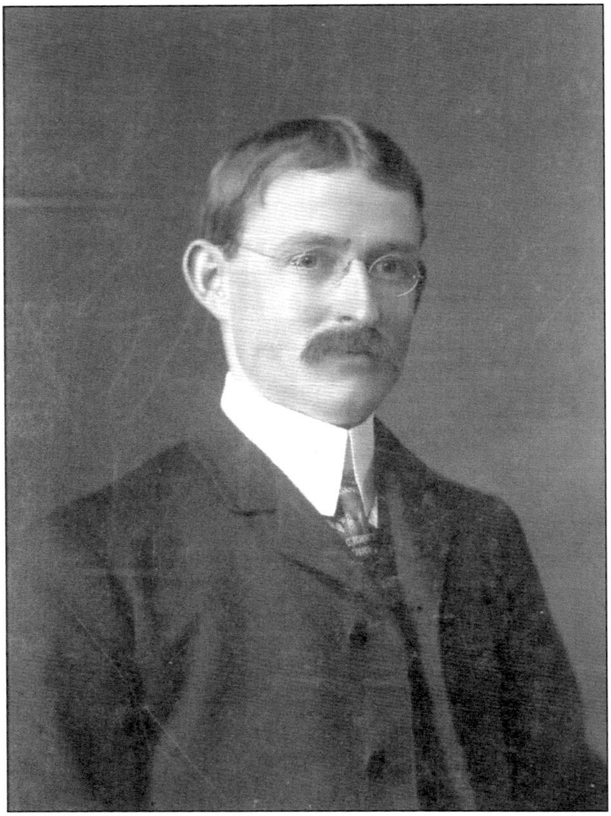

Dr. L.P. Fleming arrived in Sanger early in 1904. He finished postgraduate work in the winter of 1911–1912 and returned to Sanger to take up a partnership with Dr. T.F. Madden, which lasted until 1918. Years later, while reminiscing, Fleming mentioned early doctors in the area: "Dr. Cockrill located first in Centerville in 1868, and Drs. Hoag and Pressley coming to Sanger in 1888."

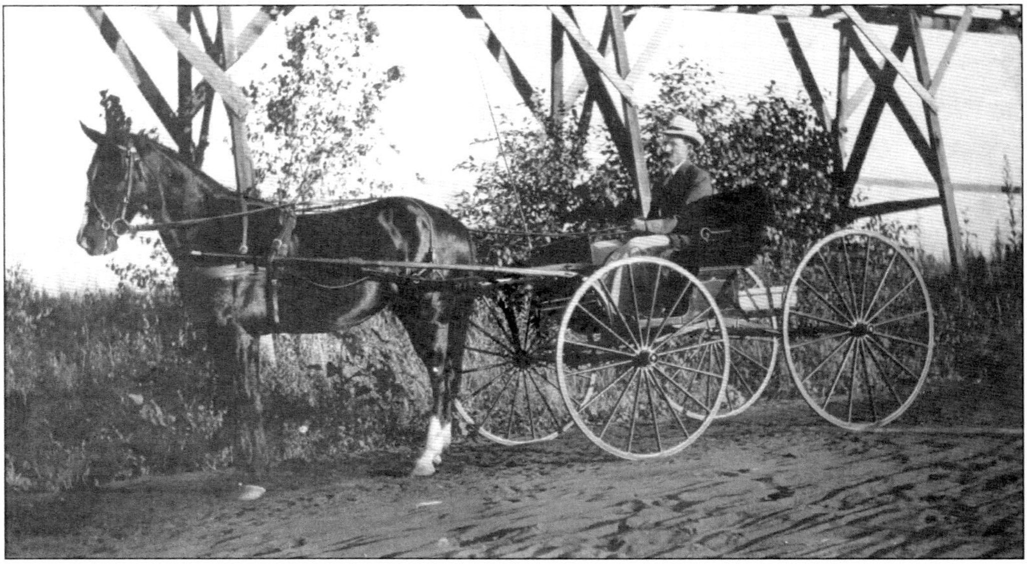

Dr. L.P. Fleming and his horse, Babe, would often be seen following the flume on rural visits to his patients. Residents also had the services of Dr. A.H. Sweeny, who in the summer worked for Sanger Lumber Company in the Sierras at the Old Millwood camp. In the winter, he resided in Sanger and was available for patients.

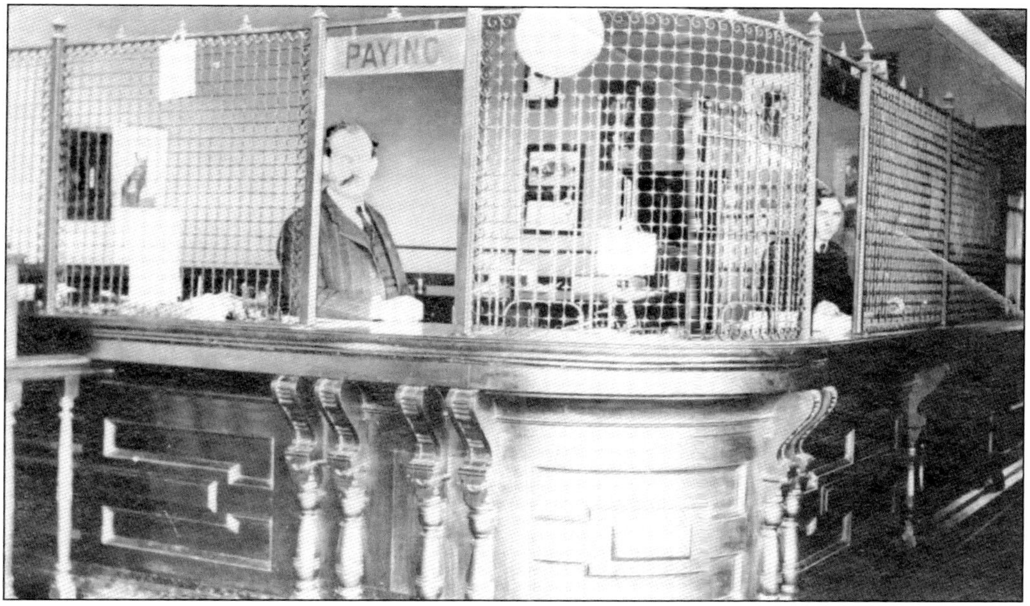

William Milton Barr arrived in Sanger in 1888. One of his first jobs was to manage the Valley Lumber Company. In 1904, he assisted in organizing the First National Bank and was its first vice president. In 1906, he was named cashier and manager of the bank.

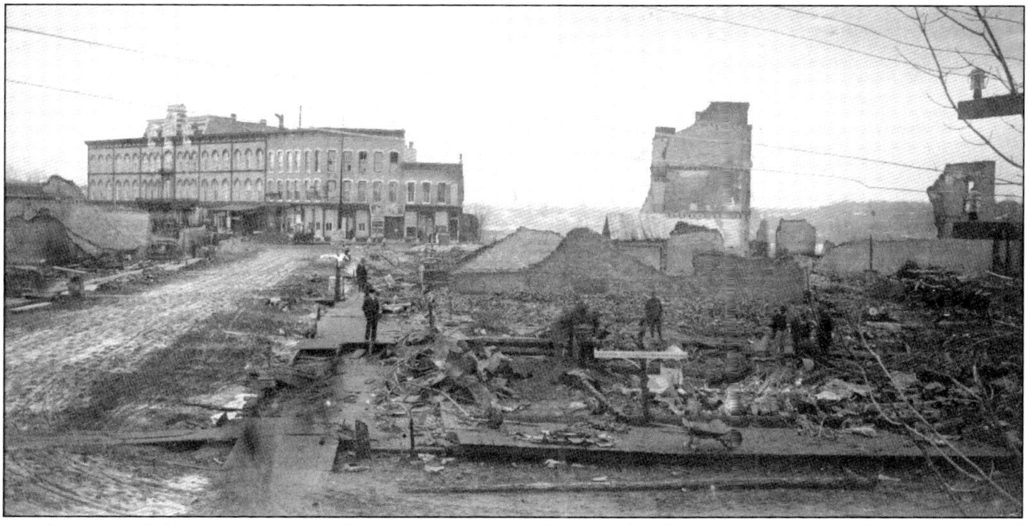

At the turn of the 20th century, fire was a major problem. Most buildings were made of wood, and gas and kerosene lamps were the primary means of lighting. This combination of material and lighting source was responsible for many blazes. The horse-drawn fire engines and the volunteer firefighters were often not adequate to meet the firefighting needs.

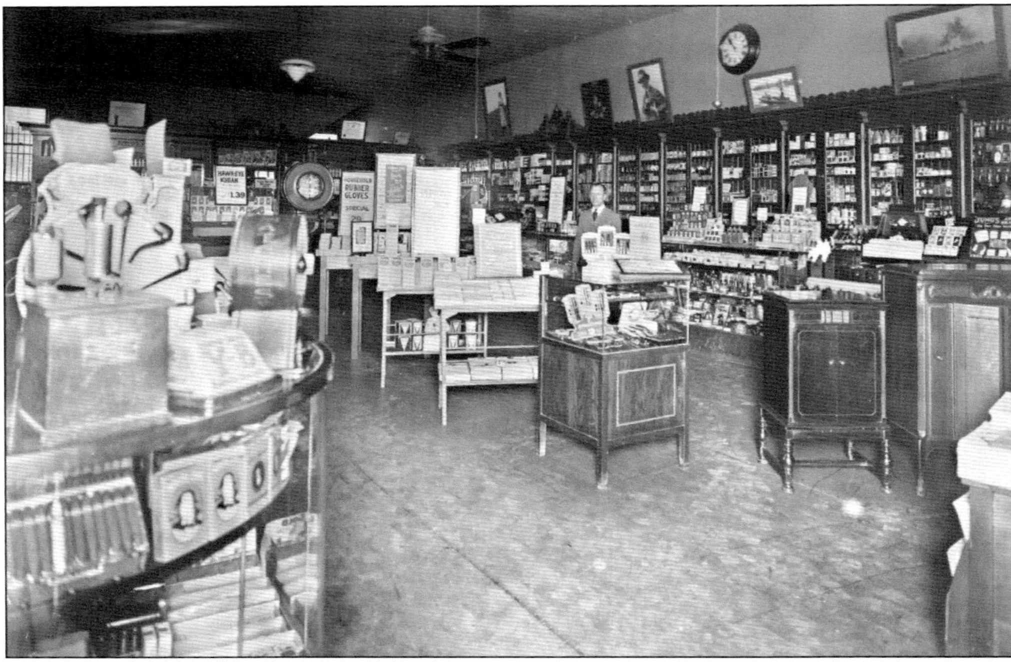

This is the Brehler Drug Store in 1905. In that year, Oscar A. Brehler bought the store from H.F. Messer. As business grew, Brehler, in 1909, moved his business to the Rogallo building, at the corner of N and Seventh Streets. In addition to pharmaceutical products, Sanger residents could purchase a Victrola, a Kodak camera for $1.39, and even a good cigar.

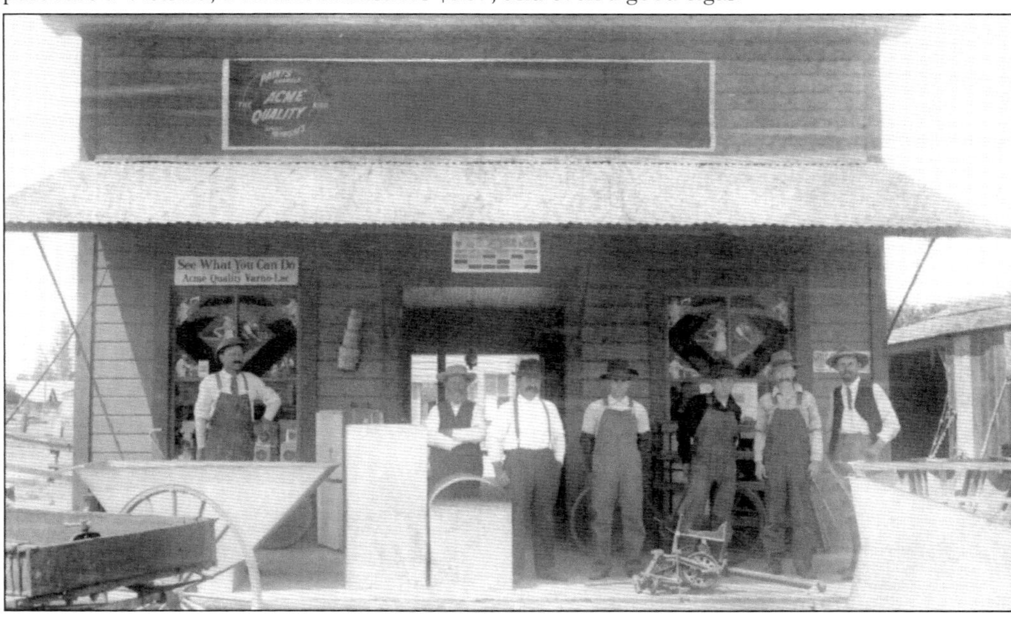

This is an early photograph of the Sanger Iron Works, which was owned and operated by George C. Owens (third from left). All types of metalwork were produced, but the company's largest volume of business was in the installation of pumps. Posing in this photograph are, from left to right, H.P. Friend, J. Suderman, ? Owens, Dillard Fike, John McEwan, George Gates, and Dr. Karrar.

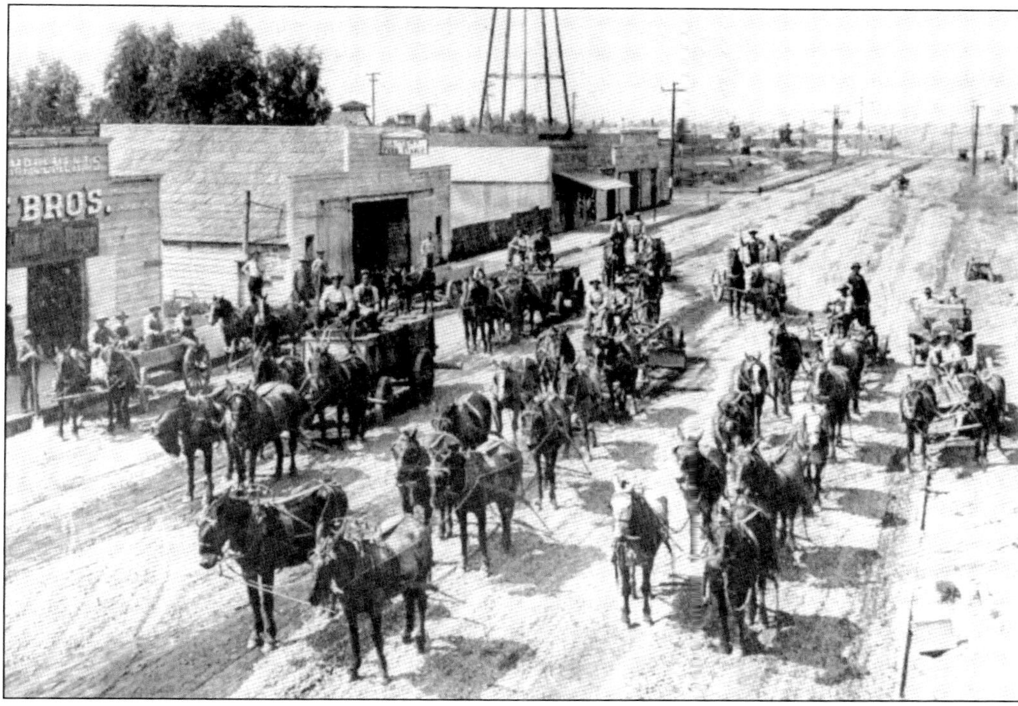

In 1916, a major grading operation was begun on M Street. R.J. Imrie, Foley Kanawyer, and George Dockery are prepared to start their teams pulling graders. Wagons filled with road material are also standing by. To the left is the blacksmith shop owned by the Burnett brothers, Robertson, and Dan Evinger. The old ball park grandstand can be seen in the distance.

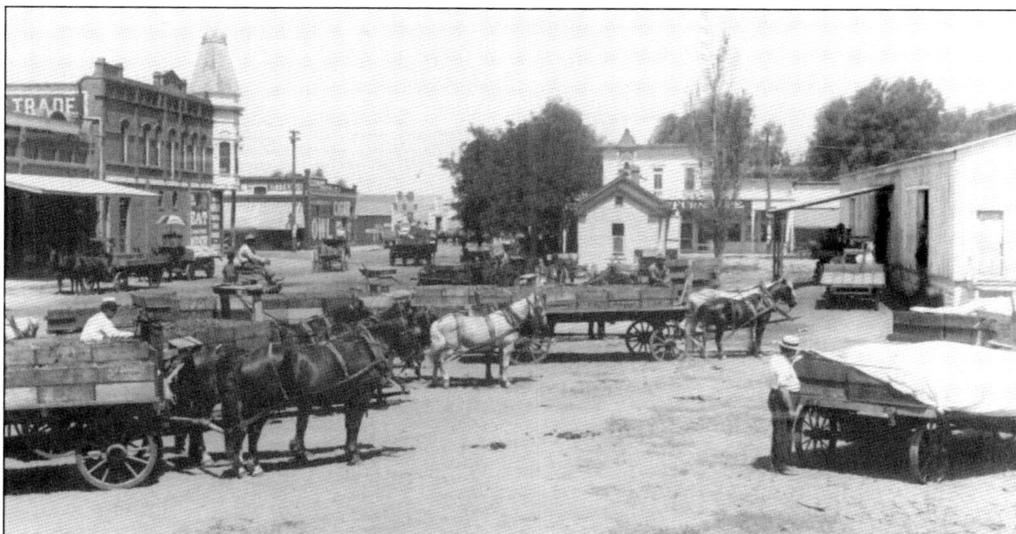

The intersection of Academy Avenue and Seventh Street is seen here in 1914. On the right is one of the local packing sheds receiving the summer harvest. The building with the bell tower right of center is Sanger's firehouse. On the other side of the firehouse is Seventh Avenue. To the left, at the northwest intersection of Seventh and Academy, is the Old Billiards Hall.

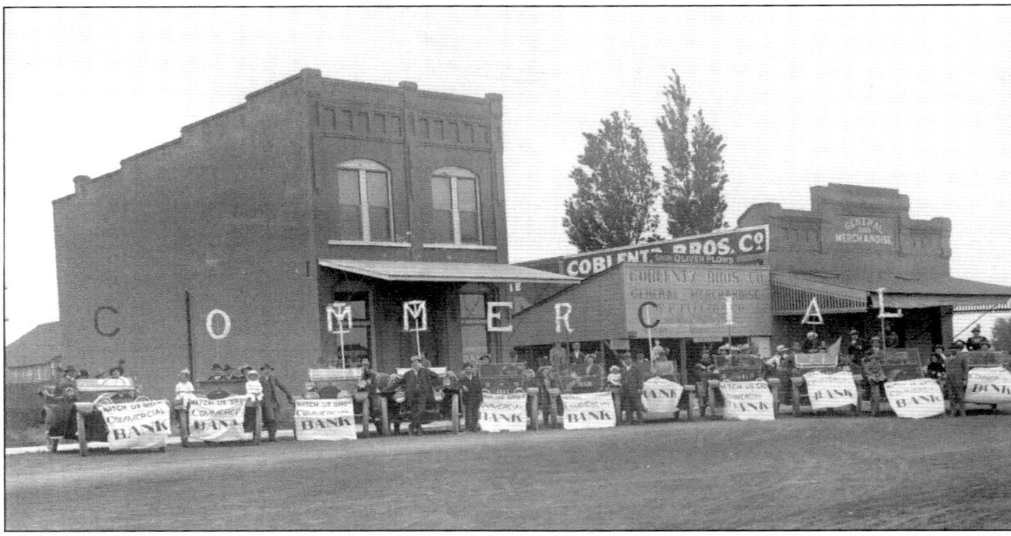

This 1914 photograph depicts the grand opening of Commercial Bank, located on L Street. On this day, a parade led by the Powers family, Dick Cameron, Frank Paden, the Oliver family, and Frank Kummeth rode through the streets of Sanger to mark the great occasion. These individuals are the founders of the bank.

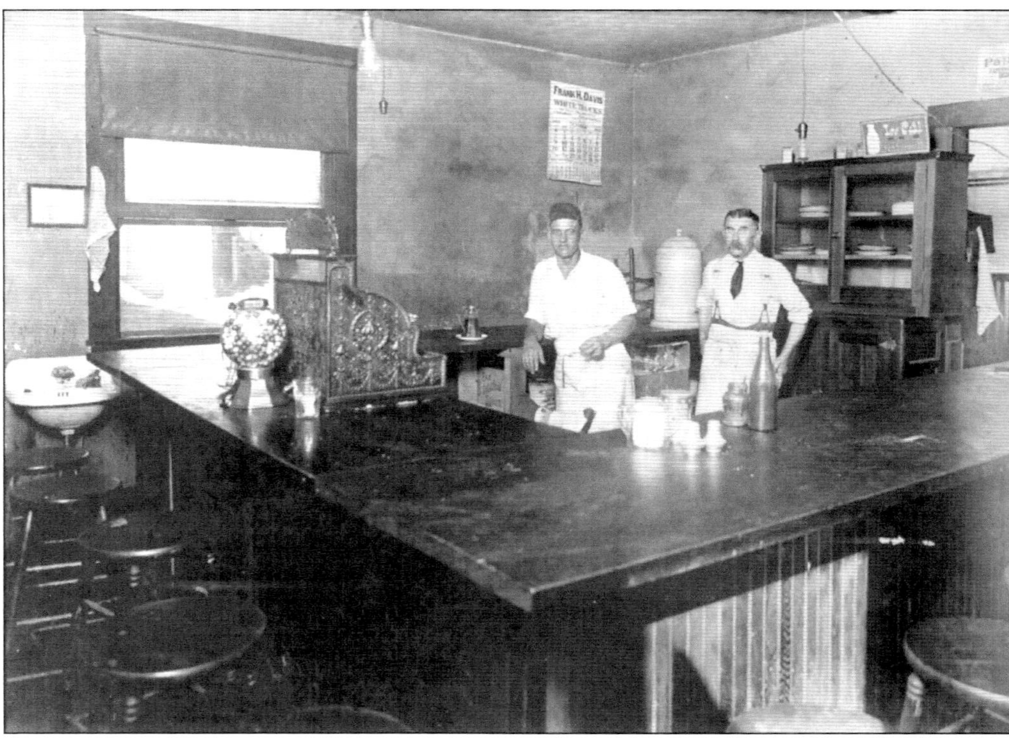

Turn-of-the-century dining in Sanger left much to be desired. However, rumor had it that Larson's restaurant had the best chili in Sanger. Owner and operator L.J. Larson is pictured at left. Homemade pies, coffee, and even jawbreakers could be purchased at Larson's.

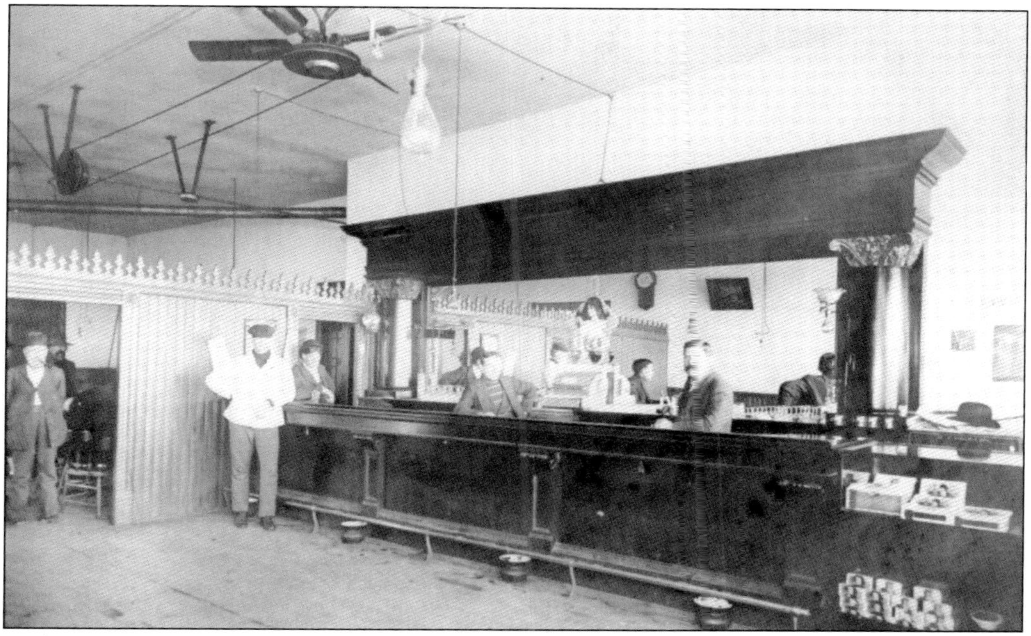

In this interior photograph of Rodgers Bros.' Sampling Room, Henry Rodgers is at left in the white jacket and George Rodgers is behind the bar with a mustache. The sampling room (another term for a bar) was located on the northeast corner of Academy Avenue and Seventh Street. Known as "Hell's Corner," it burned down in 1926. Note the system used to turn the fan.

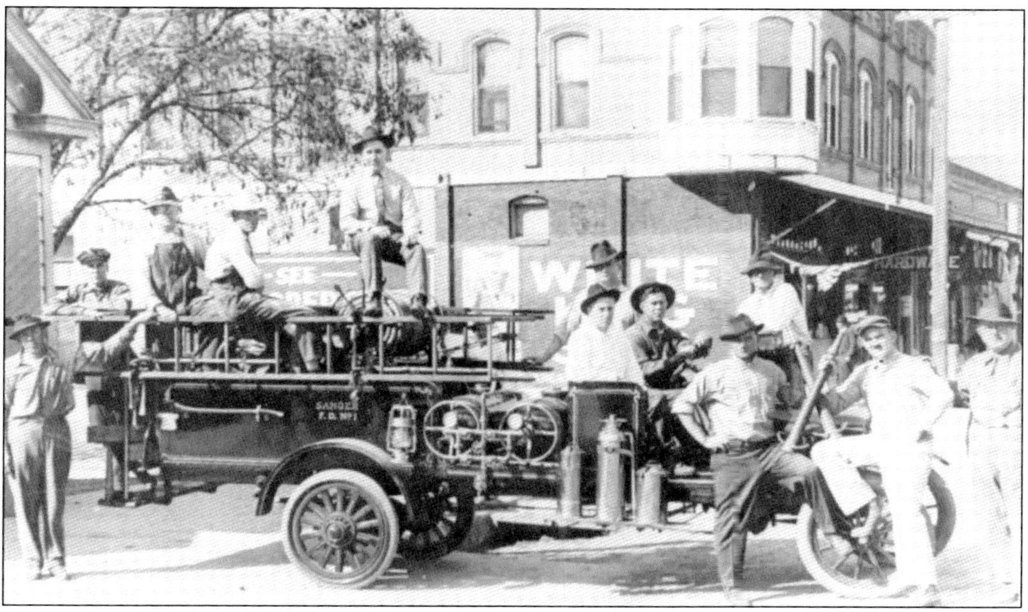

It was not until 1921 that Sanger had its first motorized fire engine. It was manned by Sanger's volunteer fire squad. Members of the squad are, from left to right, Ray Chrismer, Eddie Lewis, A.F. Warner, Kenneth Bosserman, Max Petersen, Leslie Brandon, L.N. Petersen, Dick McCann, Virgil Brumbaugh, Lillard Craig, Dick Carisle, and Bill Jones. When a fire broke out, the mill whistle would blow to alert the volunteers.

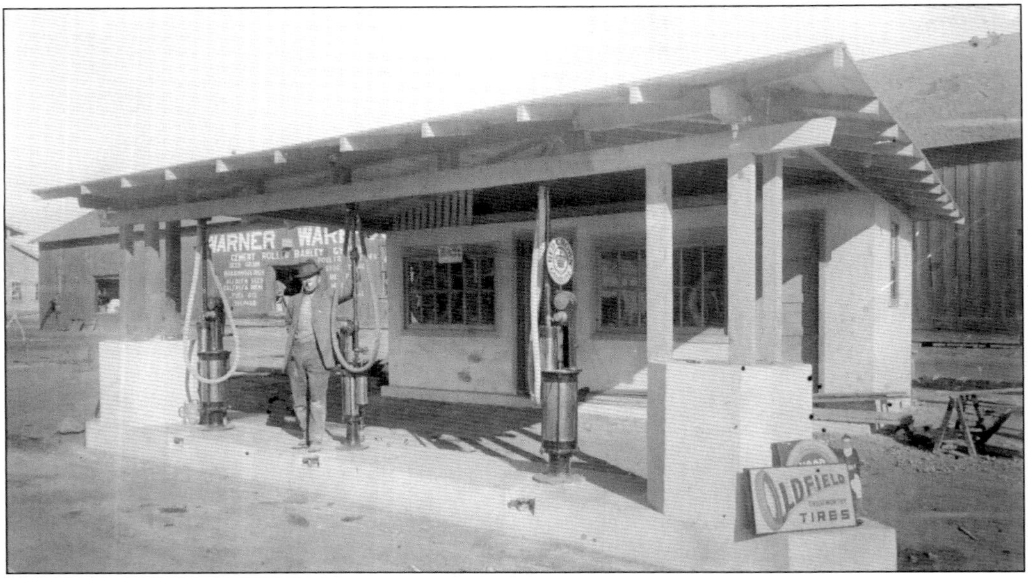

Bert Warner is pictured in front of one of Sanger's early service stations. Motorists could buy Red Crown gasoline and "trustworthy" Oldfield tires. The station was located in front of Warner's warehouse, where he also sold seed, grain, cement, sulfur, and agricultural equipment to the farmers in the area.

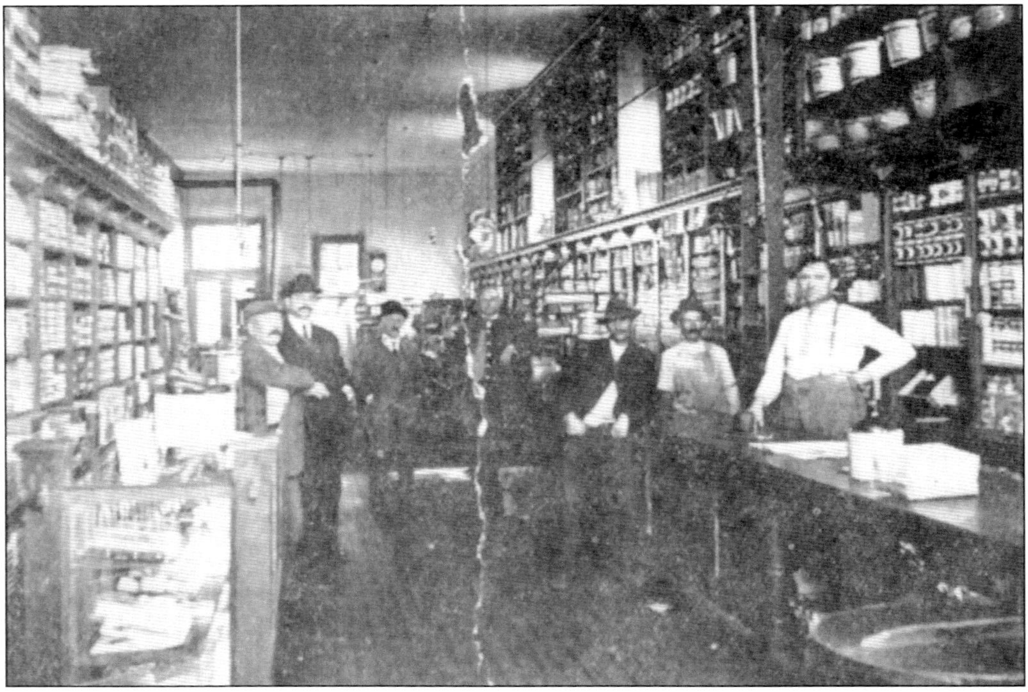

The Frankenau Merchandise store was established in 1889. Its inventory ran from the front of the store to the rear, from bottom to top. On the right is the sliding ladder used to reach the higher shelves. The individuals in this photograph are, from left to right, R.M. Wood, Jules Coblentz, Sig Frankenau, George Coblentz, unidentified, Frank Paden, and Frank Perry.

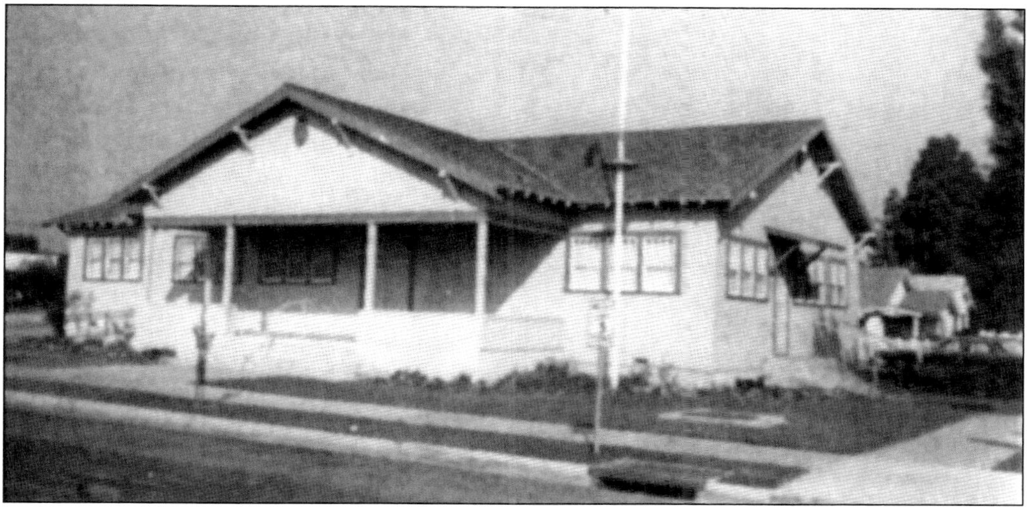

The YMCA building was located at Seventh and P Streets. In 1927, the building was purchased by the Civic Improvement Club for $727 in back taxes and penalties. Later, in 1953, the group's name was changed to Sanger Woman's Club. This organization has over the years provided many services to the community, helping to make Sanger a better place to live.

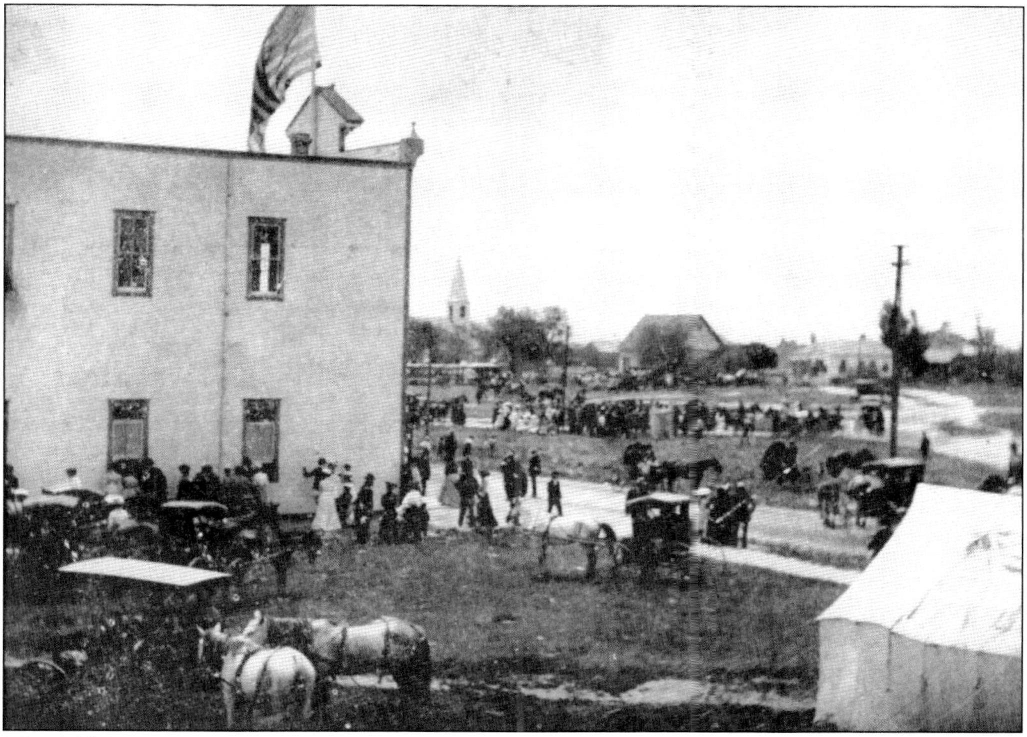

The Old Opera House is the white building on the left. Owned by the Odd Fellows, it had many uses: all-night dances, plays, meetings, and other social gatherings. This photograph was taken on one of Sanger's annual May Day celebrations. The event was so popular that people came from all over Fresno County to attend. They came by horse, wagon, and train, and many of them camped out in the open through the holiday.

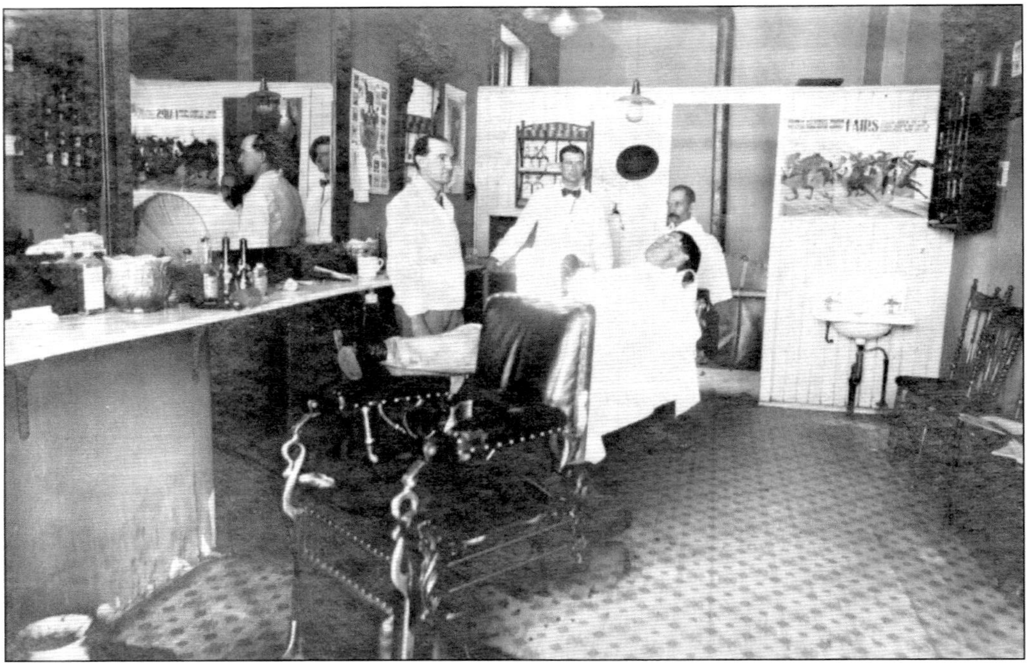

Two barbers and their customers pose for the camera. A poster on the back wall of the shop advertises the "Central California Circuit Fair, Sept 20th to Oct 3rd." Sanger had a number of barbershops such as this one. Note the spittoon in the corner for the customers who chewed tobacco.

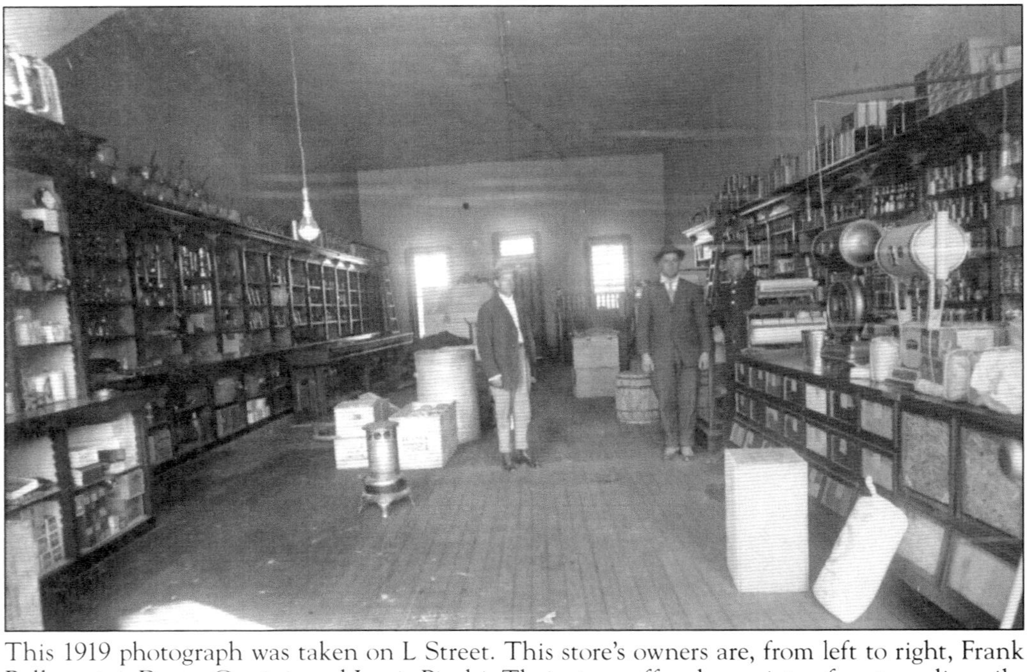

This 1919 photograph was taken on L Street. This store's owners are, from left to right, Frank Belluomini, Dante Carsini, and Louis Picchi. Their store offered a variety of pastas, olive oils, seasonings, cooking utensils, dried condiments, and canned goods. Many of Sanger's residents enjoyed this little "Italian" venture.

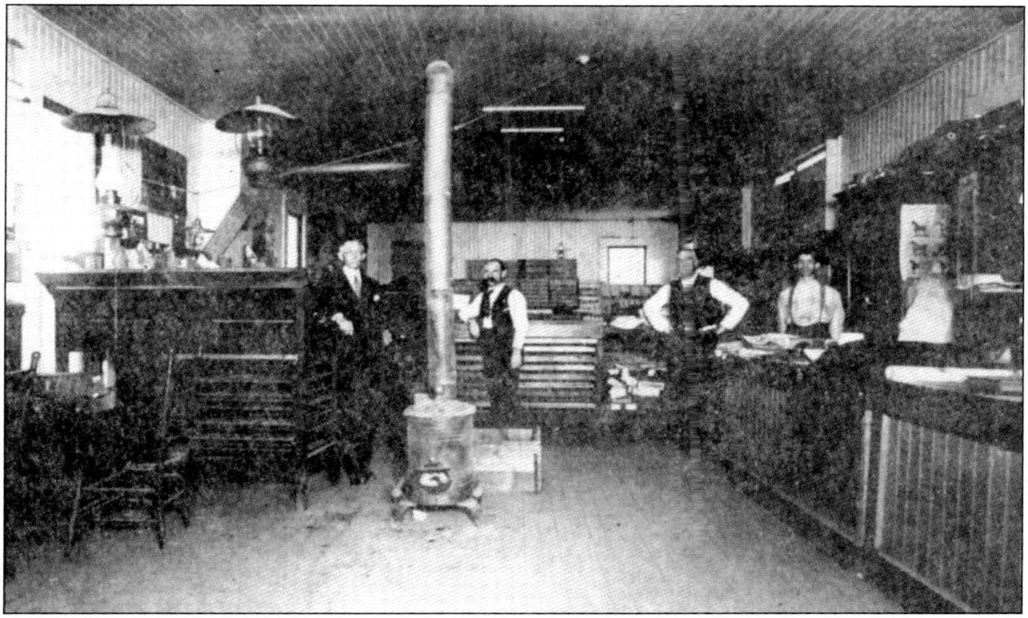

This is the *Sanger Herald* office in 1908. To the left is the Washington hand press, which enabled the workers to get the news out. Shown here are, from left to right: an unidentified visitor to the print shop; W.J. Tostevin, a member of the editorial staff; E.P. Dewey, founder of the paper; and Jesse Adams, a member of the mechanical staff. The *Herald* was the main source of information for the people of Sanger.

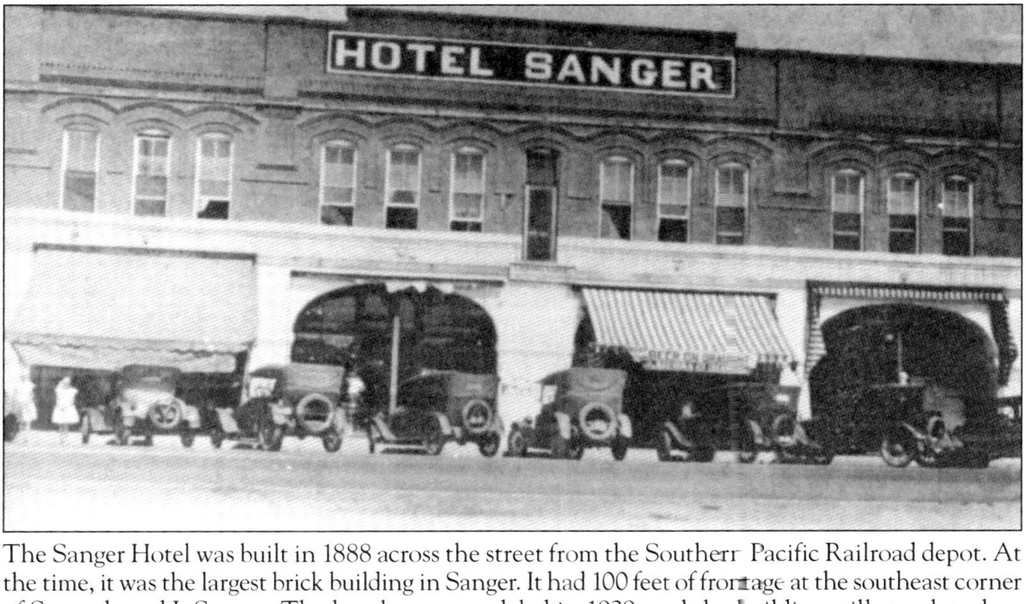

The Sanger Hotel was built in 1888 across the street from the Southern Pacific Railroad depot. At the time, it was the largest brick building in Sanger. It had 100 feet of frontage at the southeast corner of Seventh and L Streets. The hotel was remodeled in 1929, and the building still stands today.

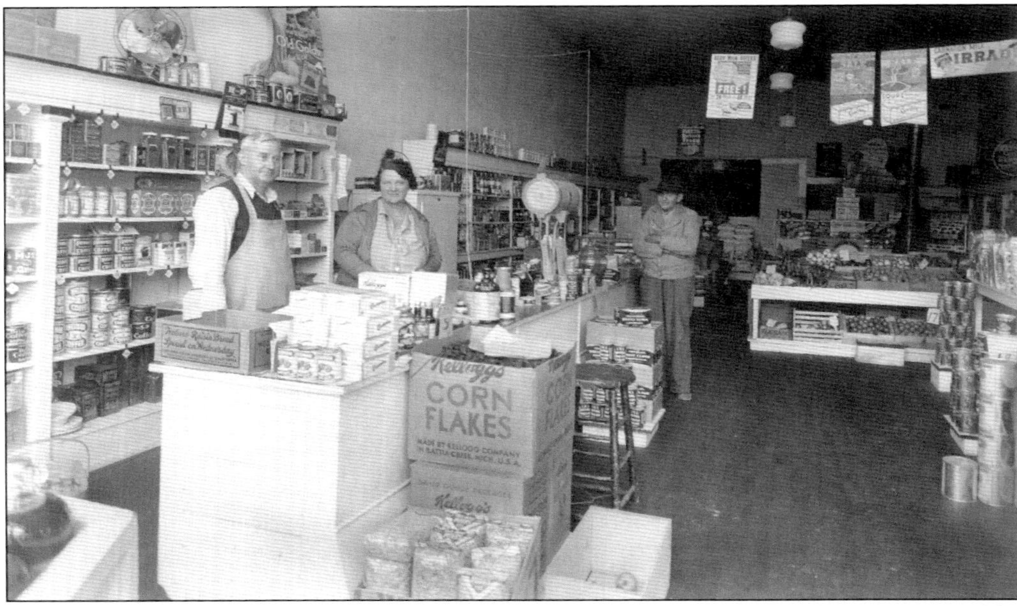

This is the Jones Grocery store as it looked in 1930. On the left are owners Charlie Jones and his wife, Dora. At the time, Charlie was the mayor of Sanger. The store seems to be supplied with everyday items needed by families. The Corn Flakes box seems to be filled with something else, possibly raisins.

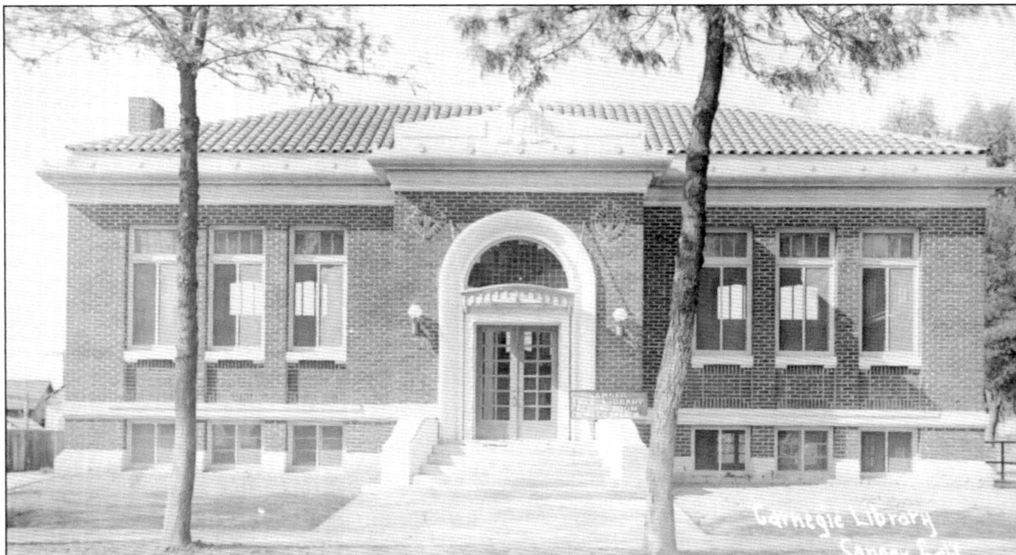

Sanger was incorporated in May 1911, and its first mayor was Dr. E.E. Baird. Early on, the library shared space in the Mission Guild Hall. Concerned patrons sought to establish a permanent home for the library and began to raise funds and finally settled a lengthy feud on the location. An appeal for funding was then made to the Carnegie Corporation, and an agreement was made. The agreement called for the city to purchase land for the new library. In return, the Carnegie Corporation would donate a new $10,000 library building to the city. The Carnegie library was completed in 1916, at the corner of Seventh and O Streets.

Seven

Churches

With the establishment of new communities in the Sanger area, residents felt the need for the same spiritual guidance that they had known before settling there. The Catholic missionaries, who had a long history in California, were the first religious group to respond. As early as 1883, missionaries were baptizing people in Tollhouse, Centerville, Squaw Valley, and Dunlap. Records from St. Mary's Church record a Father Fasionotti making regular missions to the Clovis, Sanger, and Reedley areas. Because of the long history of the California missions, the Catholic Church was the first to bring its ministry to the Sanger area. The first official Catholic church was St. Mary's, built in 1901.

As early as 1910, Yonetaro Masuda offered a building on his ranch, located near Bethel and McKinley, to be used by Buddhists in the thriving Japanese community.

Sadly, the church was closed when the Japanese were sent to internment camps during the war. Japanese Americans living north of Kings Canyon Road were sent to camps in Poston, Arizona, from the Clovis Railroad depot in July 1942. Those living south of Kings Canyon were sent to camps in Gila, Arizona, from the Sanger Railroad depot on August 6, 1942. Longtime residents recall August 6, 1942, as the busiest shopping day in Sanger, as those about to board the train went from store to store, purchasing items they might need in the camps. No one knew what the future held, what life in the camps would be like, and if they would ever be allowed to return to their homes. Many did not return to Sanger. Those Buddhists who did return after the war met in the Sanger Japanese Community Hall, which was located at 800 K Street.

St. Paul's Lutheran Church was founded in 1907 by Rev. Roehmer of Fresno. A group led by John T. Walton was instrumental in founding the First Baptist Church in Sanger. Many other churches were formed to meet the spiritual needs of the diverse and growing community. Sanger once had a least 20 different churches serving the community. Among these were three Baptist churches, the Christian Science Society, Church of Christ, Four Square Gospel, Latter-day Saints, Pentecostals, Seventh-Day Adventist, Nazarene Church, and many others. Today, 125 years after its founding, Sanger still has a diverse and thriving religious community.

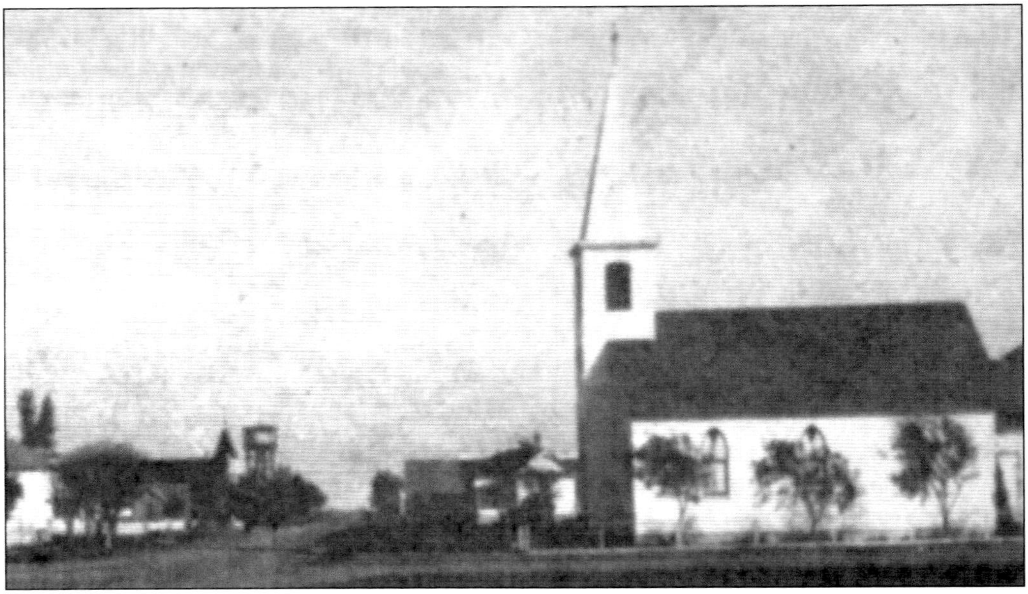

The first Catholic church in Sanger was St. Mary's (above), built in 1901. Prior to that date, parishioners met in the home of siblings Mary and Dan Lafferty. Mary raised money from the community for a church, and Dan did the construction. It was located at Ninth and O Streets. In 1935, the church was moved to the rear of the lot, and in 1947, a new church (below) was built where the first church had been. This structure holds many memories for the older Catholic families in Sanger. Even though a new church has been constructed at North and Bethel Avenues, members return to the old church.

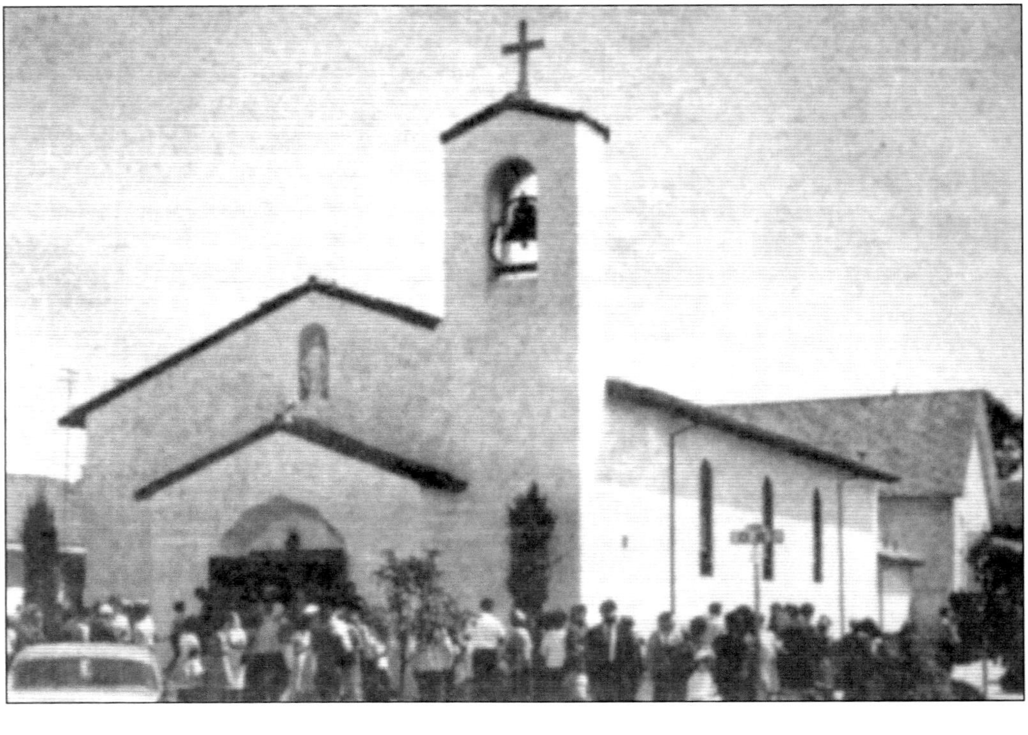

The First Baptist Church in Sanger was formed in 1890 when a group of 10 charter members, including Mr. and Mrs. John T. Walton, met to organize a congregation. The first building (right) was erected in 1892 on the corner of Seventh and O Streets. In 1910, the original church was moved to the back of the lot and converted into classrooms. In 1910, an auditorium (below) was built at the original site, facing east on O Street. This combination of classrooms and an auditorium to handle church services was sufficient until 1947. By then, Sanger's population had grown, and the Baptist congregation razed the old church and replaced it with a new church, built in the 1950s at the corner of Fourteenth and O Streets.

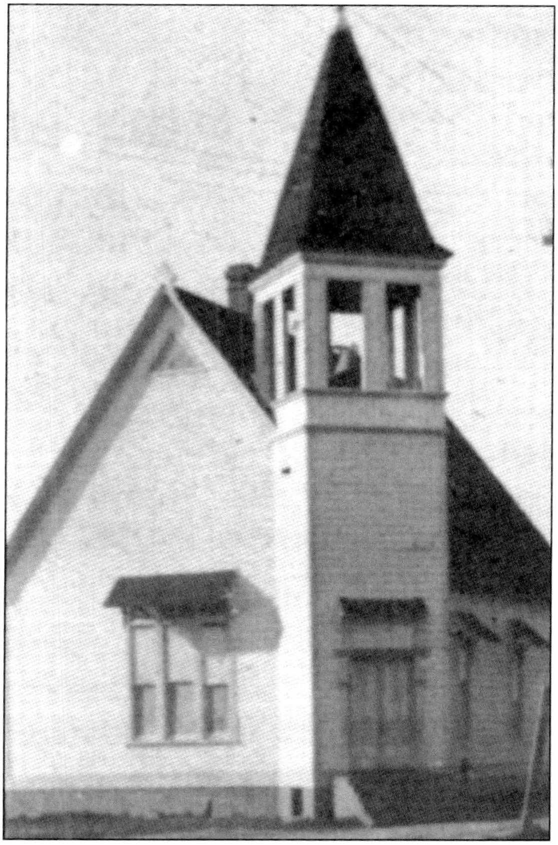

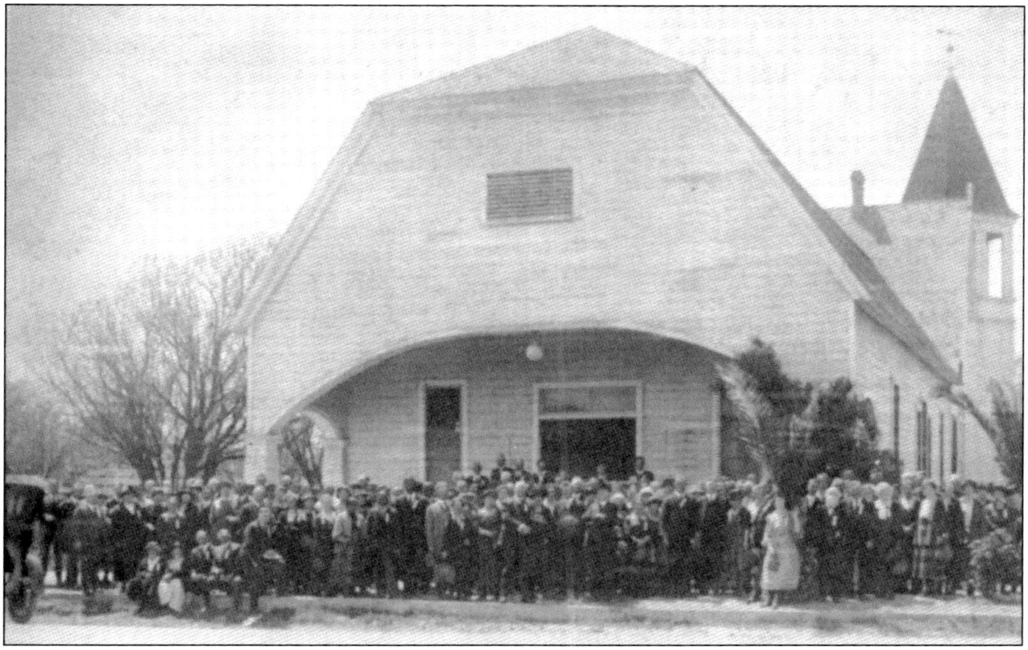

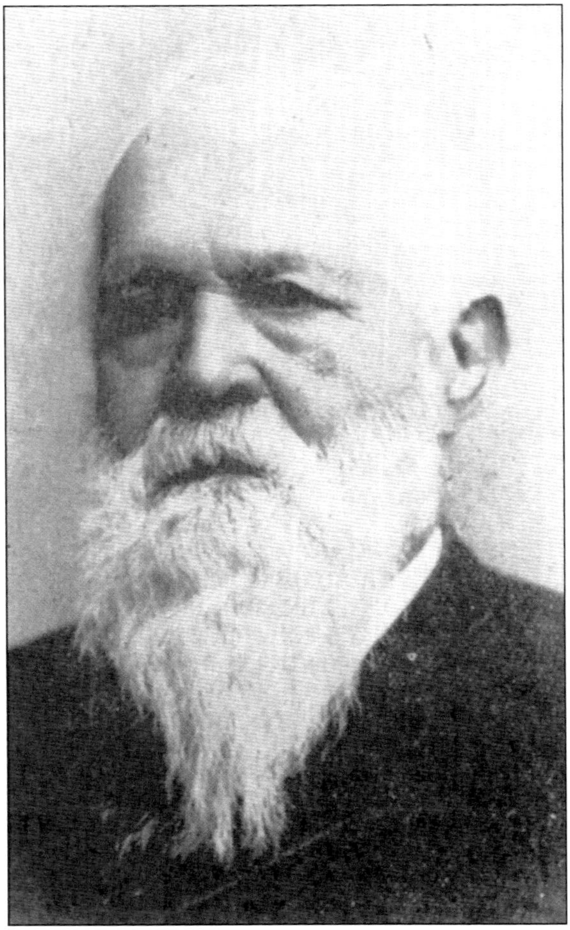

In the early 1880s, Fr. Cornelius Yager (left), a Presbyterian minister, arrived from Cumberland. He brought many settlers with him, and they became the founders of the Presbyterian church in Sanger. In 1888, these early settlers, meeting in the home of Frank Giles, started a Presbyterian Sunday school. In 1890, under the direction of Rec. George Giffen, the first Presbyterian church was incorporated. Building began, and the Presbyterian sanctuary was completed in 1892 at a cost of $1,000. Over the years, a manse was added, a Sunday school was built, adjoining property was bought, and the original church was moved. Then, in 1952, a new church (below) was built at Jensen Avenue and P Street.

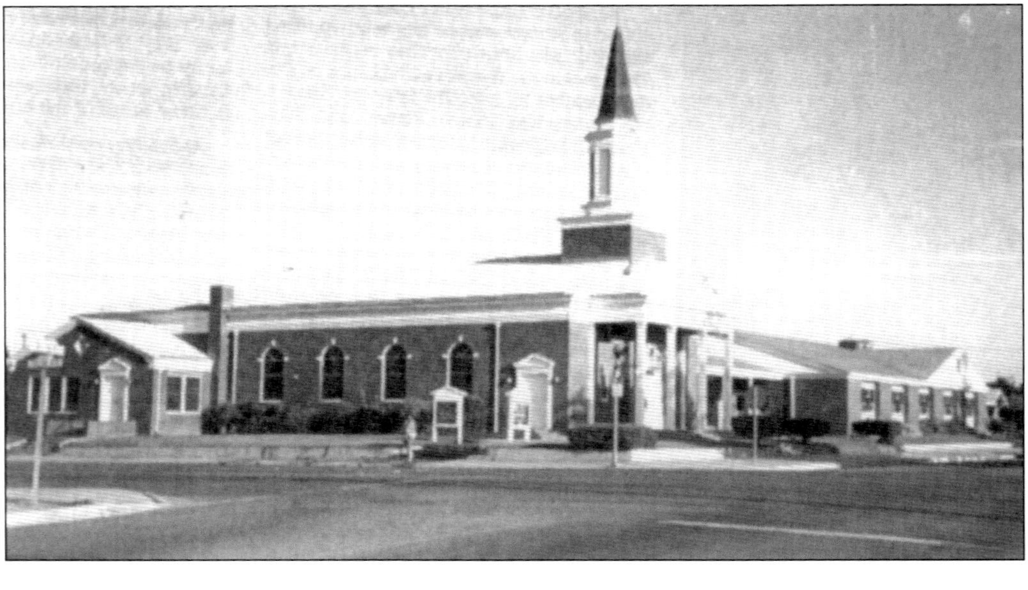

In 1881, a South Methodist Church preacher began holding meetings in Centerville. In 1888, the church moved to the Sanger Junction area. At first, services were held in the French Hotel. Then, in 1890, the congregation erected its own building (right) at Ninth and P Streets. Among the early members were Emma Conklin, Addie Potter, and Uriah Edgar. Another group, the Methodist Episcopal Church North, also built a church in Sanger, at Eighth and P Streets in 1892. Among its members were H. Cramers, J. Pottles, J. Skoonburgs, and R. Walton. The young members of each church began to socialize in their local schools, and the adults decided they should merge the two Methodist churches. A new church was built at Ninth and P Streets. This Gothic Revival structure (below) was unique among the many churches in Sanger.

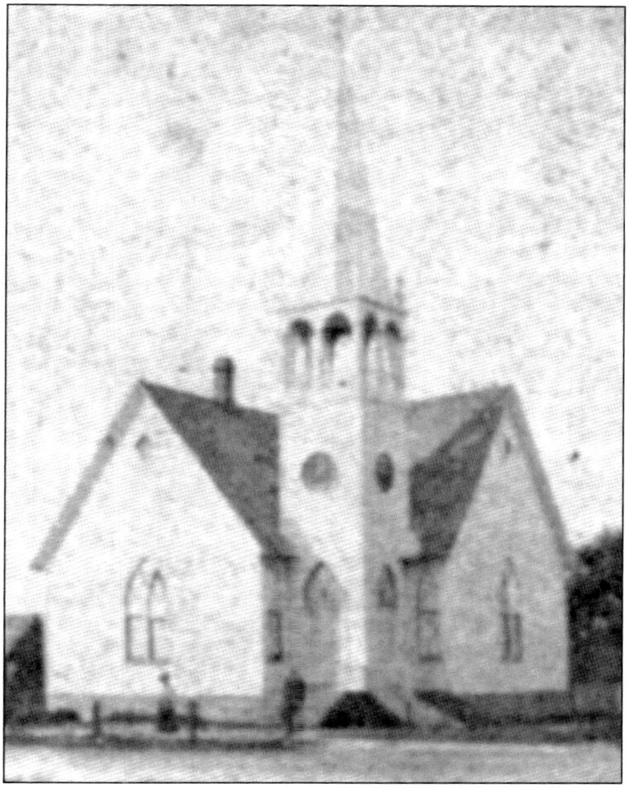

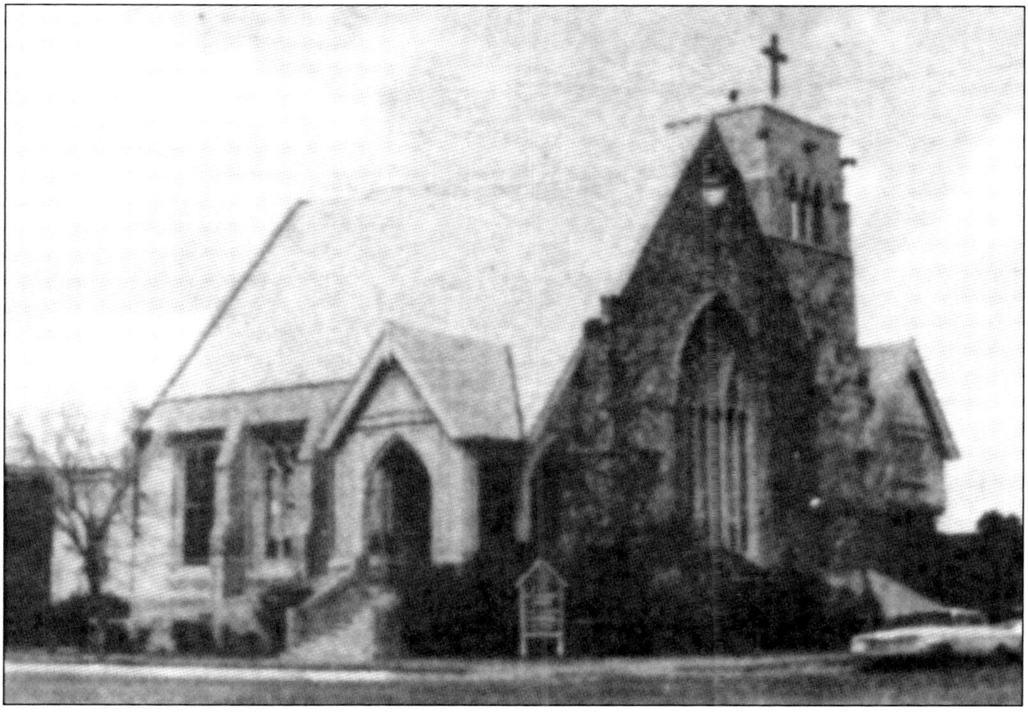

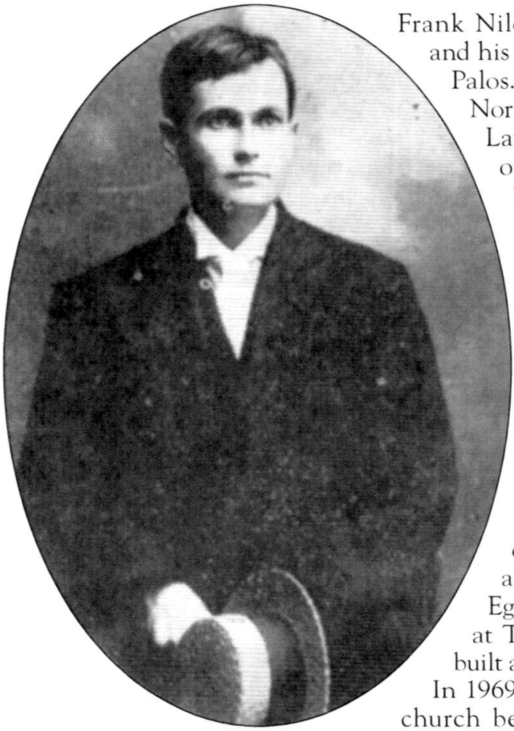

Frank Niles emigrated from Tennessee to California, and his first position as a Methodist pastor was in Dos Palos. At the time, there was a Methodist Church North and a Methodist Church South in Sanger. Later, Niles moved to Sanger and served as pastor of the Methodist Church South from 1908 to 1911. In Sanger, he also worked as city clerk for many years and ran his own business.

The Salem Congregational Church, pictured here in 1907, was started in the area by a group of German immigrants from the Volga River area of Russia. Their first pastor was Rev. Franz Egerlund, and the congregation's first church was at Thompson and North Avenues. In 1917, they built a new church at McCall and Annadale Avenues. In 1969, after a split because of political reasons, the church became the Salem Evangelical Free Church.

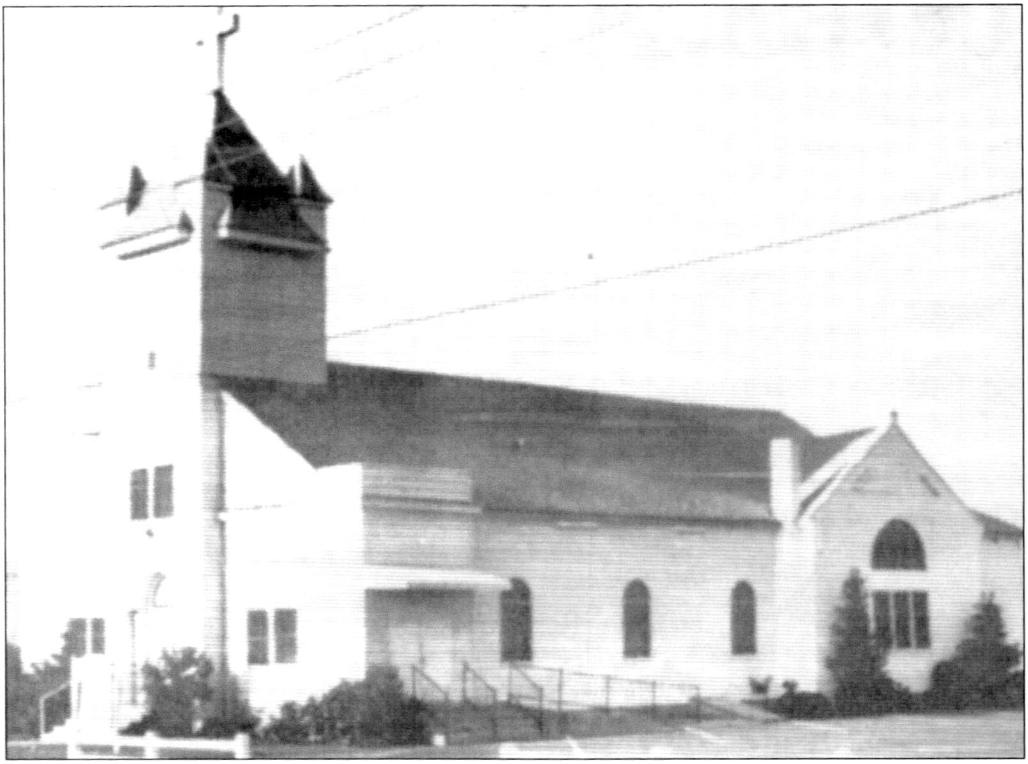

St. Paul's Lutheran Church was founded in 1907 by Reverend Roemer of Fresno. Under the leadership of Reverend Gutleben, the first minister stationed in Sanger, a Lutheran church was built at Twelfth and M Streets and later moved to the corner of Twelfth and N Streets. In the 1950s, the church was removed, and the new church was constructed on Jensen Avenue.

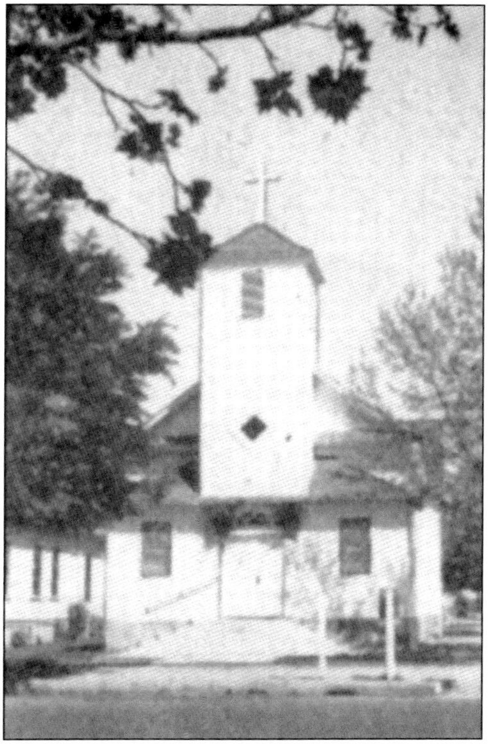

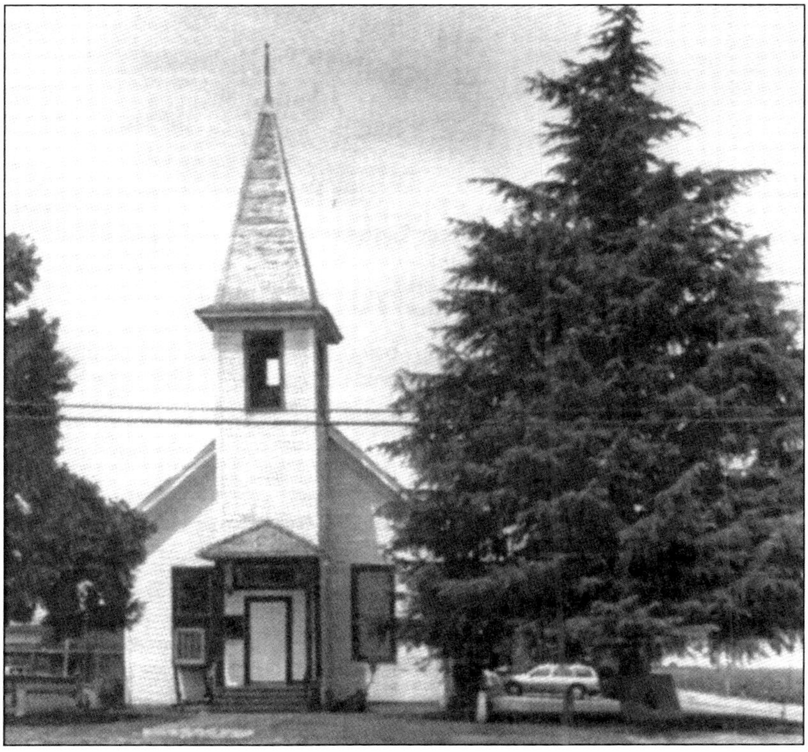

The Del Rey Baptist church, shown here, was located at the corner of Del Rey and American Avenues. The original Baptist church in Del Rey was built around 1896. At that time, most of the social life of the town was centered on the church. In addition to the Baptist church, there was a Methodist church in Del Rey.

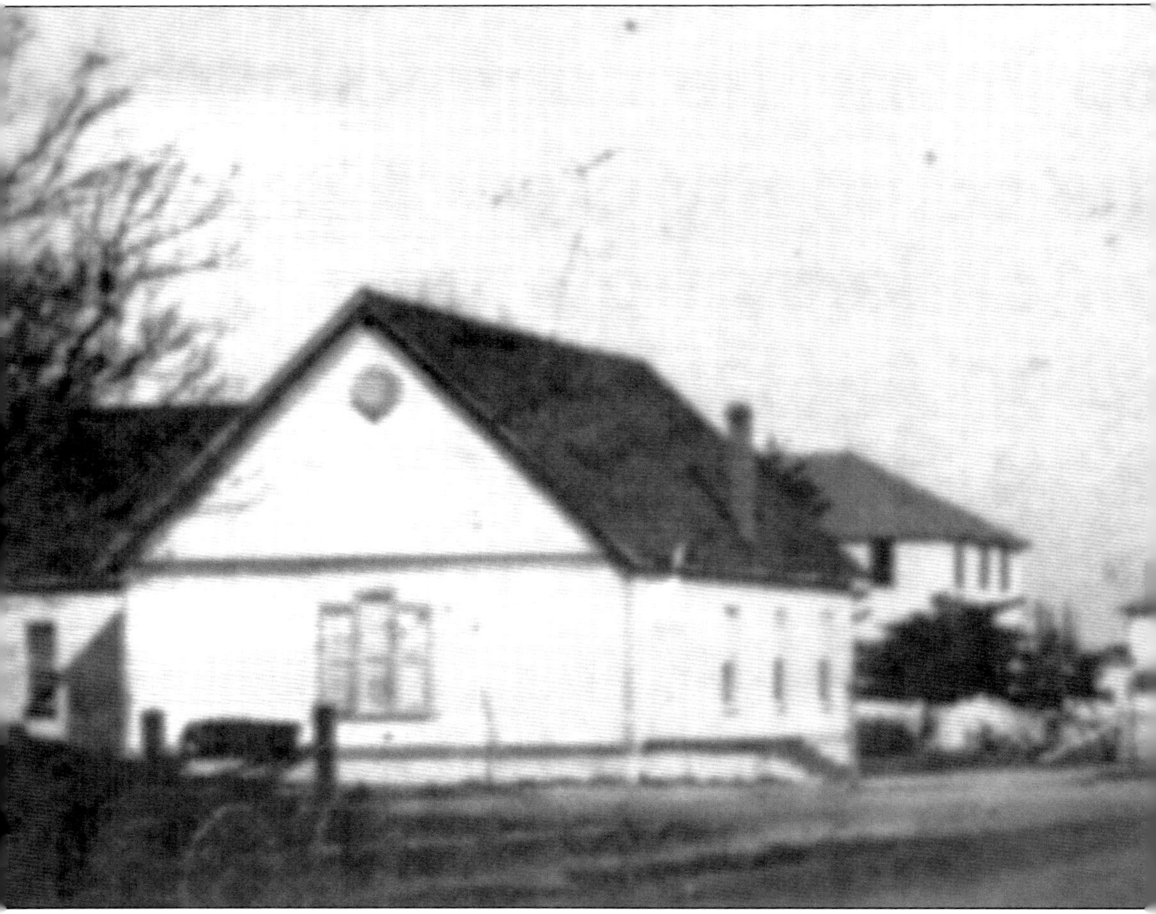

First Christian Church of Sanger was organized in April 1893. Initially, the congregation held its meetings under tents, in the room above the Sanger Meat Market, and at the Methodist church. In 1893, land was bought and one large room was built at the corner of Eighth and P Streets. It caught fire in December 1923 as services were under way, but it was rapidly rebuilt. In 1960, a new church was built.

Eight

Schools and Sports

The 1849 Gold Rush brought thousands of immigrants to California. Initially, the arrivals were men looking for gold. They were followed by merchants, farmers, religious groups, and their families. Wherever they settled, new residents wanted markets, churches, legal systems, social organizations, and schools.

One of the first schools in Fresno County was the Big Dry Creek Academy, north of what was to become Sanger. This school was founded in 1872. J.D. Collins, its first teacher, had come to Academy in 1869 from Tennessee. The small community of Academy was located along the stage line connecting Visalia and Millerton.

Before the founding of Sanger, the town of Scottsburg, now known as Centerville, was a thriving community. As early as 1887, children from the area attended Centerville School, the oldest school in the Sanger Unified District.

In early 1889, the first grammar school, composed of about 25 children, was organized in the Hotel De France, with J.W. Evans as the teacher. A few months later, the Sanger Elementary School District was formed, and a four-room, brick building was constructed. Known as the Sanger School, it was later named Taft School, after Pres. William Howard Taft. A second school was built during the Wilson administration and named Wilson School.

The first high school in Sanger was organized in 1899, and classes were held in the Sanger Opera House. A. Clyde Olney was the first principal and teacher. The freshmen learned English literature, algebra, Latin, and English history. More advanced students were taught geometry and Caesar's *The Gallic War.*

In 1901, the first Sanger High School was built on the site of the old high school tennis courts. Classes were taught by principal R.Y. Glidden and the first teacher, Edith Taber. In 1903, the first class of eight seniors graduated.

In 1914, the wood frame school was replaced with a brick building. This was enlarged and remodeled several time over the years until the year 2000, when the new high school was occupied and the old building became Washington Academic School. As of 2013, the land has already been bought for a second high school in the near future.

The three R's have always been important in Sanger; however, from the earliest days, sports has played an important part in the schools. For over a century, Sanger boys and girls have competed with neighboring schools. They did not always win, but they always gave their best. The following pictures tell their stories.

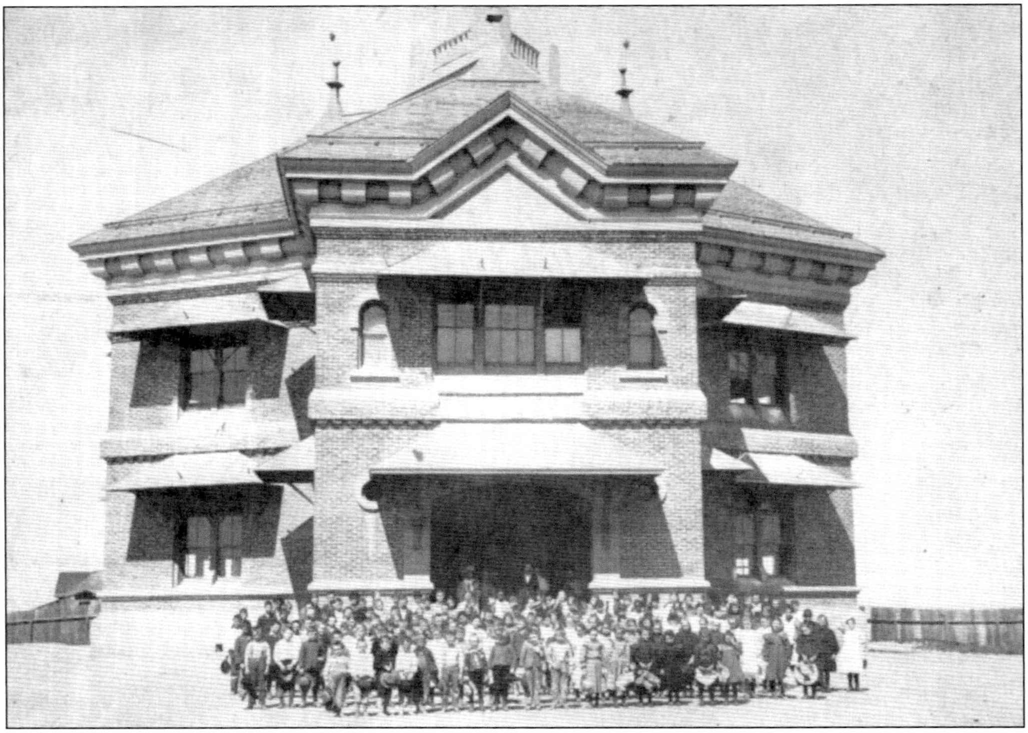

Sanger Elementary, also known as the Sanger School, was erected in 1889. It is seen in the 1897 photograph above. Miss Mary Allen, who later married W.M. Barr, was a teacher at this time and Dr. E.E. Baird was the principal. In 1914, a second school was built on the east side of Sanger, named Wilson School, after Pres. Woodrow Wilson. In the same year, Sanger School District changed the name of Sanger Elementary to Taft School in honor of Pres. William Howard Taft. The tradition of naming Sanger schools after presidents had begun. In 1891, the school had 120 students, and there were only three teachers to provide the instruction. Allen is shown in the 1892 photograph below with her Sanger Elementary class. Sadly, this school building was demolished in 1929.

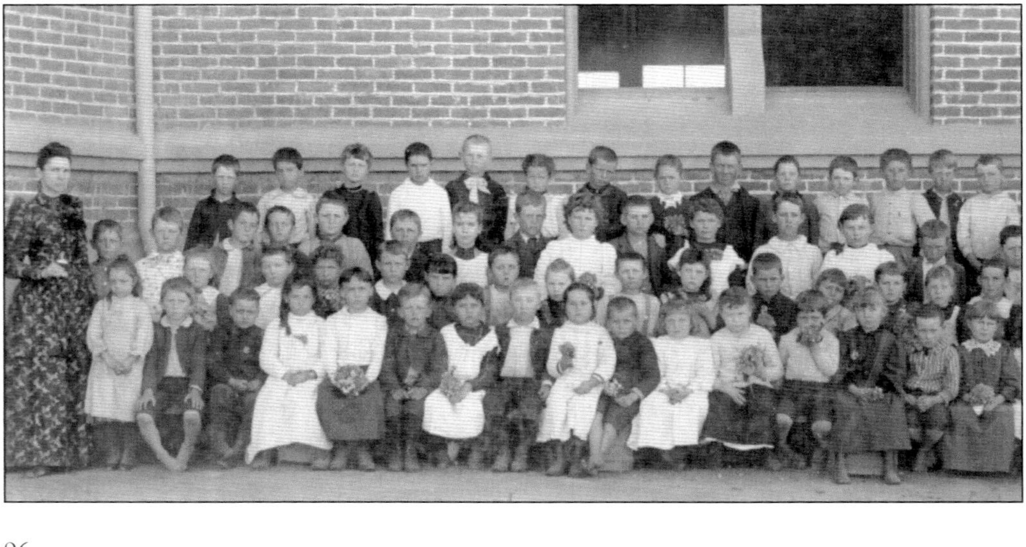

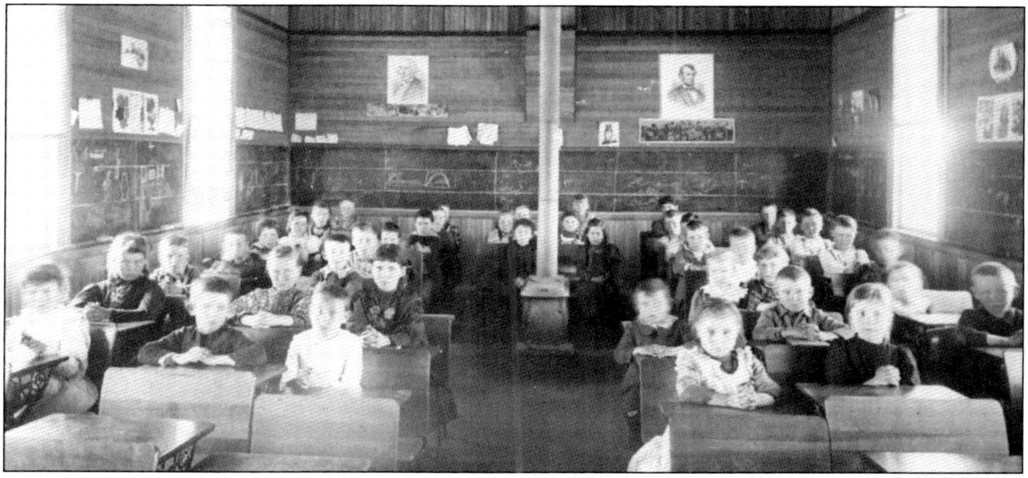

In this 1894 photograph, Sanger Elementary first-, second-, and third-grade students are gathered in one room. Presidential portraits can be seen on the back wall. Also visible are chalkboards, folded hands, and a potbellied stove. There were seven other classrooms in the building, as well as an administrative office. The teacher taught multiple subjects at different grade levels.

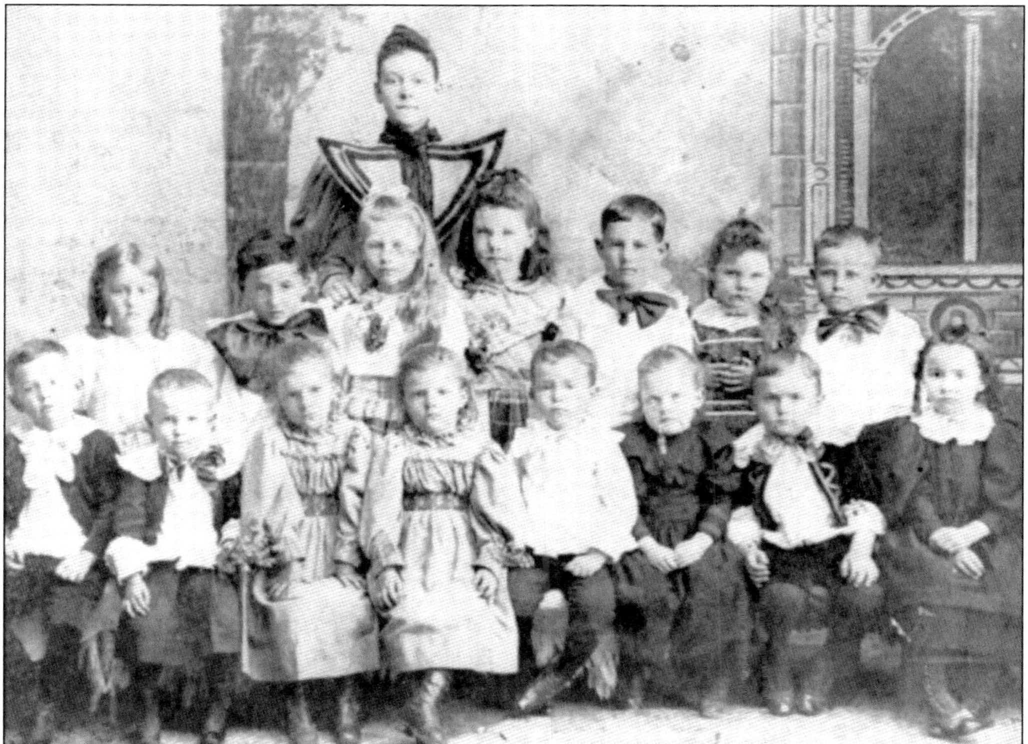

Shown here in 1894 is the first private kindergarten class in Sanger. Florence Brurns McAllister is the teacher. The students are, from left to right, (first row) Earl Ingles, Strother P. Walton, Iris Whitmore, Inez Whitmore, Artis Armuth, Jennie Grahm, Dwight Burnett, and Hattie Sayre; (second row) Edna Durgin, unidentified, Alice Southworth, Bessie Shaw, James Shaw, Ethel Chick, and Sam O'Neal.

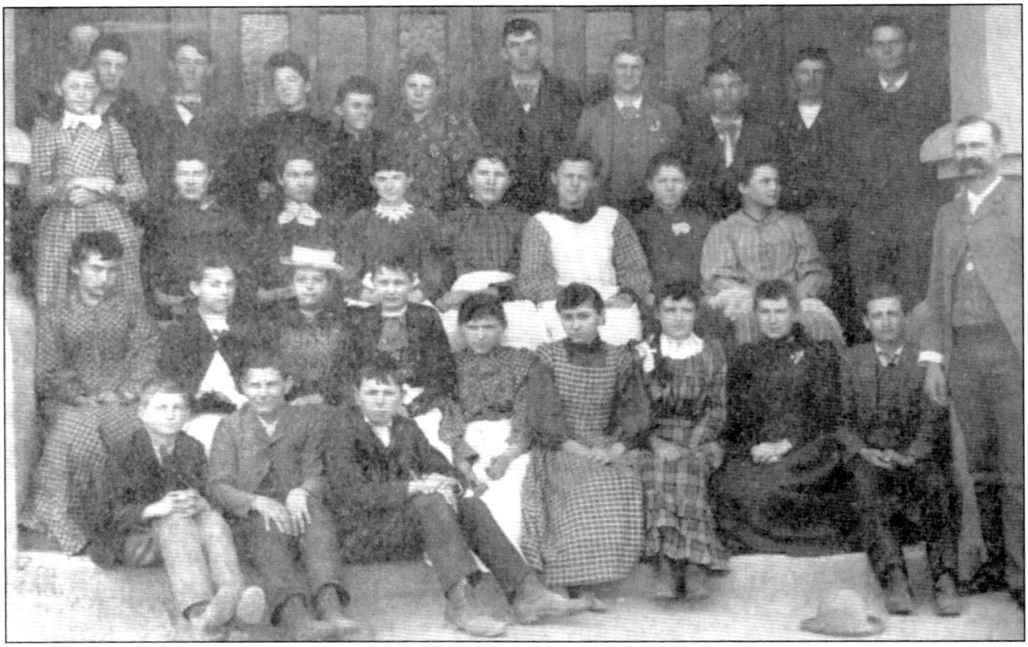

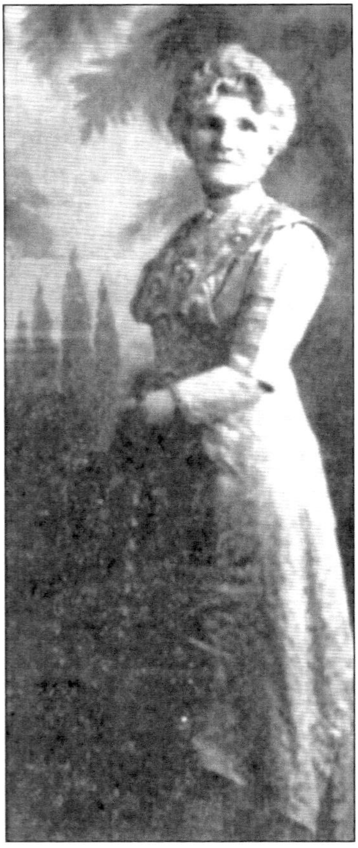

In 1891, T.J. Updyke (standing at far right) was the principal of these seventh and eighth graders. The students shown here are, from left to right, (first row) Al Joy, S. Pattison, and W. Foster; (second row) M. Winkleman, B. Martin, H. Joy, M. Paden, E. Blood, V. Giles, N. Thomas, M. Goss, and B. Stevens; (third row) J. Bornman, A. Walton, Culver, unidentified, C. Culver, M. Durgin, J. Reese, and M. Holmes; (fourth row) F. Holt, A. Akers, C. Durgin, N. Williams, B. Shaw, L. Joy, J. Qualls. A. Walton, F. Rodgers, E. Winkleman, and H. Ball.

Mattie Garrison, born in Tennessee, traveled in a covered wagon to Parker County, Texas, and then moved on to settle in the Sanger area. She taught school for over 40 years and became one of the first principals in the Sanger area. She was married to Will Garrison, a Visalia publisher.

In 1882, Lone Star School began as a one-room schoolhouse. It was located on the De Wolfe Ranch, west of what would later be Sanger. When a rail depot was built nearby, the village of Lone Star was established on Fowler Avenue. In 1898, the beautiful Lone Star schoolhouse shown here replaced the old one. In 1965, Lone Star School joined with other schools to form the Sanger Unified School District.

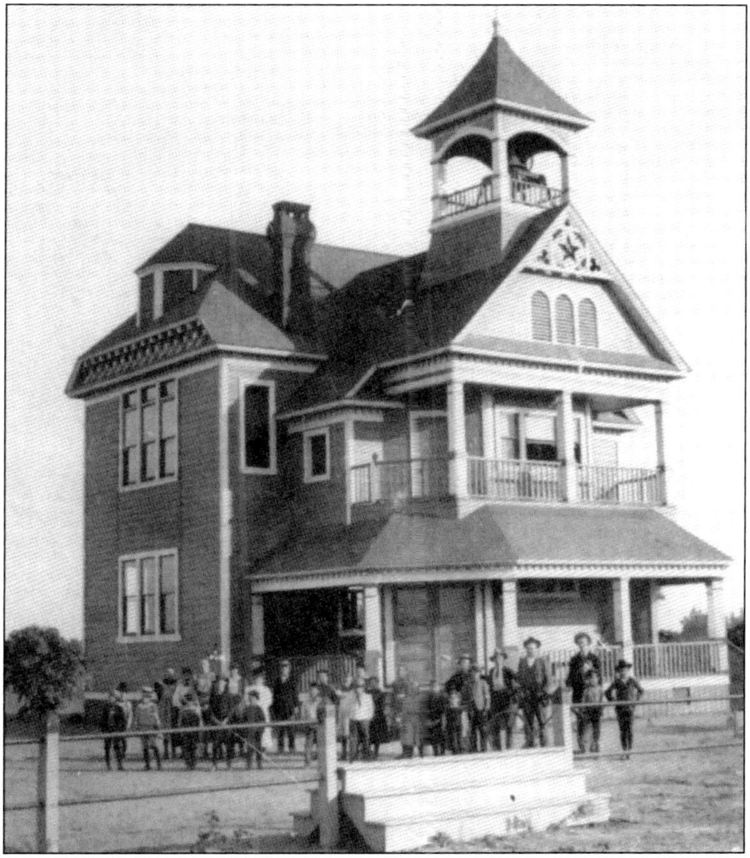

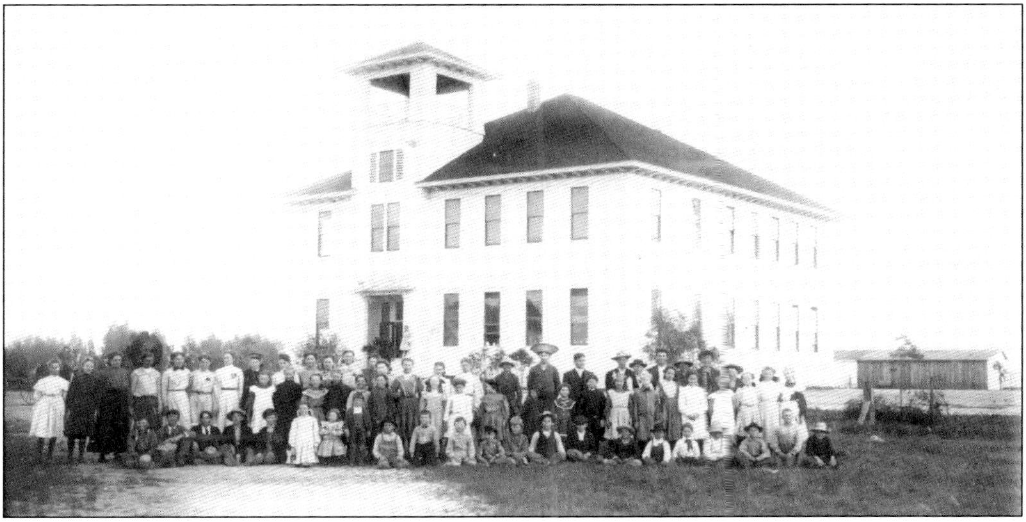

Sanger's first high school was organized in 1899, and classes were held in the upper floors of the opera house (shown here). Its first principal was Clyde Olney. He served as the only teacher of the first class of 20 students. In 1901, the town built a white frame building as its permanent high school. R.Y. Glidden was its new principal.

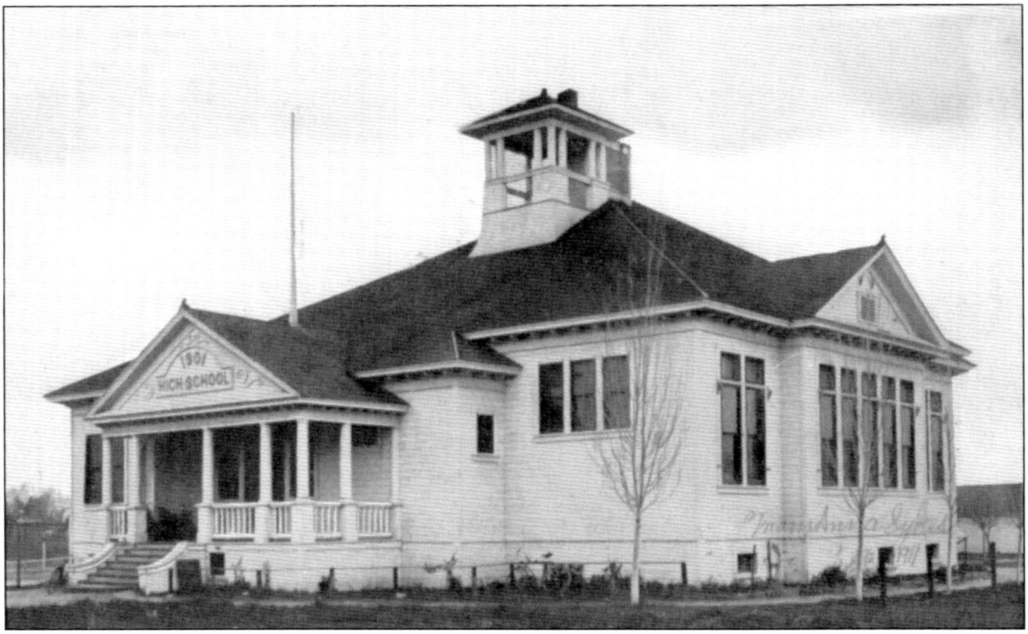

In 1901, the new Sanger High School provided space for classes that had previously been held in the opera house. The new school was built at Date and Dewitt Avenues, with the entrance facing north. The teaching staff was Edith Ackworth, W.C. Tabor, and R.Y. Glidden. This photograph came from a 1910 postcard sent to Cota Norris in Shelbyville, Indiana. A message on the back refers to "Mr. Norris and his frozen finger."

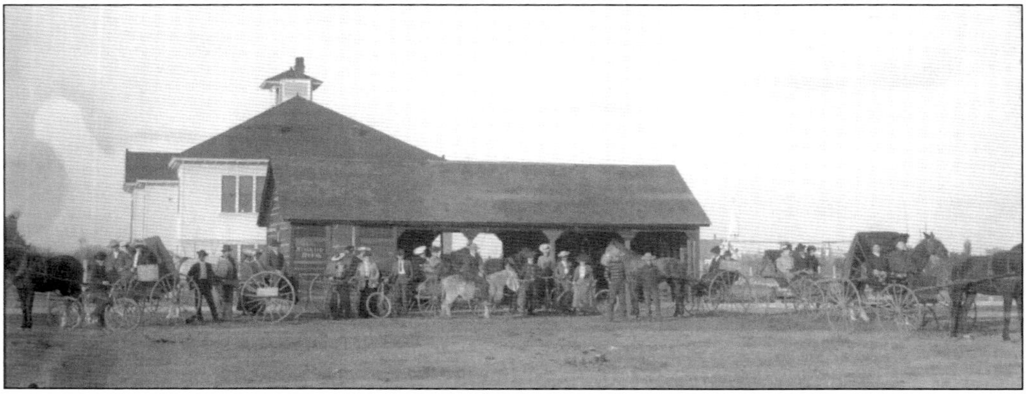

Modes of transportation in 1901 to the new high school included bicycles, wagons, horses, walking, and, as seen here in the case of one student, a donkey. Laurel and Joe Moody are at left in the buggy, Elbert Askin is on the donkey, William Savage is right of center in a striped sweater, and Frank Sayre is next to Savage. This photograph shows the back of the high school and its athletic fields.

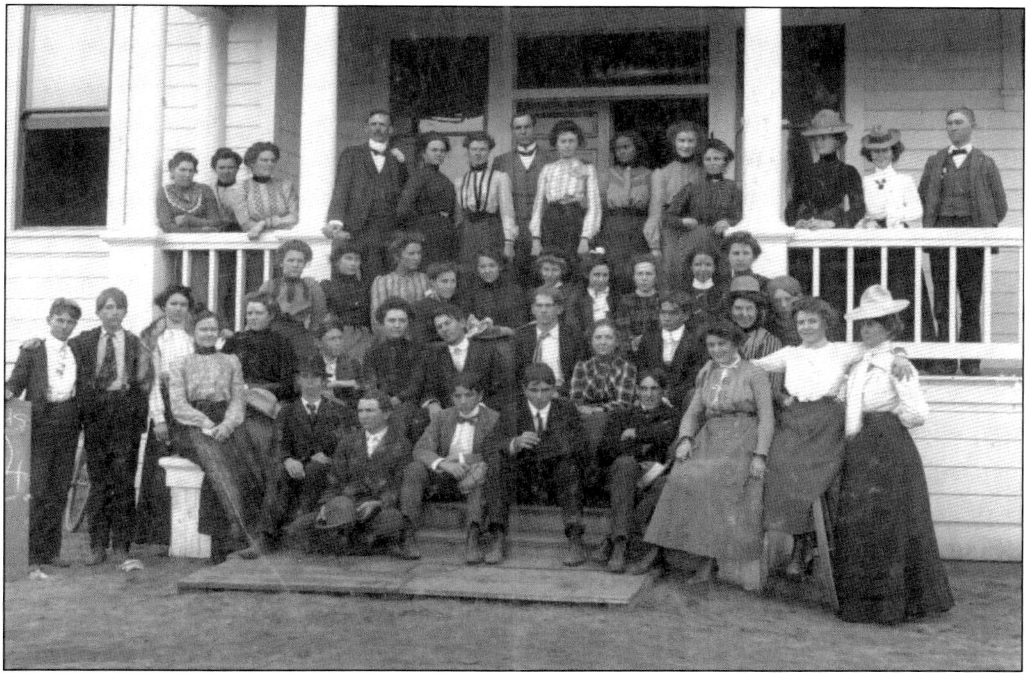

Shown here is the entire enrollment and faculty on the front steps at Sanger High School in 1903. The young man on the left is putting in a word for the class of 1904. The "class yell" at Sanger High School was, "Zip, Zap, Knowledge / Bing Boom Clee / Dauntless Seniors / Rhee, Rah, Rhee!"

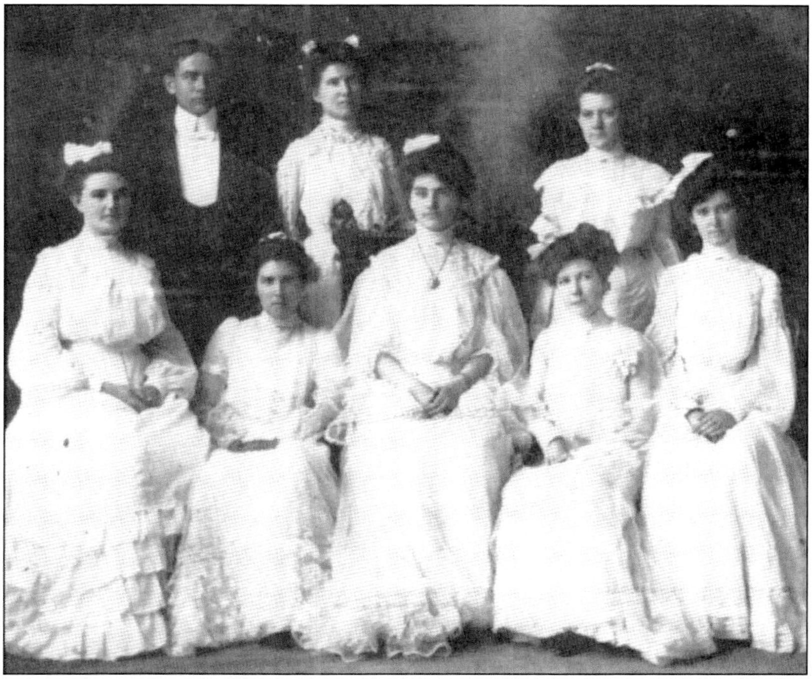

This 1903 image shows the first graduating class from Sanger High School. Shown here are, from left to right, (first row) Mamie Swank Smith, Maude Martin Burney, Mamie Lindsay, Ovella Richardson, and Viola Douglass Speers; (second row) James Black, Josie Friend Bacon, and Ida Hanke Simpson.

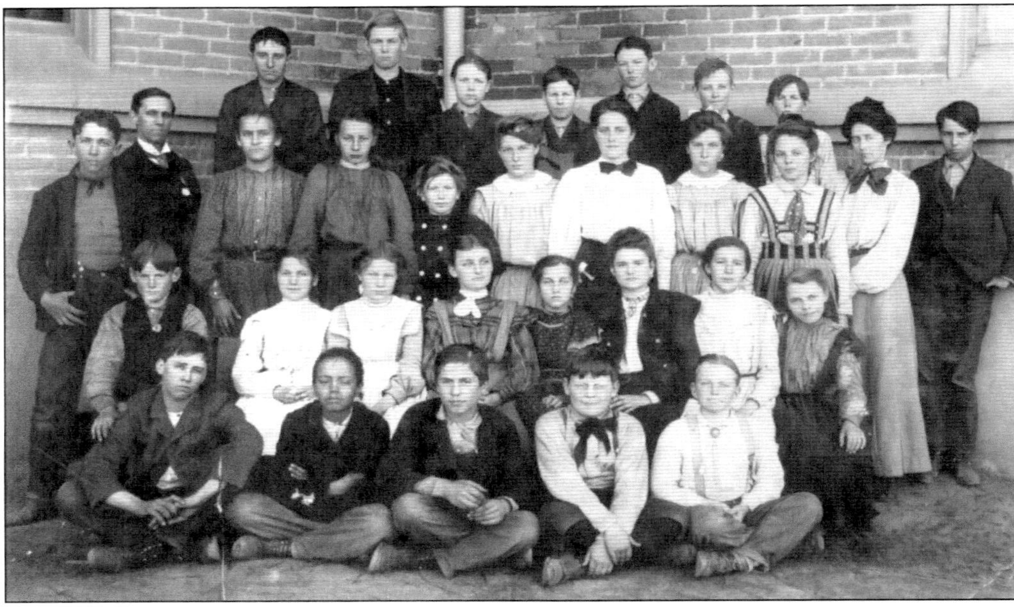

In 1938, Al C. Joy was reminiscing about attending Sanger's first school. The conditions were similar to what these students found in 1907. The principal believed that a good whipping helped maintain discipline. A later principal, Mrs. M.E. Garrison, found a more reasonable way to discipline the children. Everybody in the community loved her, and she was regarded as a splendid teacher and a fine character.

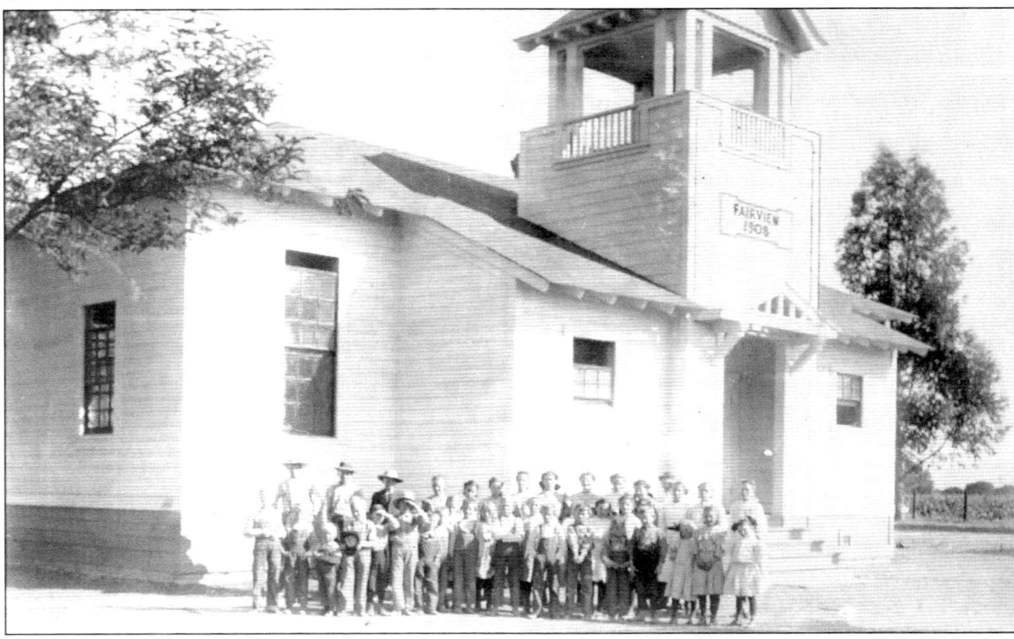

Fairview School District was established in 1873. Though classes were held between 1873 and 1908, no records can be found. This schoolhouse was built in 1908 on the north side of McKinley Avenue, about a mile west of Academy Avenue. As of 1995, Fairview School, minus the bell tower, still stands at this location.

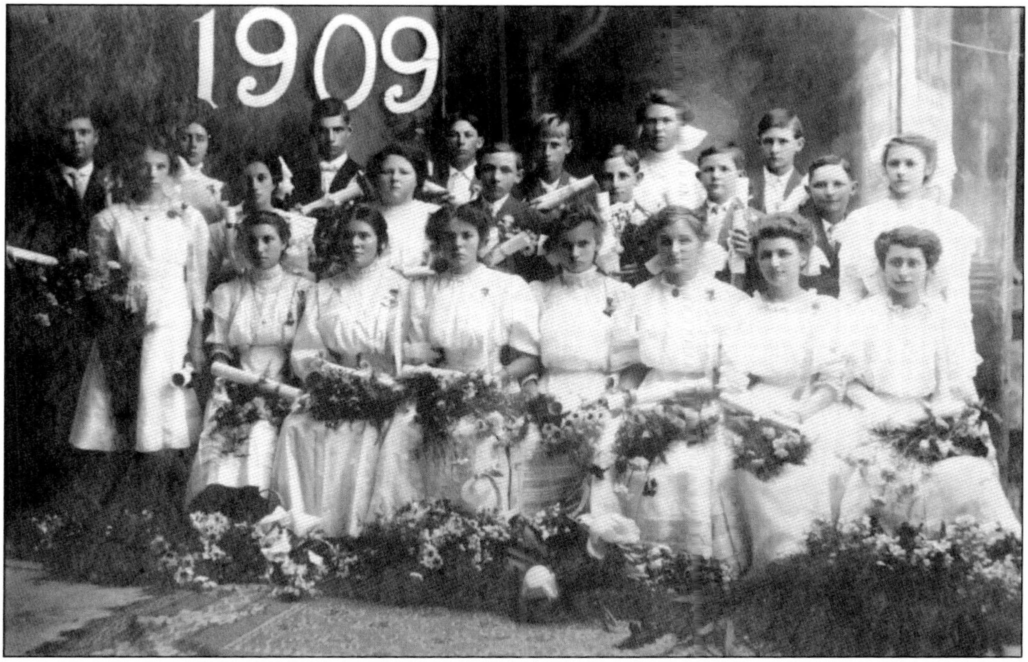

The Senior Grammar School graduating class of 1909 earned the right to this beautiful occasion. Over the years, the demand for more rigorous schooling and more years of schooling helped prepare these children for their futures. The only student identified here is Lola Bradford Gore, who is somewhere in the second row.

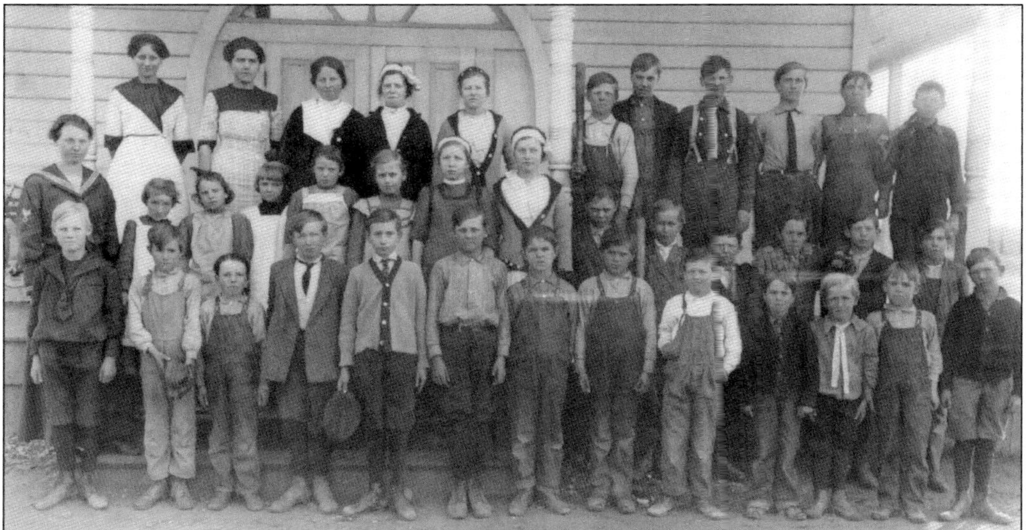

Round Mountain School was formed in 1873. By 1900, the school had been moved to Ashlan and Madsen Avenues. Standing in the first row, fourth from right, is Clint Vernon, grandfather of Bonnie Krum. In the back row, second from right, is Glenn Vernon, another relative. In 1947, Round Mountain, Gray Colony, and Fairview united to form Fairmont Union District. This photograph was taken in 1913. (Courtesy of the Bonnie Krum family.)

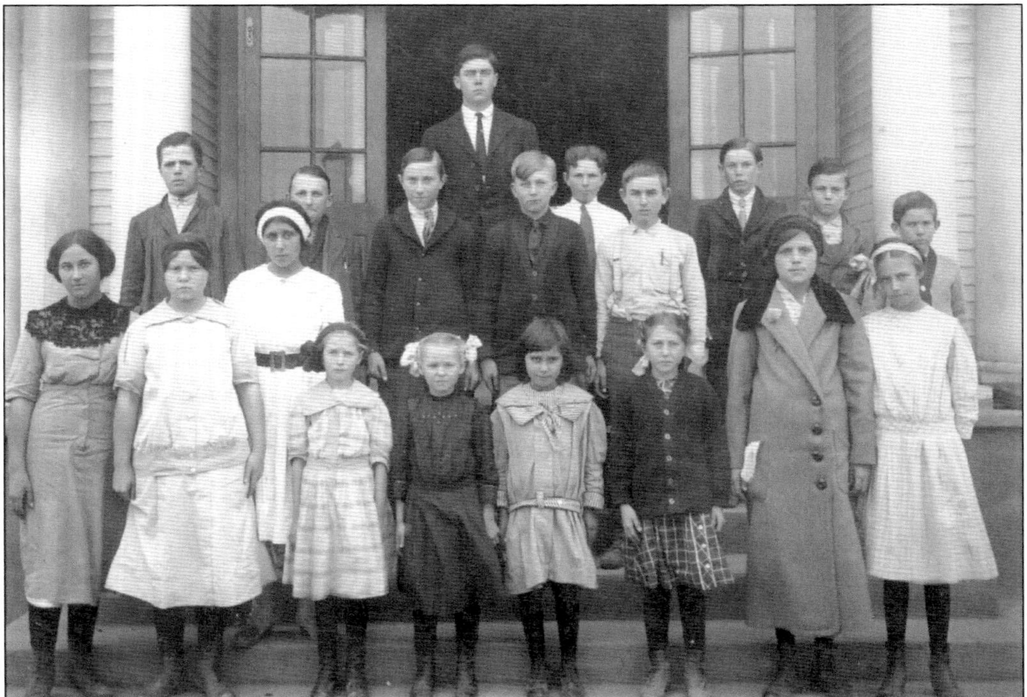

Granville School was named after Granville Kimball, who owned land in the area. This 1913 photograph is of the new school, which is still standing at East Kings Canyon Road and Indianola Avenue. Standing behind the students is Charles Leroy Walton, the principal and teacher. The bell from the bell tower was donated to the Sanger Depot Museum and is still proudly displayed there.

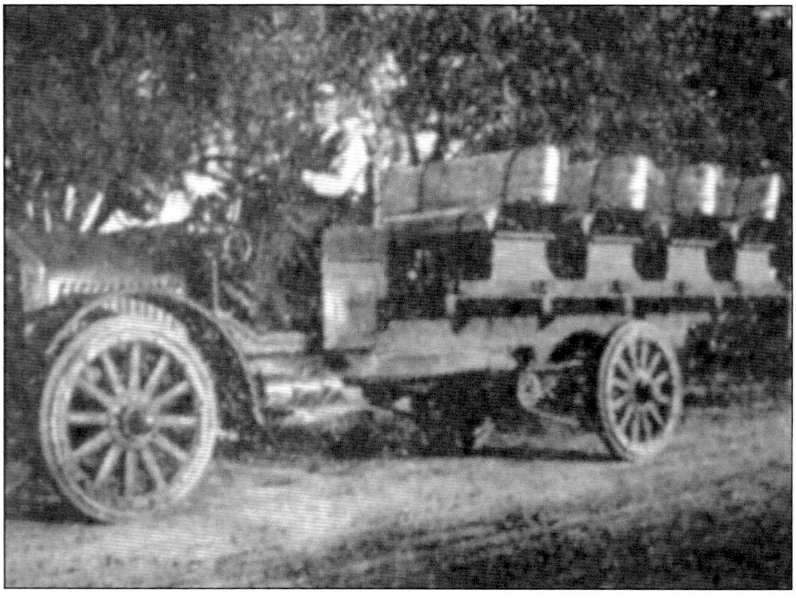

Bob Bosserman is seen here in 1913 driving a Seldon truck. Owned by M.W. Bacon, it had many uses, including as a coach for private hire, for taking high school students on trips, and, with its removable seats, as a commercial vehicle. A round trip to Fresno was $1. The truck's services were always in demand.

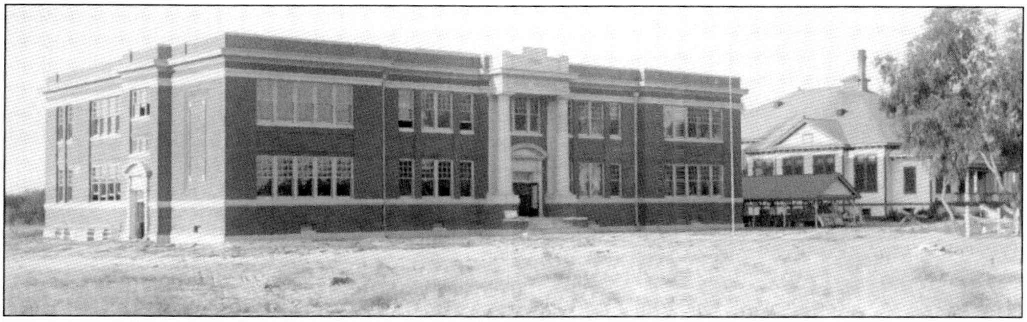

The original 1901 high school was too small for the district's needs. The brick building shown here was constructed in 1914 just east of the old school. Both buildings were used until 1928, when the brick building was expanded and the white wooden building was demolished. This photograph was taken in 1914.

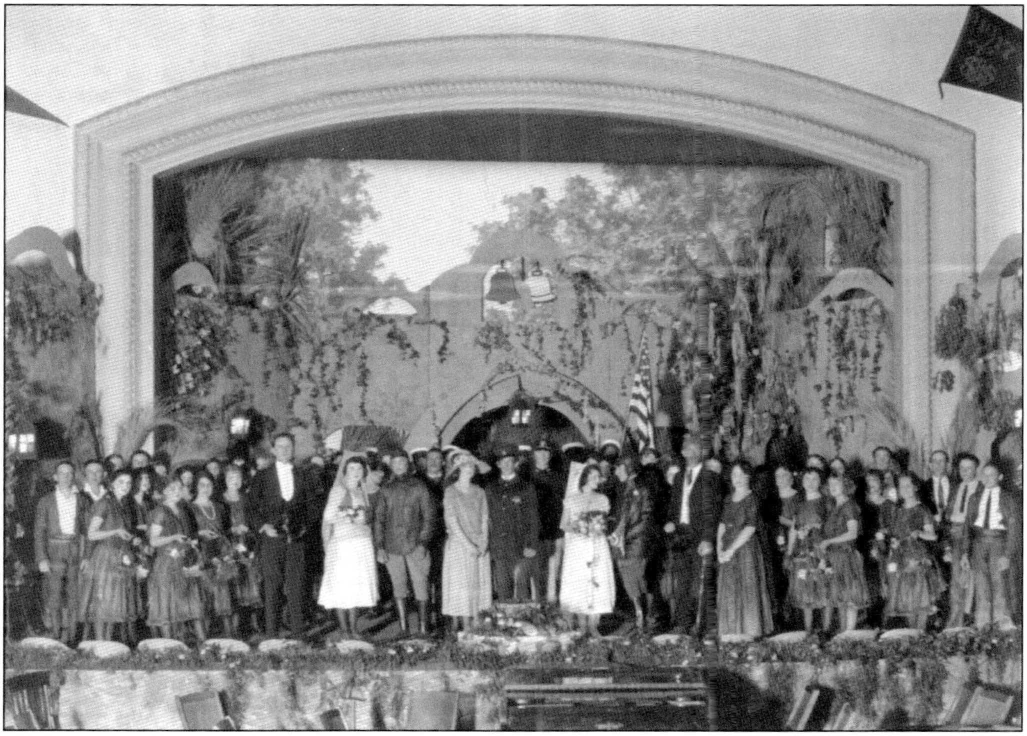

In 1914, Sanger High School students presented a play in the auditorium. The costumes, backdrop, and magnificent display were provided by the teachers and students. Within this building, an auditorium still stands, but without its balcony, which was removed for safety reasons. For almost 100 years, students have displayed their artistic skill and endeavors therein.

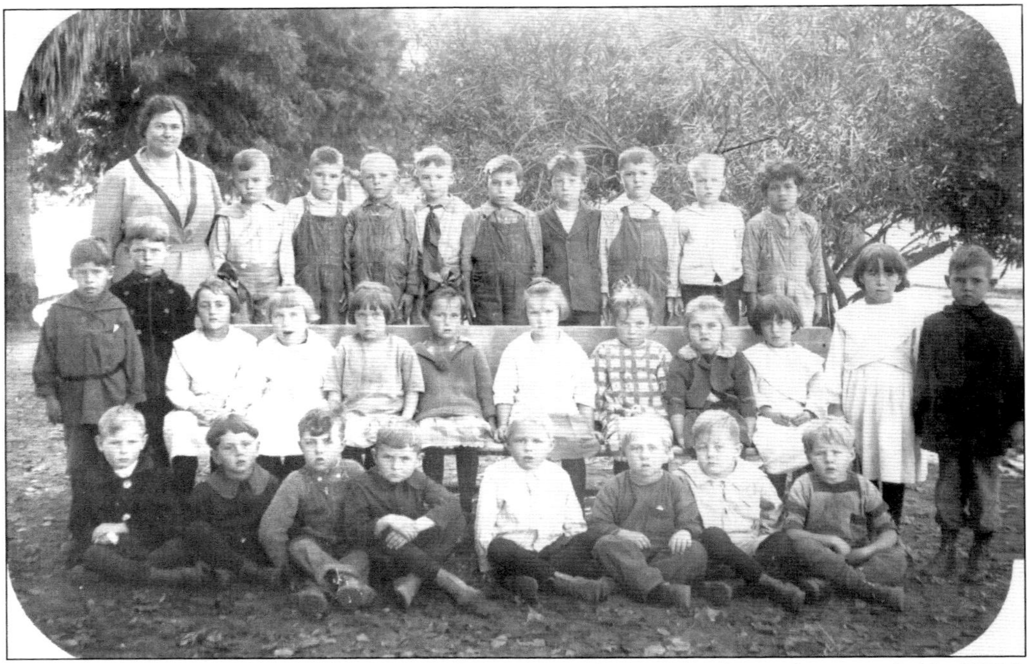

A first-grade class poses in 1920 with its teacher, Mary Miles. Among the students is a child of W.M. Barr. The pioneer families put great importance on schools. It there was none for their children, they would gather together and provide a building and hire someone qualified to teach.

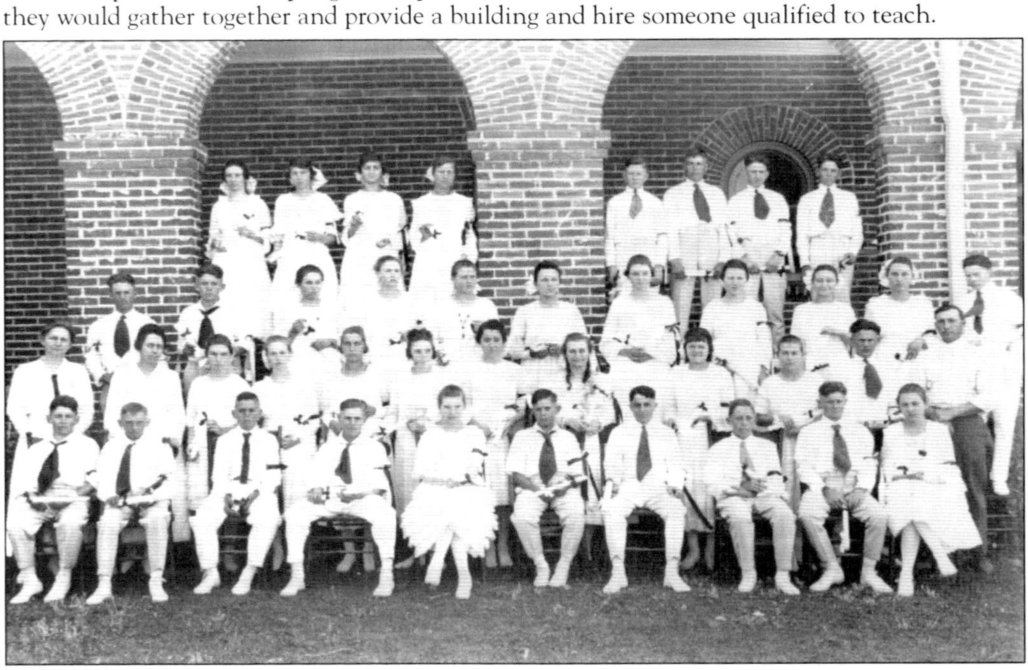

This 1922 photograph shows eighth-grade graduation at Wilson School. The principal was a Mrs. Radley, and the teachers were a Mr. Basset and a Miss Radley, daughter of the principal. This brick school with arches was built in 1914. It was on the east side of Sanger and was named after Pres. Woodrow Wilson. In 1952, a new school was built to replace this one.

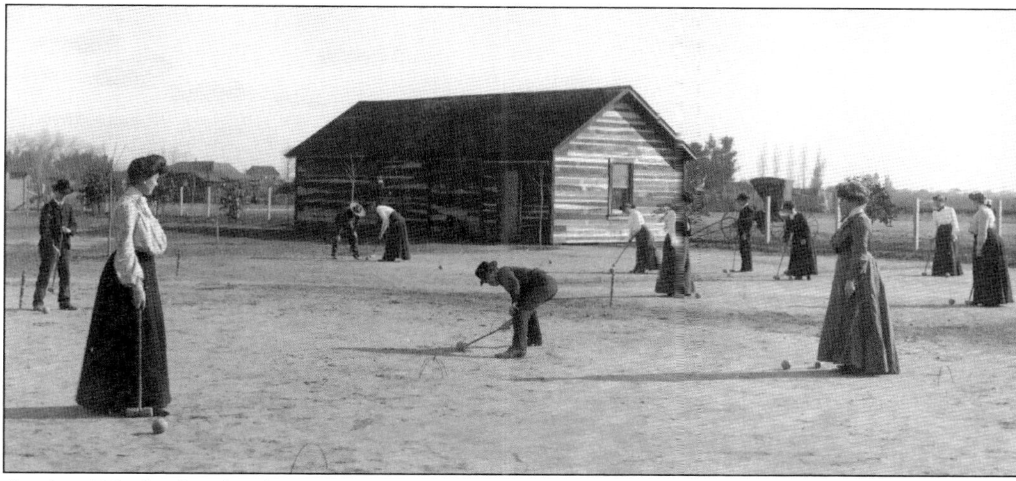

At the 1901 high school, croquet was a sport both males and females enjoyed. This field was adjacent to the track field; at times, the track athletes would participate in croquet. The students participated while wearing their regular school clothes. The game was more of a social gathering than an athletic competition.

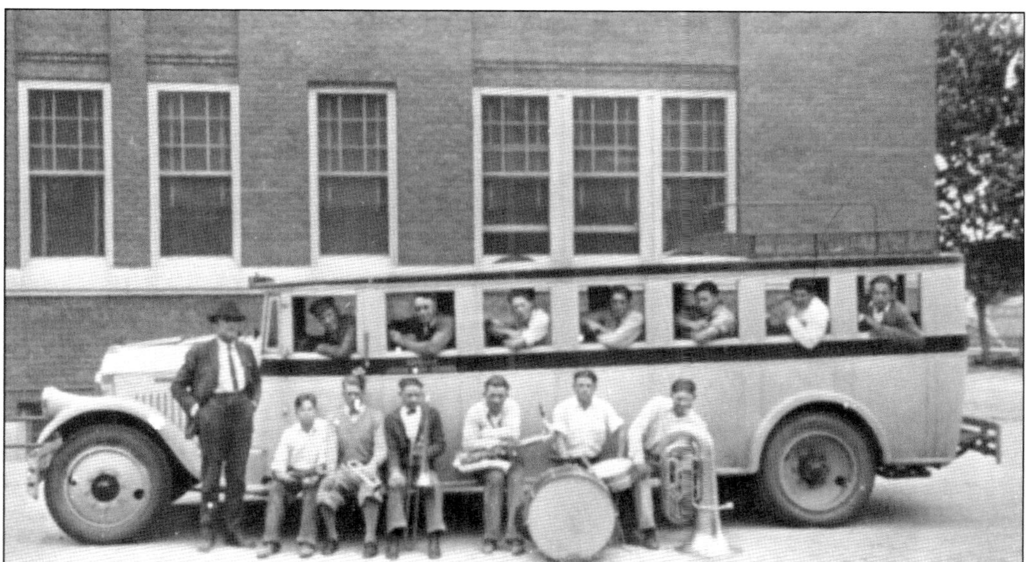

Parked in front of the high school is a Pierce Arrow school bus, getting ready to transport the Sanger High School band to one of its functions. The same vehicle was used to take students on field trips and athletes to competitions. The driver is R.L. "Bob" Bosserman.

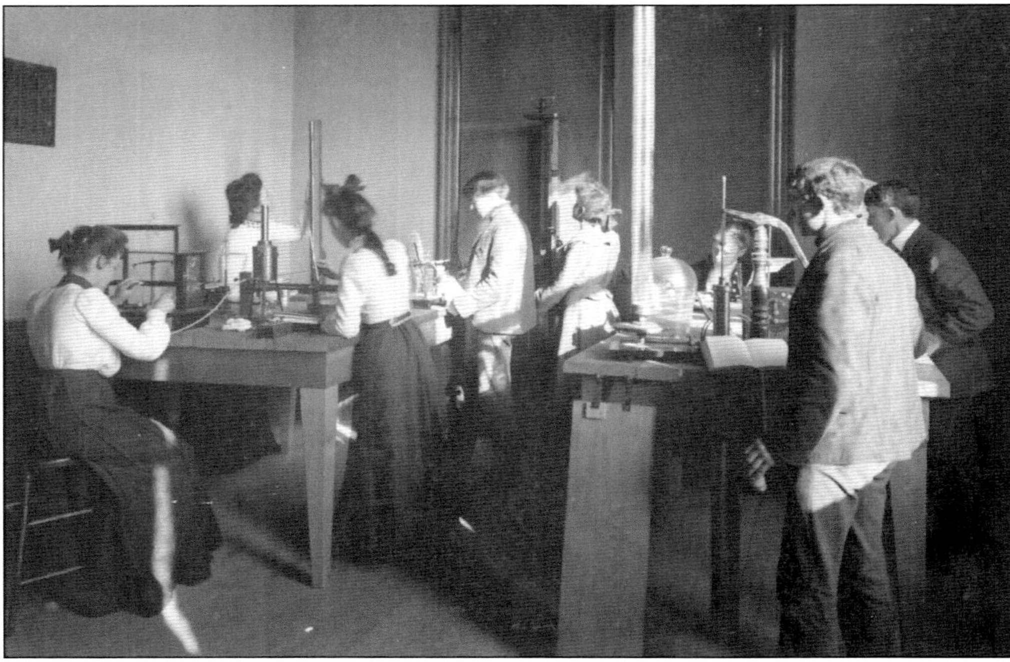

Shown here is a science class at Sanger High School. The students are, from left to right, Pearl Burns, Bernice (Roberts) Savage, Mande Price, Will Savage, Carrie Maxwell, Carrie (Barr) Olson, and Frank Sayre. The teacher, Franklin Schott, is at far right. Most of these students were required to take Latin and the higher math classes to prepare for college.

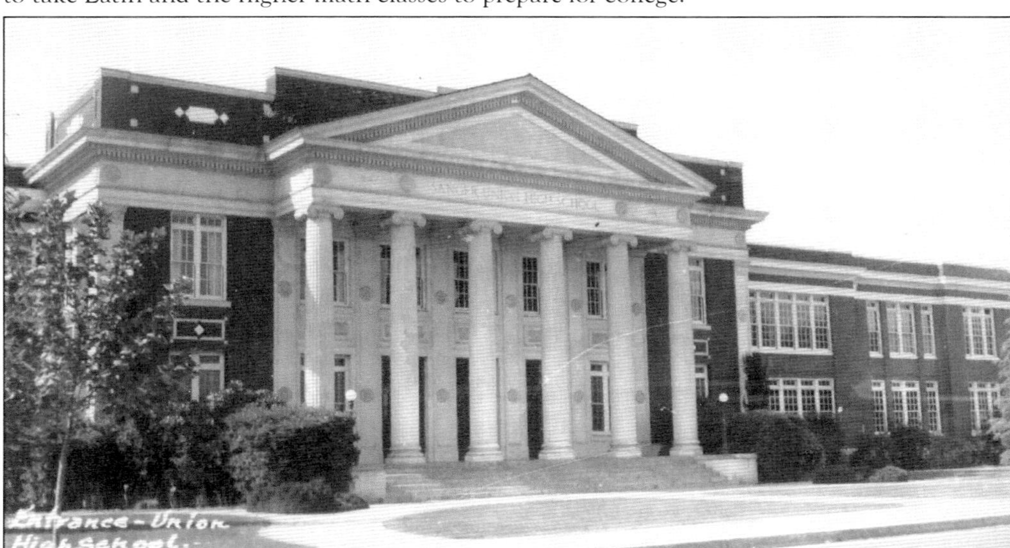

In 1928, Sanger High School was remodeled. The front entrance was extended forward, columns were erected, and hallways on the left and right were extended. A girls' gym was added in 1936. Another remodeling took place in 1957. Then, in 2000, a new high school was built at another site, and the building shown here became a middle school. Sanger is still growing, and in 2013, land has already been bought for a future second high school.

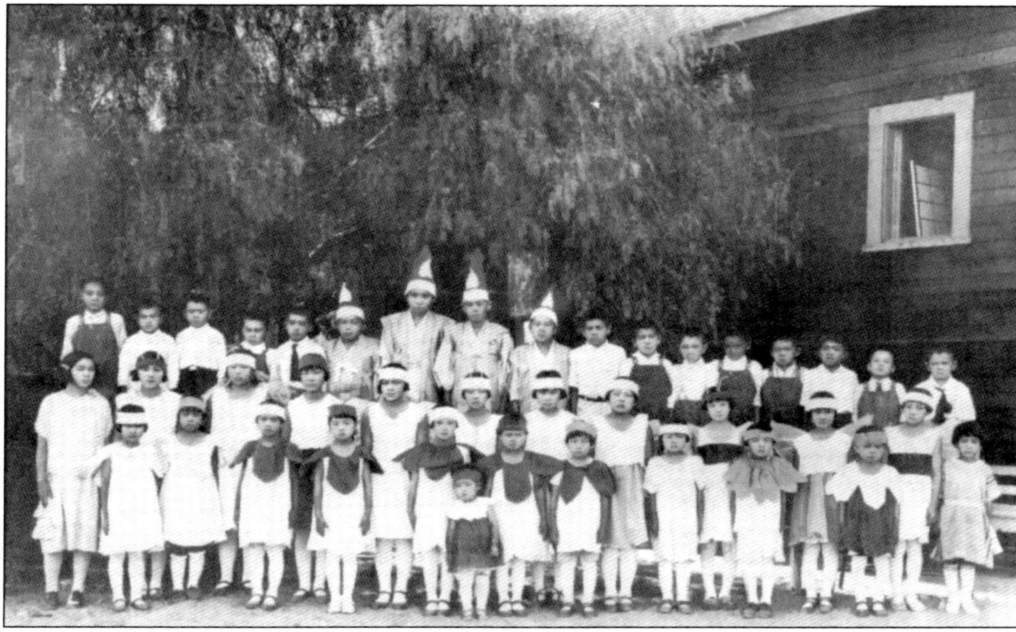

The Sanger Buddhist School is seen here in the early 1930s. The Japanese came to the Sanger area in the late 1890s. The various cultures living in Sanger accepted this group of hardworking people. In 1927, the Japanese built a social hall and used it as a place to educate their children. The students attended this school on the weekends to learn to speak and write Japanese. They were also taught standards of conduct and moral judgment.

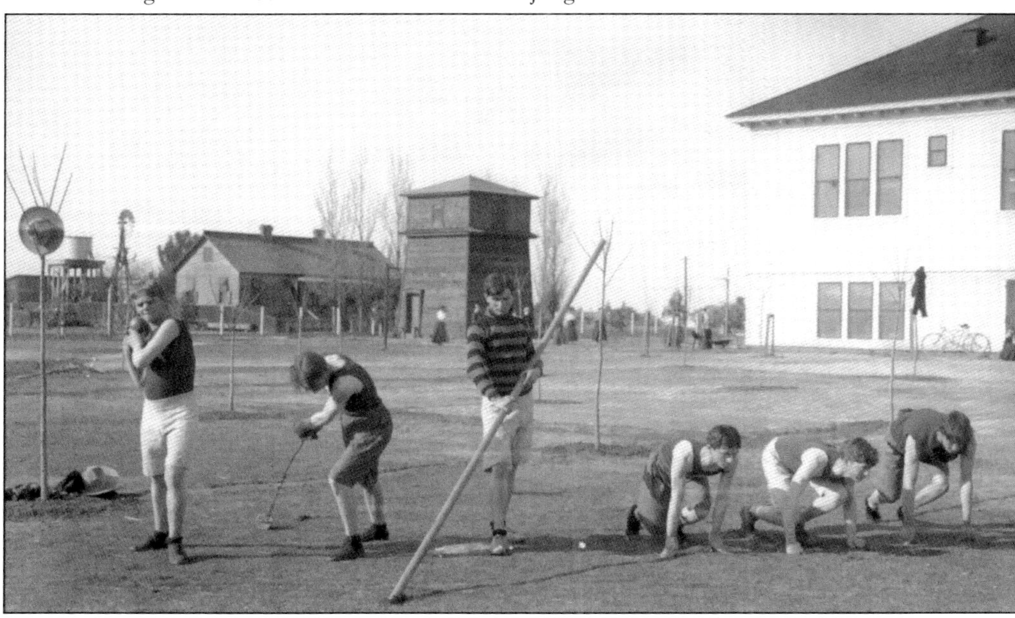

Sanger High School's 1903 track team includes, from left to right, Harold Savage, Ora Hudson, Will Savage, Frank Sayre, Joe Moodey, and Chester Tackaberry. In the background are female students playing croquet. Shot put, pole vault, the hammer, and races were standard for track competition at the time.

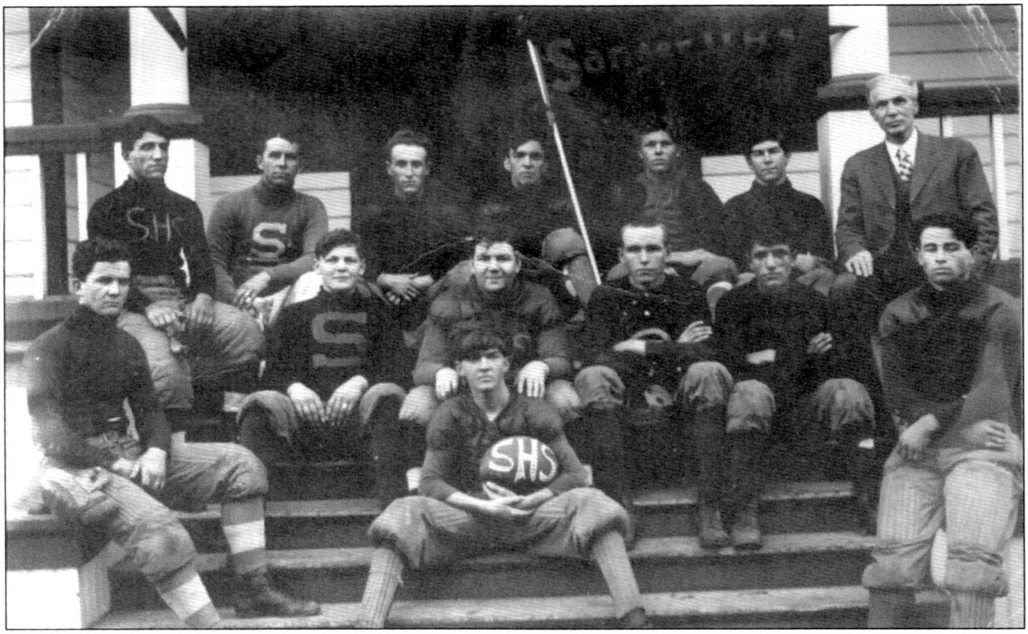

In this 1909 photograph, Sanger football teammates pose with coach Estey Walton (top row, right). No helmets are in view, but the clothing is similar to that of players today, including uniforms, padding, and sports shoes.

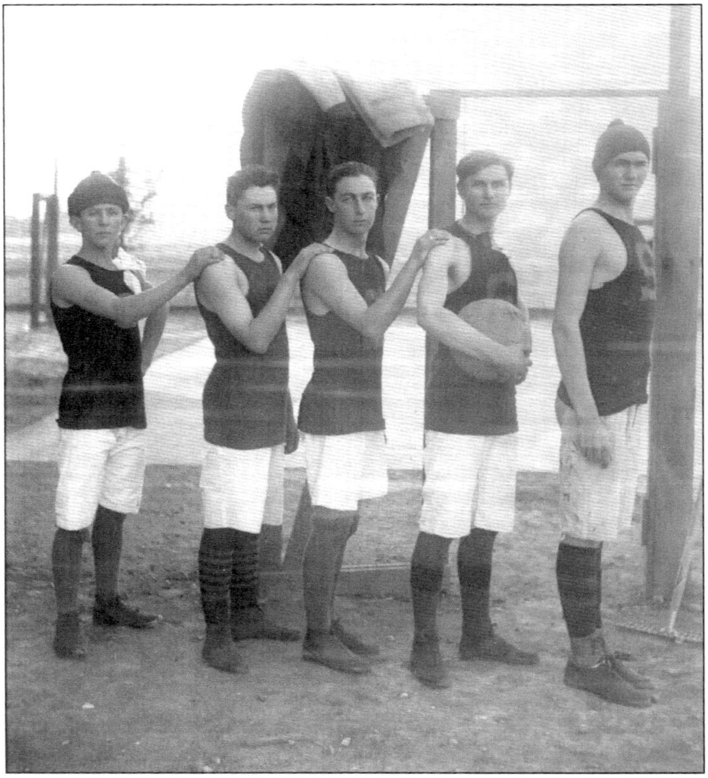

The 1911 Sanger High School boys basketball team poses for a photograph. Shown here are, from left to right, Ted Barr, Charlie Cooper. Clair Moody, Stephan ?, and Dick Carlisle. There is no record of who coached the basketball team between 1908 and 1914. Sanger was pretty much a baseball town. The first identified basketball coach was a Mr. Serfling in 1915. Sanger went on to win its share of championships under coaches Huntley Dayton, Dean Nicholson, and LaVern Lotspeich.

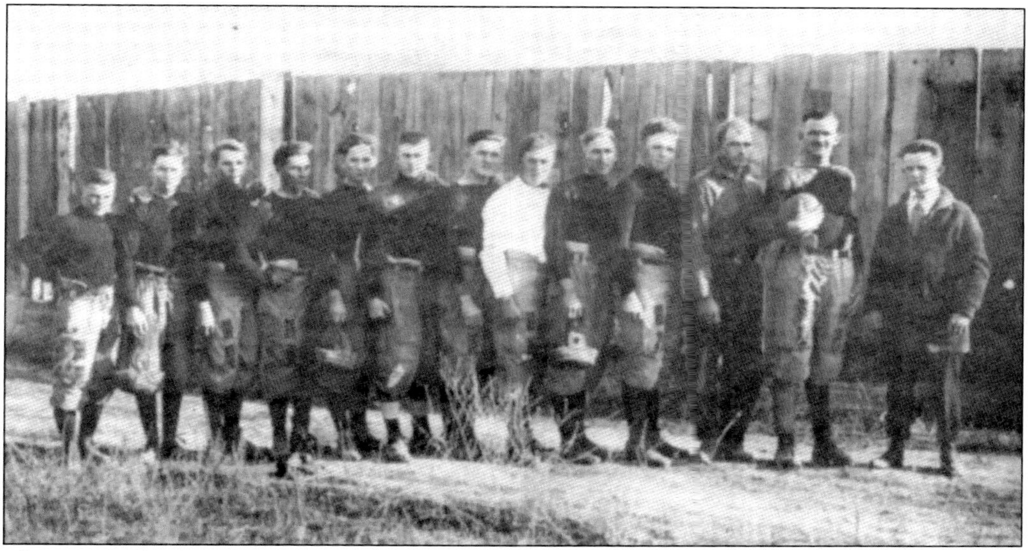

The Sanger football team poses in 1916 after beating Exeter. Fay Snodgrass is fourth from left, and coach Ted Barr is on the far right. In 1920, Selma beat Sanger 60-0, but in 1924, Sanger, coached by Frank Trine, defeated Selma for its first school championship. In 1951, the school, under coach Clare Slaughter, won its first Valley championship.

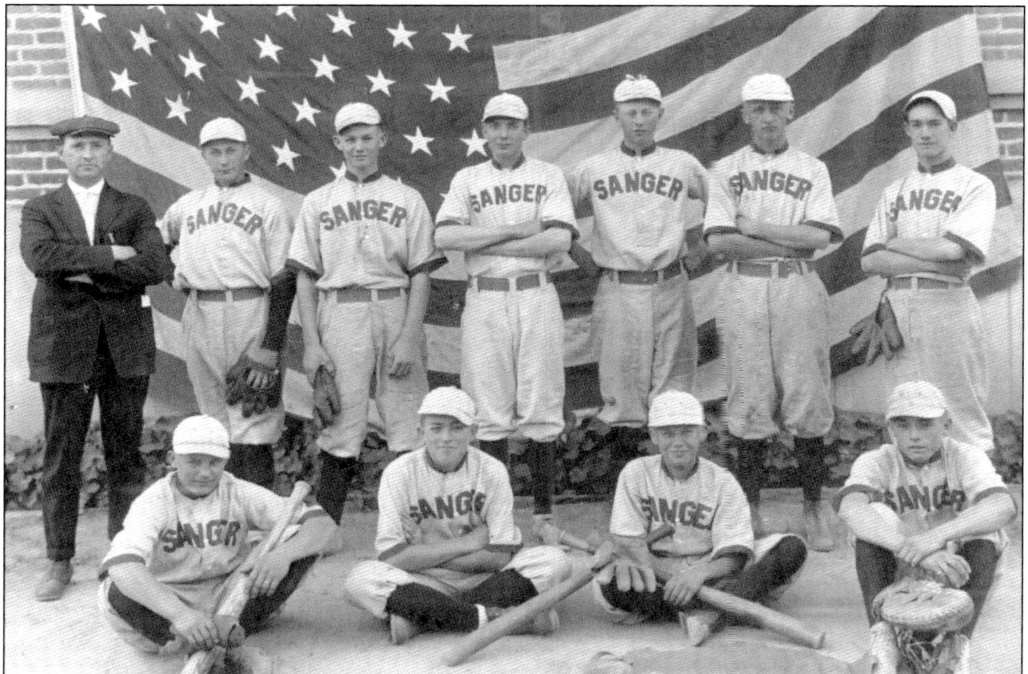

This is an early baseball team at Sanger's Taft Grammar School. Shown here are, from left to right, (first row) G. Mise, L. Jones, E. "Billy" Merker, and F. Adams; (second row) Coach Bassett, D. Merker, F. Lester, C. Demant, P. Petersen, H. Southhard, and F. Kelley. Billy Merker was the only left-handed shortstop around.

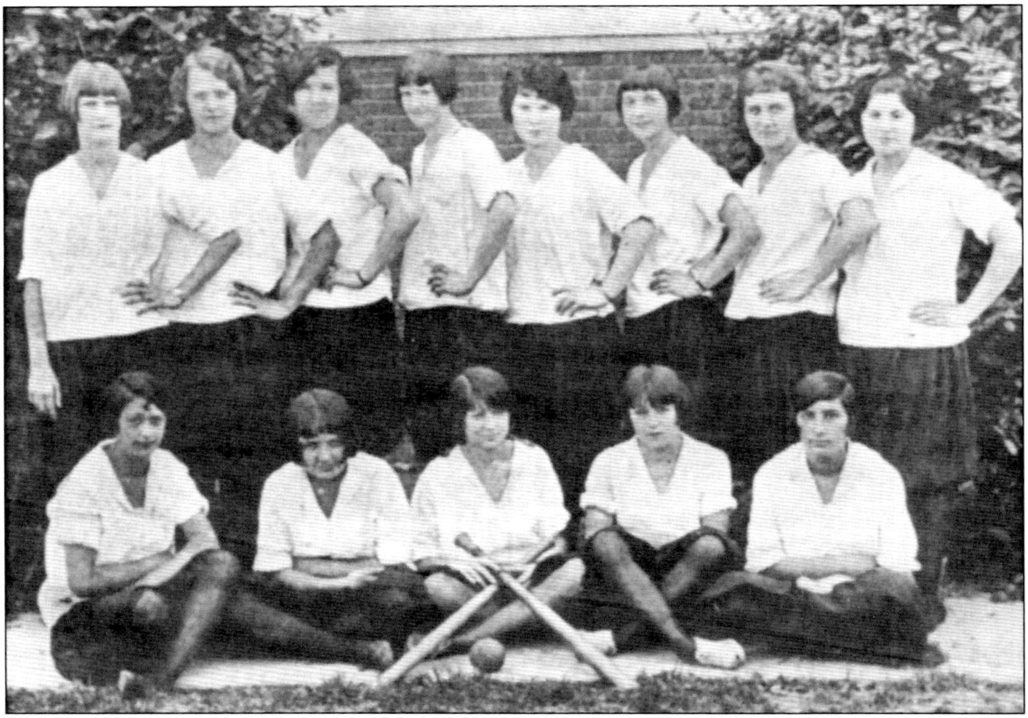

This is one of the first girls' softball teams in Fresno County. In the days when it was considered unladylike for women to participate in sports, Sanger's softball team was ahead of its time. Sanger girls have always had that competitive spirit, demonstrating it in softball, tennis, and track.

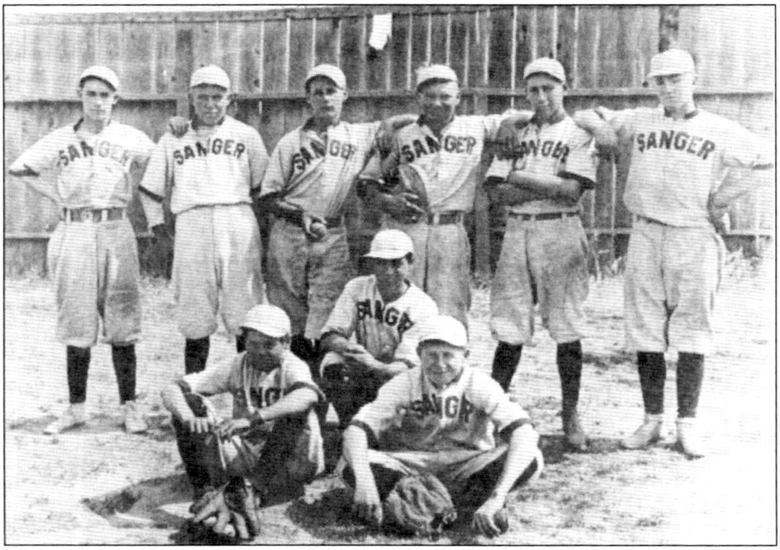

An early-1900s baseball team poses for a photograph. Shown here are, from left to right, (first row) J. Stanley, J. Jarvis, and Ted Johnson; (second row) F. Kelley, L. Crismer, L. Stanley, E. Crismer, E. Bosserman, and R. Stevenson. Many of these students played other competitive sports during the school year.

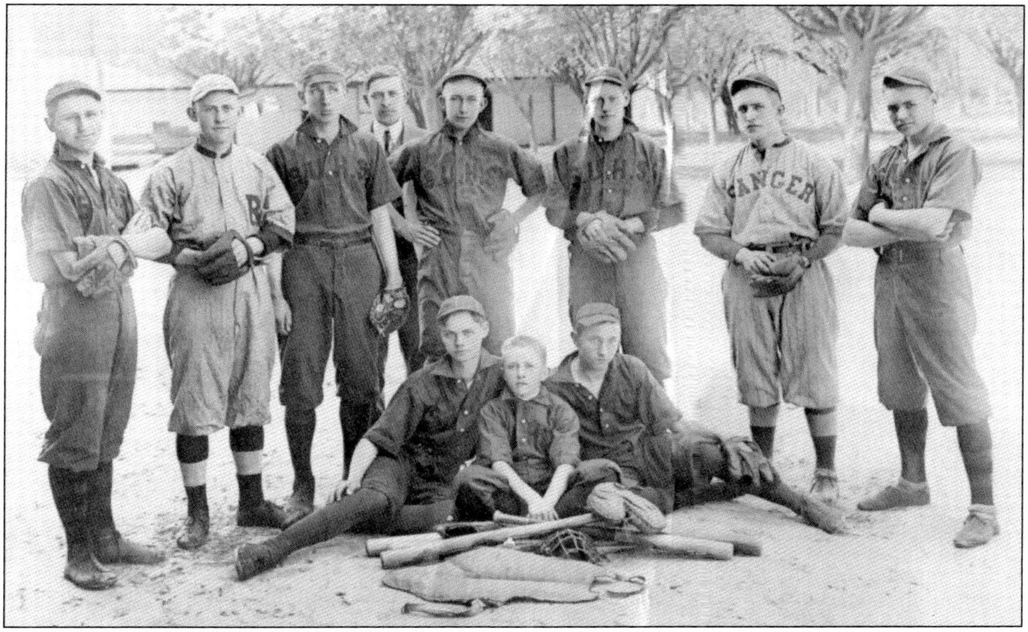

In this photograph of a Sanger baseball team, Claude Merker is standing second from left. There is no record of the first coaches of the baseball or football teams. The first record of a coach is in 1915, when a Mr. Serfling helmed football and basketball for one year. In 1921, J.W. Cook arrived in Sanger to coach the baseball and football teams.

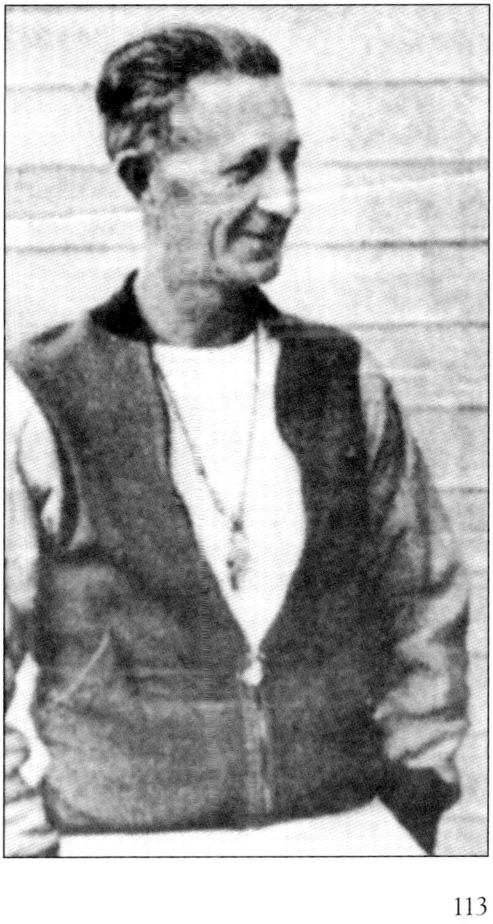

"They don't make them like that anymore" is probably the best tribute printed about coach Huntley Dayton. He started coaching in Sanger in 1926 and coached football from 1926 to 1945, basketball from 1926 to 1949, and baseball from 1927 to 1954. Nicknamed the "Silver Fox," Dayton became dean of boys in the mid-1950s and, later, vice principal of the high school. In 1976, he was enshrined into the Fresno County Athletic Hall of Fame.

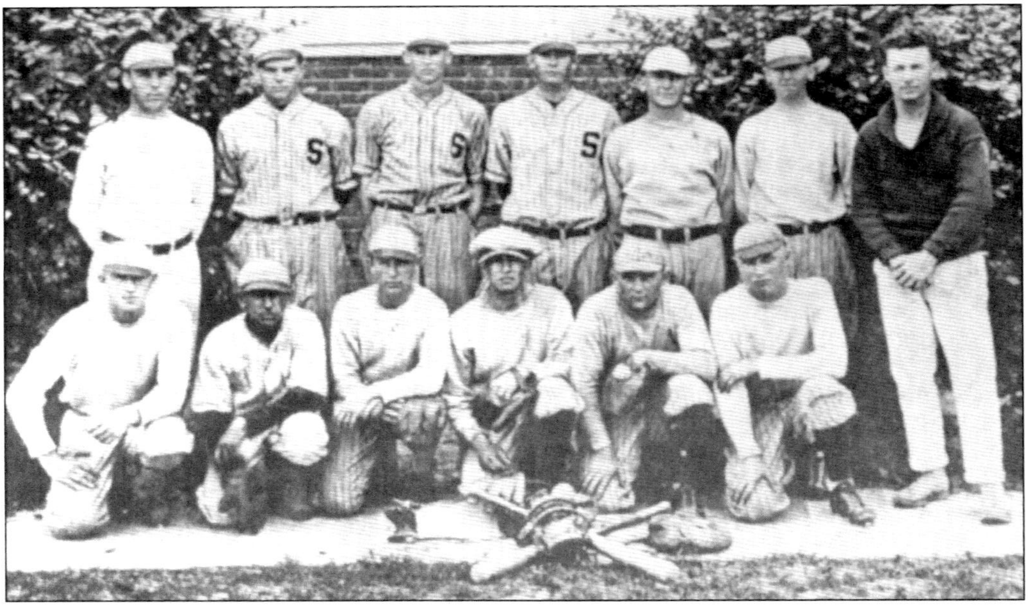

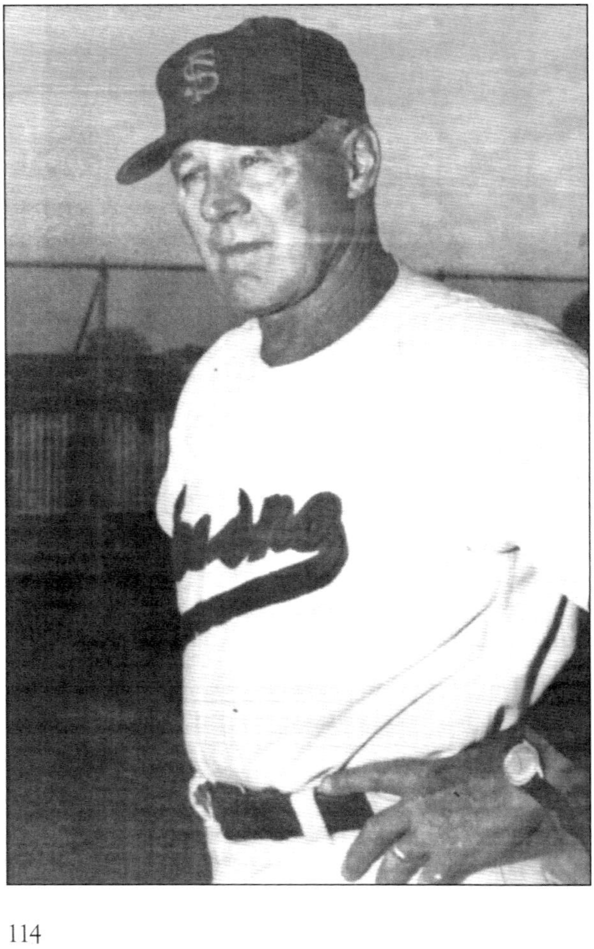

This Sanger baseball team poses in 1924. Shown here are, from left to right, (first row) unidentified, Cross Missakian, unidentified, John Jarhian, Pete Beiden, and Ray Nelson; (second row) John Boragno, Phil Krum, Leon Crabb, unidentified, Henry "Hank" Beiden, Roy Hansen, and coach Frank Trine. Pete Beiden would go on to make many contributions to the sport of baseball.

Coach Pete Beiden graduated from Sanger High with the class of 1927. He coached baseball at Fresno State College. In 1959, he took the Bulldogs to the College World Series. In 21 seasons at FSC, his teams compiled 600 wins. In 1972, Beiden was inducted into the College Baseball Hall of Fame.

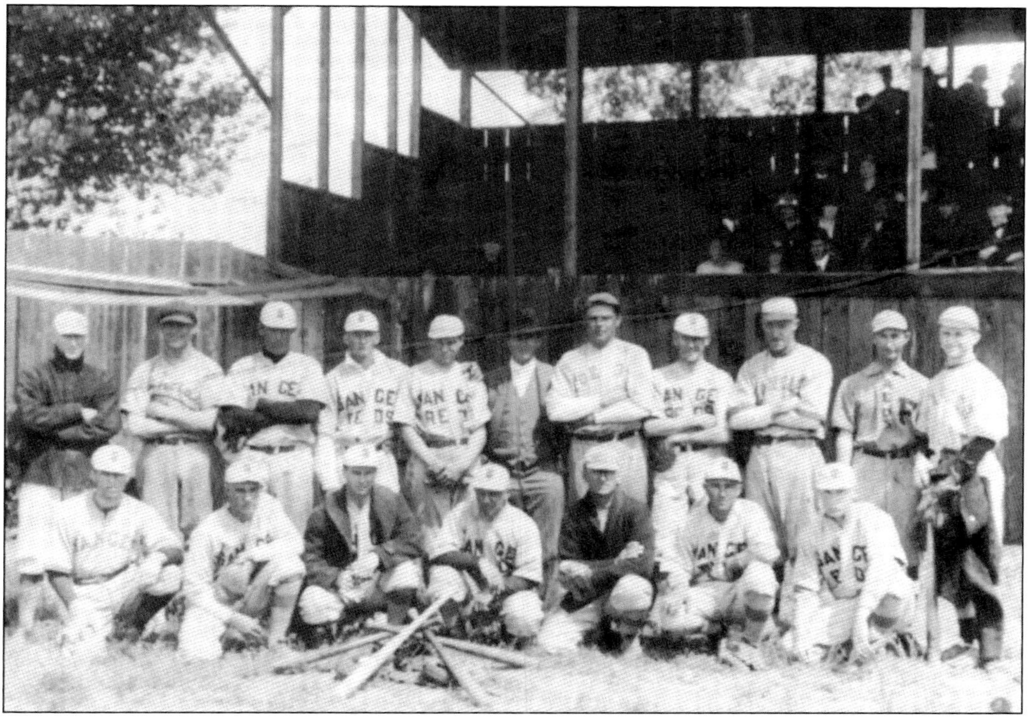

The Sanger Reds baseball team poses at the old wooden ballpark on the north side of town. Shown here are, from left to right, (first row) unidentified, F. Kelley, H. Bender, G. Mise, unidentified, F. Ferry, and B. Ledbetter; (second row) K. Bosserman, unidentified, R. Stevens, C. Atrat, J. Jarvis, ? Maltz (manager), unidentified, E. Bosserman, A. Nelson, unidentified, and Jimmy ?.

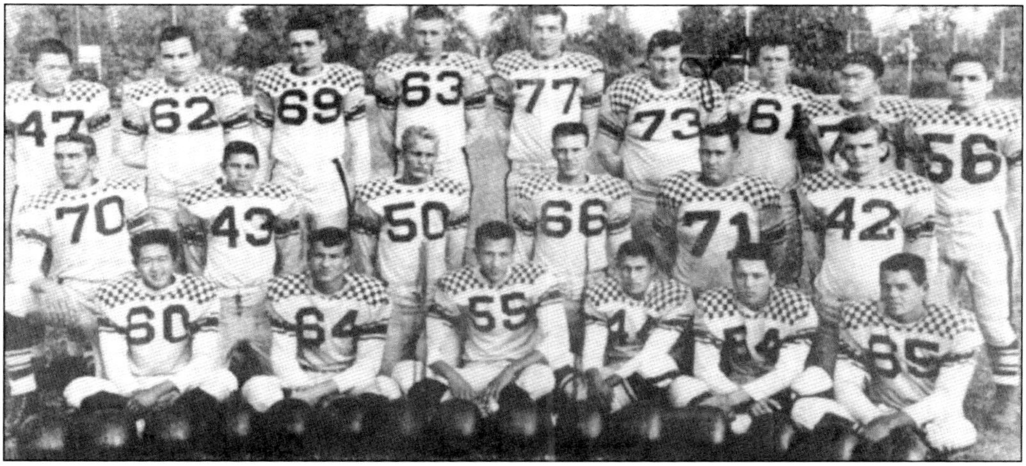

Tom Flores, under Coach Clare Slaughter, was No. 55 on Sanger's varsity football team in 1954. He was one of Sanger's best athletes, playing basketball, baseball, and football. Flores played football in college, and in 1960, he was the starting quarterback for the Oakland Raiders. He was later traded to the Kansas City Chiefs, with whom he won his first ring in Super Bowl IV.

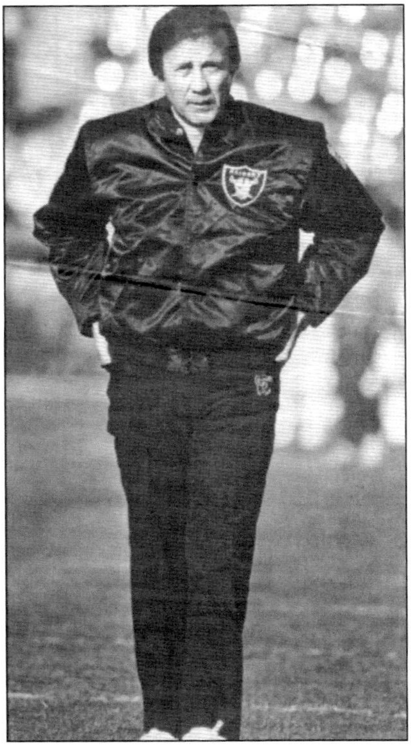

Upon returning to the Oakland Raiders as an assistant coach, Tom Flores won his second Super Bowl ring in 1977. Later, as head coach of the Raiders, he won two more championships. Flores has never forgotten Sanger. Through his Sanger Youth Foundation, he has not only raised thousands of dollars for Sanger's children, but he has earned the respect and admiration of the people of Sanger.

Sanger's 1947 Valley baseball champions, coached by Huntley Dayton, pose for a photograph. The players' names and positions are written on the image. They defeated Bakersfield 7-2 to gain the 1947 Valley crown.

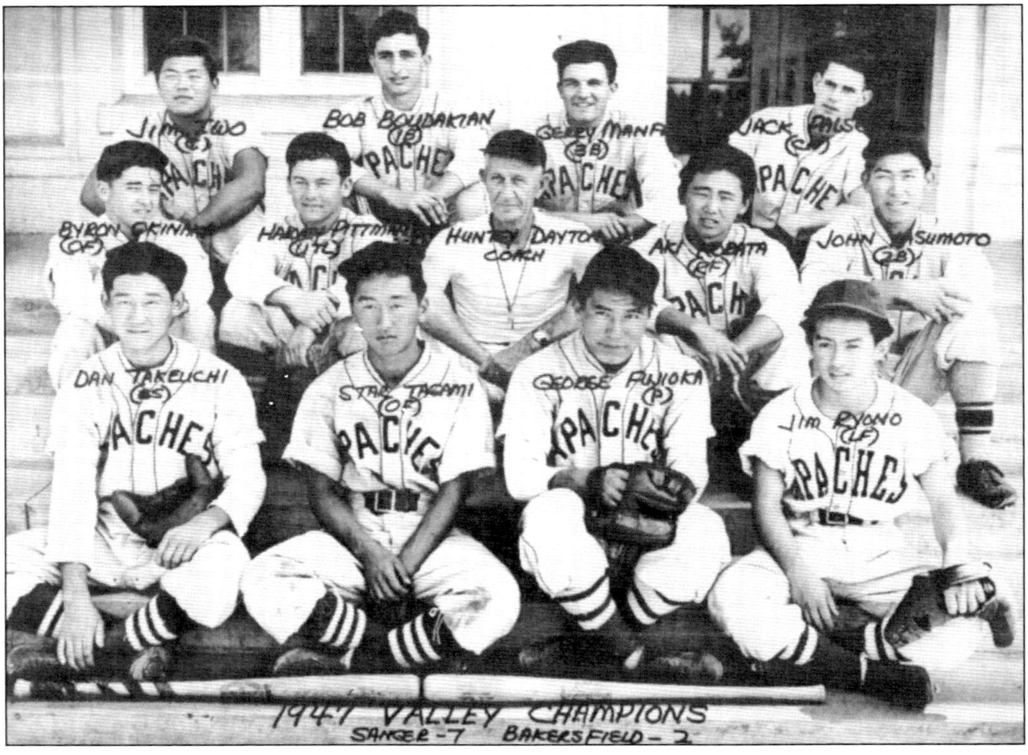

Nine

Historic Sanger

The Fresno County Registry of Historic Sites lists several buildings in the Sanger area as being of historic interest. The four that are located within the city limits and recognized as official Fresno County Historic Landmarks include the Woman's Club, the Sanger Depot Museum, the Sanger First United Methodist Church, and the Miller House. The oldest building in Sanger is the Southern Pacific Railroad depot, constructed in 1887 alongside tracks connecting Fresno and Porterville. Named for Joseph Sanger, the depot made Sanger the center for shipping grain, lumber, and citrus. The last stationmaster to call the depot home was Walter Phillips, who moved his family into the second-story living quarters in 1943. In those days, as many as 100 carloads of fruit left the Sanger station daily. Troop trains carrying soldiers occasionally passed through Sanger, as men and material were needed for the wars raging in Europe and the Pacific. With the rise of the trucking industry, less citrus was shipped by train. On November 4, 1975, the depot was closed and the last employee, Frank Lambdin, relocated to another position with the railroad. The brothers Jack and Sean Tanney purchased the depot in 1977 as an investment. When they learned that the Sanger Historical Society was looking for a site for a proposed museum, they offered the depot as a gift. The depot was then moved from Seventh and L Streets to its current location next to the Sanger library on Seventh Street. The railroad depot reopened as the Sanger Depot Museum in 1977. This institution continues to preserve and display the story of Sanger and its people.

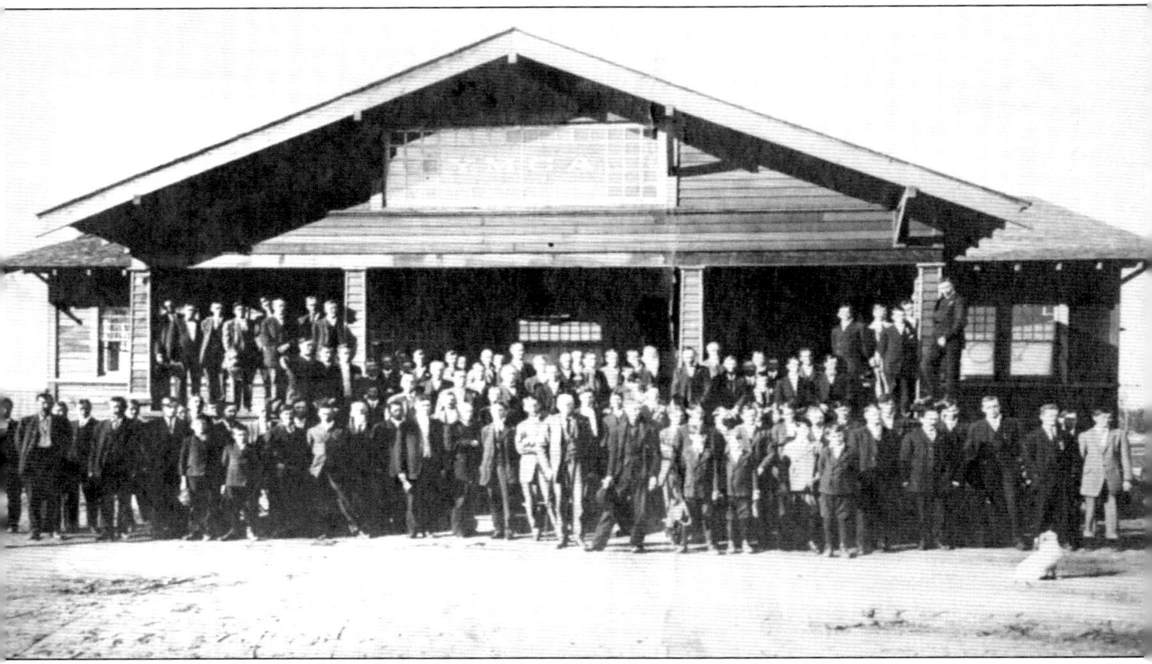

A large group poses outside Sanger's YMCA building. Constructed in 1912, it was the county's first YMCA building and was also used for business and community events. The Sanger Woman's Club purchased the building in 1927. Over the years, it has suffered the effects of age and even fire. Due to the loving care by the club's members, it has been preserved and continues to serve the community of Sanger.

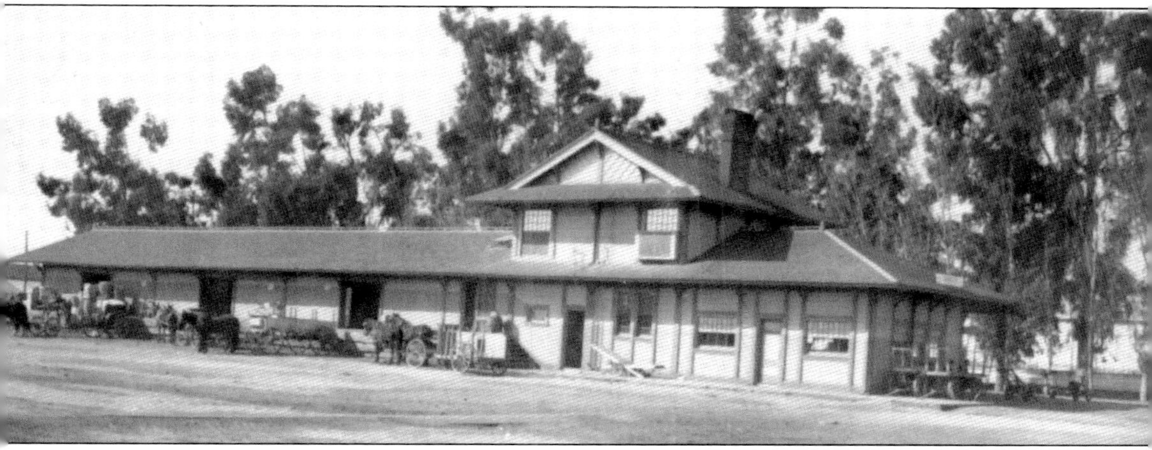

Built in 1887, the Southern Pacific Railroad depot holds the title as the oldest building in Sanger. In its heyday, it was heavily utilized for shipping lumber and, later, fruit. As time passed, the usefulness of the depot waned, and it finally closed. Some of the building was removed in order for it to fit in its new home near Sanger's Civic Center.

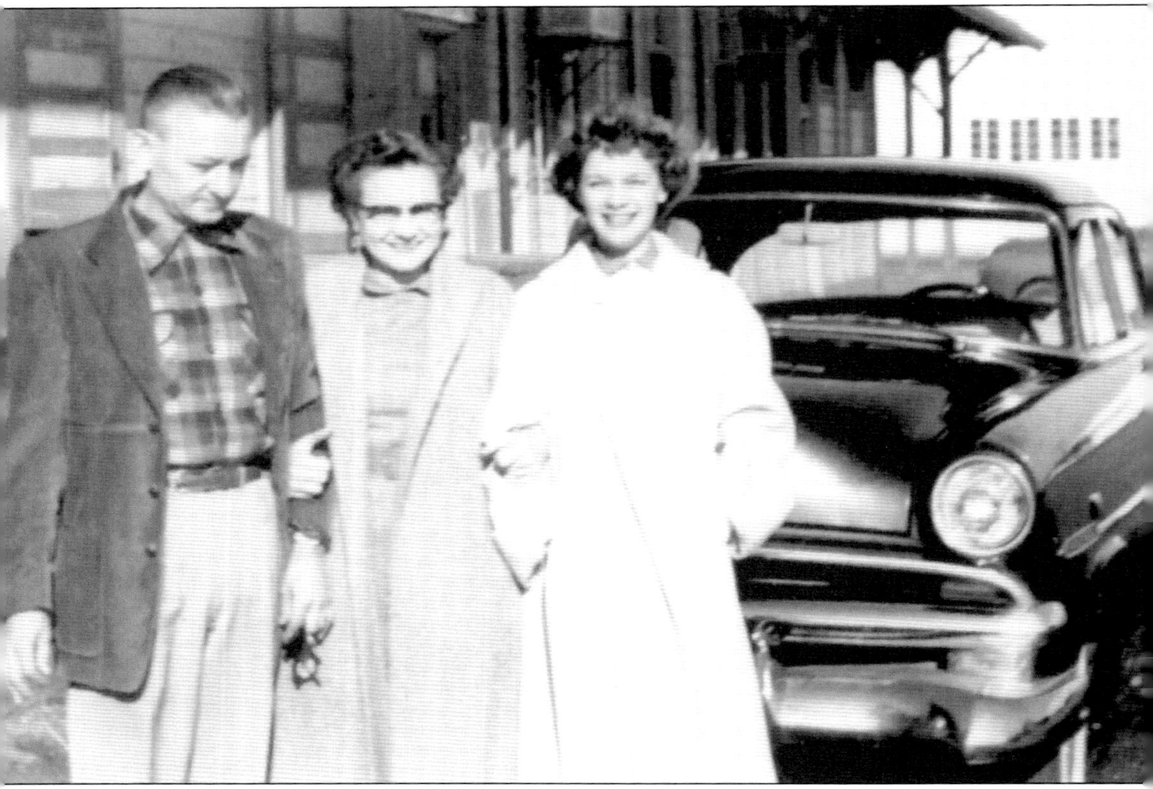

Walter (left), Pansy (center), and Arlene Phillips are shown here in front of the Southern Pacific Depot in the 1950s. The Phillips family, which also included sons George and Kenneth, was the last family to occupy the depot's second-floor living quarters. The space featured a bathroom, bedroom, living room, dining room, and kitchen. The monthly rent was $5, which was quite a deal for a couple who had lived through the Great Depression. (Courtesy Arlene Phillips-Hess.)

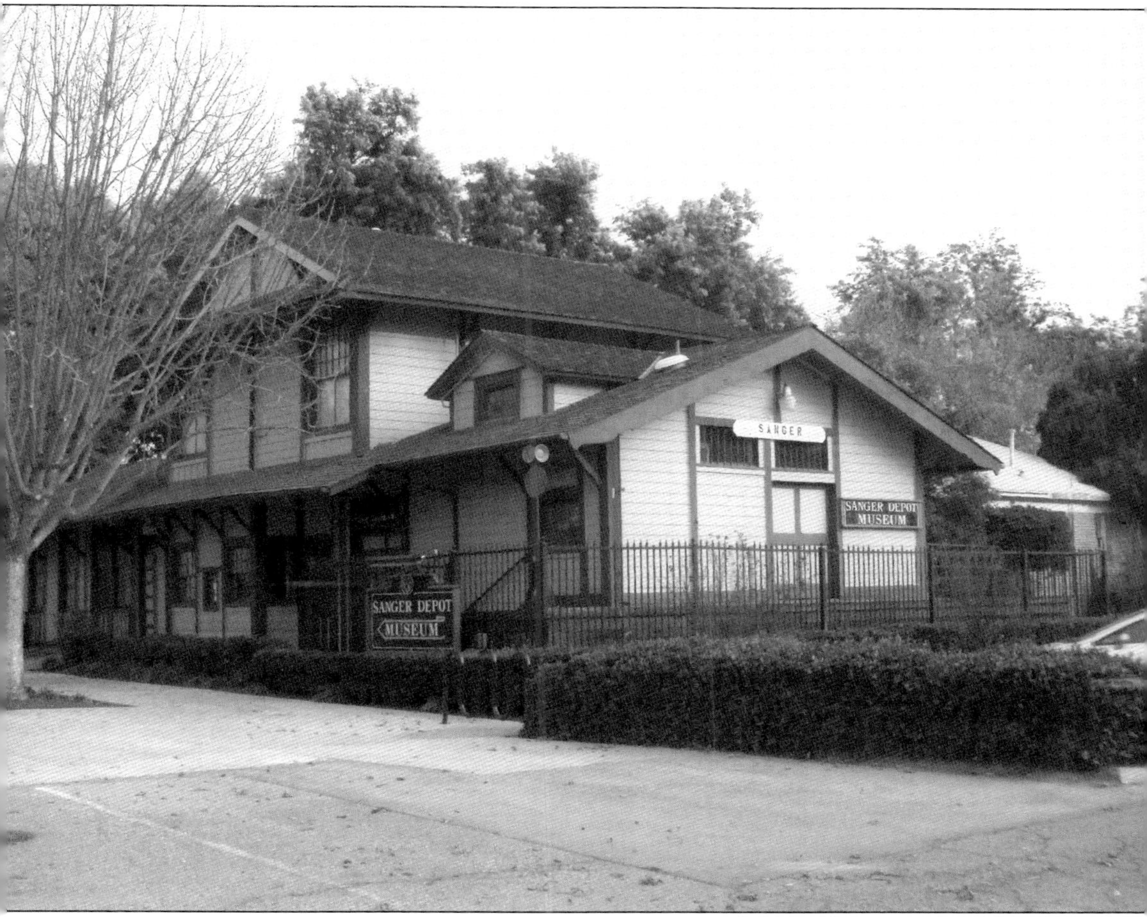

The former railroad depot is seen in a present-day photograph. Since 1983, the building has been the home of the historical society's Sanger Depot Museum. The museum is a popular field trip destination for schools. During the summer tourist season, the museum receives visitors from around the country. The museum features exhibits of local history, Native American baskets, and an extensive collection relating to the lumber industry.

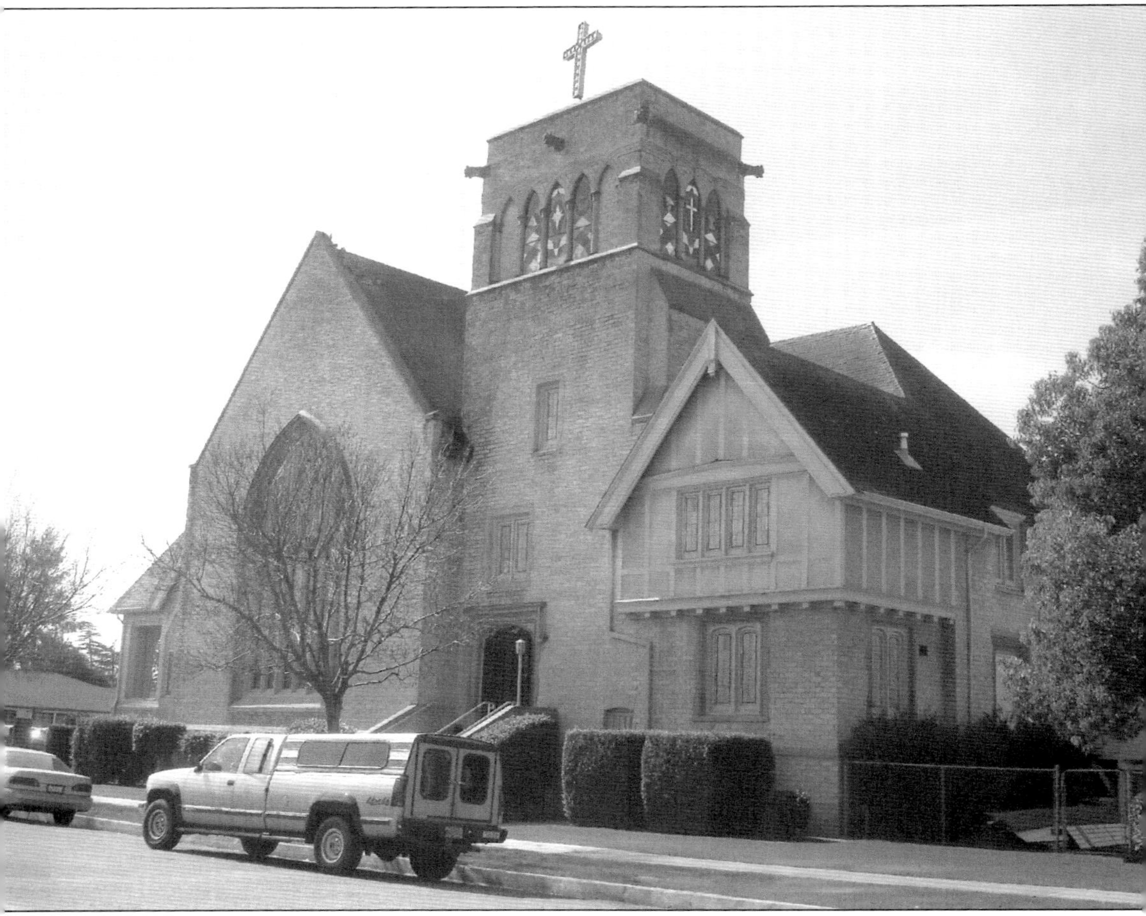

The First United Methodist Church was built in 1922. It was chartered as the Methodist Episcopal Church South. The site of the present building was purchased in 1889. In 1916, during the Reverend Luther Rice's pastorate, he succeeded in uniting the north and south churches, and money was raised to construct the present building (seen here). The Gothic Revival architectural style made it unique in the city of Sanger.

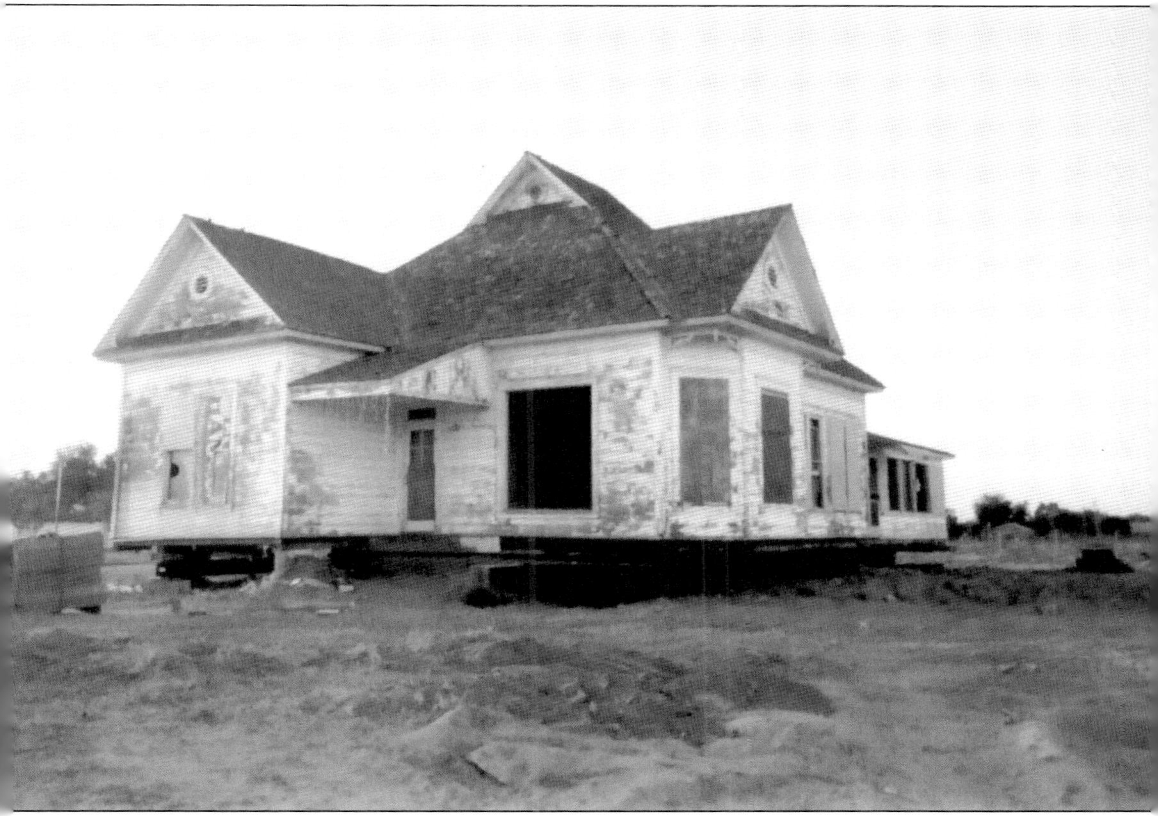

The Miller House was built by Peter Miller around 1898. He constructed the house on his 250-acre ranch using redwood that had been floated down the 54-mile flume from the lumber town of Millwood to the Kings River (later Hume-Bennett) mill in Sanger. A century later, the abandoned home had fallen into disrepair, as seen here. (Courtesy of Fred McNairy.)

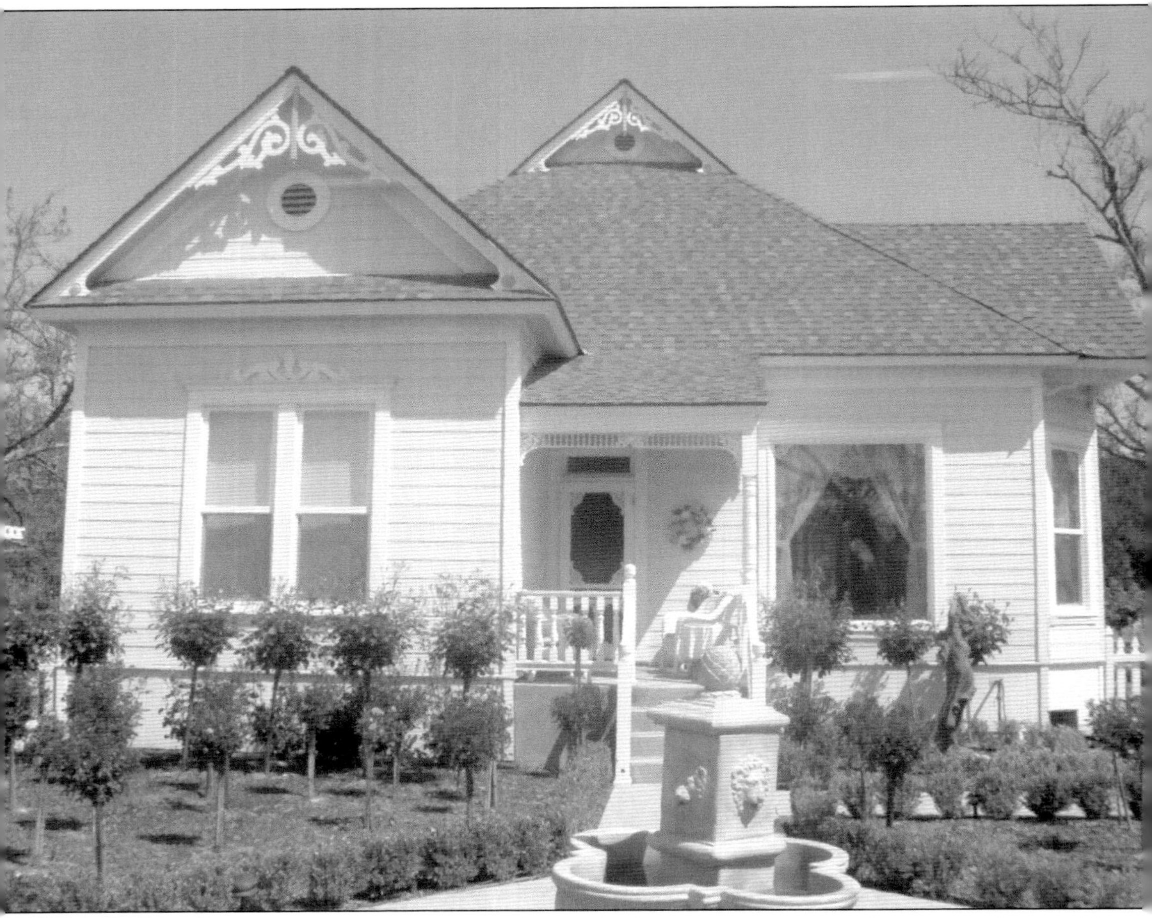

During the housing boom of the early 2000s, the land where the Miller House stood was sold to a developer and was to be cleared to make room for a subdivision. The house narrowly escaped being razed when it was purchased, moved, and lovingly restored by the McNairys. As seen here, the Miller House has begun a new life as the Blossom Trail Bed and Breakfast. (Courtesy of Scott Haugland.)

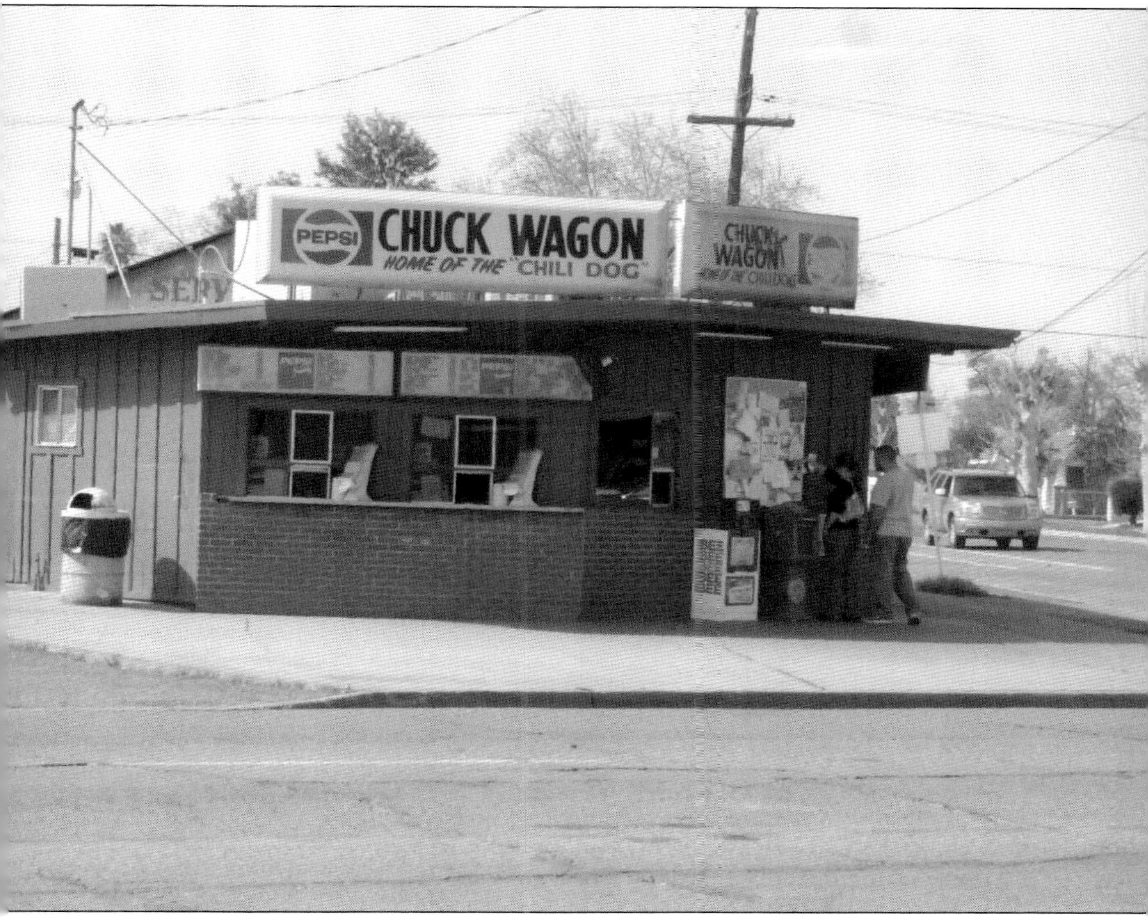

Not yet an official landmark, the Chuck Wagon is perhaps Sanger's most iconic building. The establishment has been serving its famous chili dogs, Clark burgers, and fries for almost a century. Begun by the Guffy family, the restaurant was later sold to Jack Clark, who passed it on to his son Jack Jr. Roy Furamoto purchased the business from the Clarks in 1970, and it is now operated by his daughters Joann and June. The chili recipe remains unchanged, and generations of loyal customers would have it no other way.

Sanger's Mill Whistle
by Aunt Mary Rodgers

Oh how we miss that whistle
and its old familiar sound.
It would wake the country people,
for miles and miles around.
It sounded first at half past five,
and waked you from your dream.
Then again at six o'clock.
how early it would seem.
But when 'twas seven,
the men would hurry most.
For when it blew at seven o'clock,
they must be at their work and post.
Over thirty-five years it had sounded,
from the same old place it came.
The workmen changed most every year,
but the whistle was just the same.
Now if that mill would run again,
old Sanger would feel right.
To hear that whistle sound again,
at morning, noon, and night.

(Poem from the 1938 golden jubilee edition of the *Sanger Herald*, reprinted courtesy of the *Sanger Herald*.)

About the Organization

"A town with a future, needs to remember its past."

In 1969, Oscar Brehler's stepson Jack Sayre and niece Virginia Lee entered into an agreement with E.L. Barr Sr. of Sanger. The agreement was that Barr was to receive approximately one half of Brehler's prized Native American basket collection, provided that Barr could form a nonprofit corporation to care and exhibit the baskets and that adequate housing and display cases be provided for the collection. Barr then turned the task over to his nephew, John Olson. In 1974, with the assistance of the Kiwanis Club, Olson established the Sanger Historical Society. The first directors were John Olson, Alden Knapp, Johnnie Steinert, Richard Manfredi, and James Walton.

The group then took on the task of finding a location to display the baskets. During that same period, the Tanney family had purchased the recently closed Sanger Southern Pacific depot. The Tanneys offered the depot to the historical society. Part of the purchase agreement between Southern Pacific and the Tanneys, was that the building be removed from the railroad's property. A location was found near Sanger's Civic Center, and, on the rainy day of December 7, 1977, the depot was moved to its new home. The historical society then formed a group responsible for fundraising and another group to take on the task of preparing the old depot for conversion to a museum. Thanks to the many generous people who gave financially and countless others who gave of their labor skills and volunteer time, the Sanger Depot Museum officially opened in the fall of 1983. Over the last 30 years, the historical society has continued to improve the museum and add exhibits. The museum has no paid employees, relying instead on the volunteer hours of its members, who are generous enough to serve as dedicated docents. The historical society is continually looking for new members and hopes to pass on Sanger's history for generations to come.

For information regarding museum hours, donations, membership, or questions, please contact the Sanger Historical Society at www.sangerdepotmuseum.com.